The Scriptural Temple

The Scriptural Temple

Mark H. Greene III

First Printing: May, 2000

International Standard Book Number:
0-88290-681-X

Horizon Publishers' Catalog and Order Number:
1262

Printed and distributed
in the United States of America by

Horizon
Publishers
& Distributors, Incorporated

Mailing Address:
P.O. Box 490
Bountiful, Utah 84011-0490

Street Address:
50 South 500 West
Bountiful, Utah 84010

Local Phone: (801) 295-9451
WATS (toll free): 1 (800) 453-0812
FAX: (801) 295-0196

E-mail: horizonp@burgoyne.com
Internet: http://www.horizonpublishers.com

Contents

> **Note:**
> Throughout the book, the author and editors have used *italics*
> to add emphasis to key and noteworthy ideas and statements.

Introduction

About ten years ago I tried to discover the meaning of the gospel doctrine of the "mighty change." This change seemed to occur to many prophets who testified about it in the Book of Mormon. I wasn't sure that such a marvelous change could ever occur in my life. In searching the meaning of the mighty change, I wrote an essay containing my beliefs about this doctrine and gave a church talk titled "The Great Paradigm Shift of the Gospel." While this search led to deeper understanding of the doctrine, I still did not have a clear vision about how to obtain the mighty change in this life. However, after giving the talk, I had a strong impression that more on this subject would be revealed to me if I kept searching. *The Scriptural Temple* is the fulfillment of this "strong feeling" and search.

Writing this book has not only given me priceless knowledge about temple worship as the power to produce the mighty change, but I have learned much about the spirit of prophecy and revelation. It is a process in which our talents, experiences, and beliefs are refined by the power of God. There may be moments of pure heart-felt inspiration, but mostly the process is slow distillation of pure knowledge until we recognize it in our hearts and minds.

I have watched my wife bake bread before the automatic bread-maker took her place. The dough would rise under the influence of yeast, then, with a clenched fist, she would deflate the dough, only to see it rise again. This best describes the distilling process in writing this book. When I felt the rise of the "dough" of this book to be right in my mind and heart, then it was right with God.

I cherish the moments of heart-felt inspiration. They were moments of such spiritual alacrity that overpowering feelings welled up within me and spilled on my cheeks as tears of joy. I cannot adequately describe these moments but they were real.

Donna Nielsen, who wrote the marvelous book *Beloved Bridegroom*, described her writing experience as having the companionship of "research angels." I have dedicated this book to Brian, my firstborn son, because he was my research angel. Brian was born in Brussels, Belgium, and died shortly after birth. In a cold storage hanger of the

Brussels airport, I sat alone next to his small coffin wrapped for flight to the United States. When I finally said goodbye, I had an overwhelming impression that we would meet again in this life. Years passed, but this impression never left my thoughts. I even had the feeling before I understood the importance of the temple, that I would meet him there. When my research angel came, it was in the *scriptural temple* that we met.

There are others who have encouraged this book and given helpful support. For my family's patient endurance, I am in debt. I extend my deep appreciation to Barbara Lewis, Kellene Adams, Donna Nielsen, and Claudia Greene for their editorial help. I am most grateful to Duane S. Crowther, President of Horizon Publishers, for his editorial insights and guidance, and to the staff at Horizon Publishers for their willing assistance in publishing this book. The many scholars and Church authors who have written wonderful books and articles about the temple have provided a solid foundation upon which I stood in writing this book.

To the reader who feels in reading this book what I have felt, I share a bond of joy.

Dedication

To Brian,

the son I met again in

the scriptural temple.

The Temple Paradigm

The intent of this book is to bear witness of a great view—an understanding in my mind and heart of scriptural messages about the temple. This view has changed my life. I hope it will change your life too.

Temple Dropouts and Temple Inactives

My expanding view of the temple began a few years ago with a calling to the stake high council, which included an assignment to teach a temple preparation class. I was obliged to learn about a subject that had been of occasional interest to me, but largely ignored. I was surprised when I reviewed our stake's statistics of those holding a current temple recommend compared with those having received their own endowment. I found that only one-third to one-half of our stake's members who had received their own endowment held current temple recommends, and that number may have been even better than Church-wide figures.

How many new members actually receive their own endowment? What happens between the first endowment and subsequent temple recommend interviews? Why are there so many temple dropouts? While I was not a part of this "drop-out" group, I was part of a larger, non-reported group in the Church that I will call temple inactives.

At a temple recommend interview, the stake president asked me when I last attended the temple. I told him it had been the prior month, but I didn't respond with conviction. In fact, I felt so guilty that I had to return and confess to him that it had been a whole year since I had really attended the temple. I knew that he was not asking me about temple attendance for a family wedding, but rather temple service for my own salvation and for that of the departed. I was so occupied with my profession and other secular matters that temple endowment attendance had been excluded from my calendar for a whole year. However, the real reason for my being a temple inactive was not the typical excuse of a busy life, but rather that I did not fully understand that Moroni atop the temple was blowing his trumpet for me. I did not hear his call.

Few Comprehend the Full Meaning of the Temple Endowment

My first temple experience was in Los Angeles. I was eight years old, and the Los Angeles Temple had just been completed. My parents invited me to go to the dedication. I remember walking into a magnificent room and sitting on an aisle seat. Soon, a procession of men dressed in white entered. One was tall, with white waved hair. He was such an impressive, divine figure that I could have imagined it was God himself. My mother whispered to me that the Prophet David O. McKay had just passed by.

Years later I read an interesting statement concerning President McKay's visit to the Los Angeles Temple dedication. While addressing member leaders before the dedication, he told about his niece who regarded her initiation into a sorority superior in effect and meaning to her endowment in the temple. Then he said:

> Brothers and Sisters, she was disappointed in the Temple. Brothers and sisters, I was disappointed in the Temple, and so were you. There are few, even temple workers, who comprehend the full meaning and power of the Temple endowment. Seen for what it is, *it is the step-by-step ascent into the Eternal presence. If our young people could but glimpse it, it would be the most powerful spiritual motivation of their lives!*[1]

When I read this statement by President McKay, I became uncomfortably aware that the temple had not been the most powerful spiritual motivation in my life. I did not comprehend the temple endowment as the step-by-step ascent into the presence of God. Why not? My parents attended the temple. I was taught to be worthy to go to the temple and certainly to be married in the temple. But little was said about temple worship, either at home or at church. I had a notion that it was mysterious and secret. Even after first going to the temple, I didn't fully comprehend its significance, and I considered it more as a church annex for specialized work.

I am grateful that the Lord has blessed me over the past few years with a new paradigm. This paradigm is a great change in my frame of reference towards understanding the temple. In this paradigm I have increased insight and find greater personal meaning for the temple. I hope to explain the new frame of reference by revealing the temple paradigm found throughout the scriptures.

The Term Scriptural Temple as Used in This Book

The term *scriptural temple* in this book *refers to scriptural verses that directly or indirectly reveal true temple worship.* This term may intrigue many and cause them to ask where temple worship is found in the scriptures. Perhaps too many are looking for references to the sacred ritual while missing the profound temple teachings found in the scriptures.

The temple is a marvelous template for scripture study because if we enhance what we learn inside temple walls with the rich temple teachings of the scriptures, temple worship will have great and glorious meaning in our lives. The *scriptural temple* will help us understand important concepts of true temple worship, such as the mighty change of heart, anointing with the Spirit, growing up in the Lord, the bond of perfectness, the redemption of Zion, eternal life, and many other important temple concepts and principles.

This book is a broad synthesis of scriptural relationships and messages designed to create a temple paradigm in the image of a mountain and our ascent of this mountain. However, it is not a comprehensive *scriptural temple.* I have discovered that *the scriptural temple keeps expanding as we are taught by the Holy Spirit.* Many verses of the scriptural temple are quoted in this book. In addition, references are made to many more. *It is recommended that this book be read prayerfully, with the scriptures in hand.*

By constructing a temple paradigm from the perspective of the scriptures, I bear testimony that the temple will become central in our lives and our most powerful spiritual motivation.

A Whale of a Tale and Its Message

If understanding the temple is so important, why isn't it revealed more fully in the scriptures? Previously, I rarely saw the temple reflected in the scriptures. Now the scriptures and the temple come to life in the *scriptural temple.* A major burden of the scriptures is to reveal the temple. (*See Teachings of the Prophet Joseph Smith*, p. 193.)

For example, I have been told and have read the scriptural story of Jonah many times. It was at first a curiosity, a whale of a tale, like the story of Pinocchio. But then it took on believable significance as a sign of the crucifixion and resurrection of Christ. When the Savior was challenged by the scribes and Pharisees to produce a sign from heaven, He made reference to "the sign of the prophet Jonas" (*see* Matthew 12:39-40), as a sign of His own crucifixion and resurrection.

Jonah feared for his life after receiving his mission call to the hostile Assyrian city of Nineveh. He foolishly thought he could flee from the Lord by sailing to Tarshish. En route, a tempest threatened the lives of those aboard. Jonah identified himself as the possible cause of the peril then volunteered to be thrown overboard to save the others.

> Wherefore they cried unto the Lord, and said, We beseech thee, O Lord, we beseech thee, let us not perish for this man's life, and lay not upon us innocent blood: for thou, O Lord, hast done as it pleased thee.
> So they took up Jonah, and cast him forth into the sea: and the sea ceased from her raging. (Jonah 1:14-15)

These verses imply the Atonement with the reference to innocent blood and the voluntary sacrifice of Jonah to save others.

Jonah was swallowed by a "great fish" (a whale) and taken to the depths of the sea where he "prayed unto the Lord his God out of the fish's belly . . . the belly of hell" (Jonah 2:1-2). Can the Lord hear our cry from the belly of hell? From the depths of the sea? Yes! Oh, yes, He can! Thus, we should all pray to the Lord in the depths of our despair, in our most miserable conditions.

Can we run or hide from the Lord? Like Jonah, Adam and Eve learned that Satan will try to convince us that we can, but the Lord will find us wherever we go, even in the belly of hell (*see* Deuteronomy 30:4).

In the story of Jonah and the whale, we see a reflection of Adam and Eve being cast out of the Garden of Eden. To be swallowed by a whale and cast out of the sight of the Lord is a description of the depth of the Fall, yet even while he was in the belly of the whale, it was the thought of the Lord's temple that sustained Jonah. "I am cast out of thy sight;" said Jonah, "*yet I will look again toward thy holy temple*" (Jonah 2:4). *It's this key verse that first alerted me to the temple significance of the book of Jonah.*

Adam and Eve did the same thing, looking back to the garden, which represented the temple, for direction from the Lord.

And Adam and Eve, his wife, called upon the name of the Lord, and they heard the voice of the Lord from the way toward the Garden of Eden, speaking unto them, and they saw him not; for they were shut out from his presence.

And he gave unto them commandments, that they should worship the Lord their God, and should offer the firstlings of their flocks, for an offering unto the Lord. And Adam was obedient unto the commandments of the Lord. (Moses 5:4-5)

What happened to Adam and Eve happens to us. Because of the Fall, we are cast out of the presence of the Lord. We must look towards the garden, the Lord's temple, and hear His voice to receive His commandments, that we may find the way to return to His presence.

For Jonah, the memory of the Lord was in His holy temple. He hallowed the memory of being in the presence of the Lord or being in His holy temple. What a contrast to Jonah's current surroundings!

Through this memory, Jonah was teaching us that Christ didn't die just to save sinners from physical death, but to draw all sinners to Him—to elevate them from the belly of hell to His level. The repentant sinner needs to make the effort to be in the presence of the Lord. "And my Father sent me that I might be lifted up upon the cross; and after that I had been lifted up upon the cross, *that I might draw all men unto me*" (3 Nephi 27:14; *see also* John 12:32). Being in the presence of the Lord is true deliverance from the Fall.

I see in the account of Jonah a broad, glorious metaphor—a whole series of comparisons between Jonah's experience and various facets of the plan of salvation.

There are many other metaphors and parallels between the story of Jonah and Christ's sacrifice. As Christ was pressed under the weight of the Atonement (as Jonah was pressed under the weight of the sea) and the Father withdrew, He cried unto the Father that He might not have to drink the bitter cup and that He not be forsaken (just as Jonah cried to the Lord). Yet Christ's sacrifice was out of love for his Father and for us. Thus, He obediently kept His vow to complete the Atonement.

Because of this obedience (because of Jonah's desired obedience to his temple vows), the Father delivered His beloved Son to His celestial presence on His right hand (Jonah was delivered to dry ground, a celestial place compared to the belly of hell). The Lord can take each of us from the belly of hell to this celestial realm if we are obedient to Him.

The waters compassed me about, even to the soul: the depth closed me round about, the weeds were wrapped about my head.

I went down to the bottoms of the mountains; the earth with her bars was about me for ever: *yet hast thou brought up my life from corruption, O Lord my God.* (Jonah 2:5-6)

This description of the increasing depth (bottoms), the pressure (bars), the darkness (weeds) is vivid. Jonah is on the verge of drowning. These verses are symbolic of our great fall, the depth of corruption in this life. Jonah knew that only one person could save him and bring him up from corruption—that person was his Savior.

Do we sense our impending drowning in this world of carnal security? Do we realize there is only one person who can save us? Jonah would have rejoiced at the words of Jacob: *"My soul delighteth in proving unto my people that save Christ should come all men must perish"* (2 Nephi 11:6).

When all hope was apparently gone, Jonah remembered the Lord in the temple: "When my soul fainted within me I remembered the Lord: and *my prayer came in unto thee, into thine holy temple*" (Jonah 2:7). I wonder if I would have thought of the temple if I were in Jonah's condition.

To be delivered from the belly of hell, we must have faith unto life and salvation. This requires sacrifice with real intent (thanksgiving) in covenants (vows) (*see* Jonah 2:9), sacrificing all things to the Lord, as Joseph Smith taught: *"Let us here observe, that a religion that does not require the sacrifice of all things never has power sufficient to produce the faith necessary unto life and salvation."*[2]

We must keep our covenants (vows) through strict obedience to the Lord. We must be willing to sacrifice anything for this obedience. We must have hope that the Lord's grace is sufficient for our rescue (salvation is of the Lord; Jonah 2:9). No wonder Jonah thought of the temple and his vows. The way of salvation is paved with repentance, sacrifice, obedience, hope in Christ, and covenants with Him. All of these are beautiful temple teachings.

"And the Lord spake unto the fish, and it vomited out Jonah upon the dry land" (Jonah 2:10). As miraculous as this seems, we should have confidence and expectation that the Lord can do something just as miraculous, if not more so, even for us.

But the Lord knoweth all things from the beginning; wherefore, *he prepareth a way to accomplish all his works among the children of men;* for behold, *he hath all power unto the fulfilling of all his words.* And thus it is. Amen. (1 Nephi 9:6)

Jonah's rescue was symbolic of the power of the resurrection and of exaltation. Do we see ourselves resurrected and perfected because of the power, work, and glory of the Lord? (*See* Alma 5:15.) I can imagine that Jonah used words and feelings similar to Nephi's psalm (*see* 2 Nephi 4:16-35) after being "encompassed about" but "preserved upon the water of the great deep" and then becoming a successful missionary to the Assyrians.

For years, I had not noticed the reference to the temple in this whale story. Now, with my new temple paradigm, this story has become not only an important witness for the Savior, but one of the most glorious accounts of temple deliverance in all of scripture.

I realized, as I studied and read, that *the temple was central to Jonah in his peril, even in his sin.* Why wasn't the temple central in my life? Why wasn't it the most powerful spiritual motivation in my life? Why had I not seen the temple in the scriptures?

The Fall, the Plan of Redemption, the Atonement, the Resurrection, the celestial potential of man, the power and grace of Christ—all taught in this whale of a tale—are central temple doctrines. *The story of Jonah teaches us that the temple should be the center of our lives, even in the moment of our greatest tribulations, because it represents the presence of the Lord and teaches us the process of true deliverance from the Fall, including our personal falls.*

The Mighty Change: The Great Paradigm Shift of the Gospel

Prior to recognizing the temple message in the scriptures, I had become intrigued with the Book of Mormon doctrine of "the mighty change," as taught by King Benjamin and the prophet Alma:

And they all cried with one voice, saying: Yea, we believe all the words which thou hast spoken unto us; and also, we know of their sure- ty and truth, because of the Spirit of the Lord Omnipotent, *which has wrought* a *mighty change in us, or in our hearts, that we have no more disposition to do evil, but to do good continually.* (Mosiah 5:2)

And now behold, I ask of you, my brethren of the church, *have ye spiritually been born of God? Have ye received his image in your countenances? Have ye experienced this mighty change in your hearts?* (Alma 5:14)

I wondered seriously if any of us really do change except by the modifications of time and experience. Does our basic nature change, our hearts, our countenance? What does it mean to be spiritually born of God?

The mighty change seems to be something quite separate from the changes imposed by the natural process of mortality. It is, according to King Benjamin and Alma, a change of heart. King Benjamin further said that *this change of heart requires putting off the natural man, acquiring the qualities of a child, and becoming a saint through the Atonement* (*see* Mosiah 3:19). I call this mighty change of heart *the great paradigm shift of the gospel.* Alma, the converted son of Mosiah, testified of this great shift in his own life, and he said further that *all mankind must make this shift to be born of God:*

For, said he, *I have repented of my sins, and have been redeemed of the Lord; behold I am born of the Spirit.*

And the Lord said unto me: Marvel not that *all mankind,* yea, men and women, all nations, kindreds, tongues, and people, *must be born again; yea, born of God, changed from their carnal and fallen state, to a state of righteousness, being redeemed of God, becoming his sons and daughters.* (Mosiah 27:24-25)

In spite of successfully going through the major events of life (birth, family, schooling, marriage, children, profession, aging) with their attendant rewards, trials, teachings, and experiences,we often continue to ask a deep, nagging question: "Have I really changed?" Perhaps it is the question that we ask ourselves when we contemplate the declaration of Amulek: *"This life is the time for men to prepare to meet God"* (*see* Alma 34:32).

What does it take to prepare to meet God? What labors are to be done for this preparation? Have I not prepared by acquiring knowledge, developing talents and character, and even striving to keep the commandments?

Yes, all of these are part of the labors and preparation to meet God, but Amulek had something more profound in mind. He even implied the nature of this mighty change when he referred to a witness in the heart (*see* Alma 34:30-31). *The mighty change is the core, the crux, of the gospel of Jesus Christ because it requires Christ and His Atonement to happen for us individually. It is the great paradigm shift of the gospel—the mighty change of heart.* The Apostle Paul and Alma the Younger taught that it is a literal change in our nature:

> For all things are for your sakes, that the *abundant grace* might through the thanksgiving of many redound to the glory of God.
> For which cause we faint not; but *though our outward man perish, yet the inward man is renewed day by day.* (2 Corinthians 4:15-16)

> Therefore if any man be in Christ, *he is a new creature: old things are passed away; behold, all things are become new.* (2 Corinthians 5:17)

> And thus *they become new creatures; and unless they do this, they can in nowise inherit the kingdom of God.* (Mosiah 27:26)

I found myself wondering, like Enos, "*Lord, how is it done?*" The answer Enos received is simple yet profound, "*Because of thy faith in Christ*" (Enos 1:7-8).

Faith in Christ leads to repentance, which leads to obedience to the words of Christ. This obedience leads to the mighty change of heart. Therefore, in this life we have the choice of either a mortal suffering relieved through repentance and faith in Christ now, or else procrastinating repentance until we die and must suffer spiritually in spirit prison—with weeping, wailing, and gnashing of teeth (*see* D&C 19:4-5). This is why Amulek said, "*I beseech of you that ye do not procrastinate the day of your repentance until the end*" (Alma 34:33).

As a missionary, I saw a mighty change in some of my investigators, and certainly in myself. Most missionaries experience the same, and they testify that faith in Christ is the power behind this mighty change. *The only reason that this mighty change does not continue in our lives is that we do not continue to seek and follow the Lord with the same conviction and intensity, having faith that He can change us mightily.*

When I find myself crossing the straight and narrow, I get a glimpse of what I really want and hope to be, but alas, "O wretched man that I am!" (2 Nephi 4:17). We have only one hope to acquire this divine nature—this mighty change of heart in becoming a new creature. *This hope comes through faith in Christ, who promises to make weak things strong unto us according to our faith and His grace* (*see* Ether 12:27). For the power of Christ to work in my life, I must be meek enough to seek Him, and draw near to Him as He draws near to me (*see* D&C 88:63).

While I believe the mighty change to be a true doctrine of the gospel, I had difficulty seeing it consistently taking place within me in this life until I connected the great paradigm shift of the gospel with my changing paradigm of temple worship through the *scriptural temple*. I truly believe, as I will explain in detail, *the mighty change of heart—the change from an unbelieving hard heart to a pure heart—is the pinnacle of the temple paradigm. It is the highest peak of Mount Zion, the Temple Mount, that we can climb in this life.* It is the pure heart that is needed in preparation to meet God. This preparation, the mighty change of heart, is possible in this life by the power of the Atonement manifest through the ordinances and covenants of the temple. As stated by Joseph Smith, *"being born again comes by the Spirit of God through ordinances."*[3]

Truman Madsen also placed our rebirth in the temple through the Atonement when he said,

> The birth [mighty change] that climaxes all rebirths is in the House of the Lord. The perfecting of His work (D&C 76:10) is the perfecting of His people. Are any perfected? Only those who are "made perfect through Jesus the mediator of the new covenant, who wrought out this perfect atonement through the shedding of his own blood" (see D&C 76:69).[4]

The *scriptural temple* teaches that to "be in Christ" (2 Corinthians 5:17) requires the full priesthood of God through the ordinances and covenants of the temple. The power of His order and His love can produce the "renewing of our bodies" that makes one a "new creature" both physically and spiritually (*see* D&C 84:32-33). It can even take a hard heart and make it pure.

Moroni's Heralding Call to Commune with God

In a memorable lecture on temple worship, the Apostle John A. Widtsoe said the following:

> There is at present an unusual increased interest in temple activity. Our temples are crowded. The last time I attended the Salt Lake Temple I was a member of the third company. One started early in the

morning, one late in the forenoon, and my company started about 2 o'clock in the afternoon. It was about 6 p.m. before we had completed the day's work.

The number of temples is also increasing. The Hawaiian temple has only recently been dedicated; the Cardston temple is being rushed to completion, the Arizona temple is being planned and numerous communities in the Church are anxiously waiting and praying for the time that they may have temples.

There is a renewed spirit in behalf of temple work, not because people are wealthier than they were before, nor because temples are more accessible, but because the time has come for more temple work to be done. *The spirit is abroad among the people, and those who are honest in heart and understand the Gospel of Jesus Christ, are willing to give their time and means more liberally in behalf of temple work.*[5]

This is an interesting statement, especially in the context of what is happening to temple activity in the Church today. If Elder Widtsoe were alive now, I believe he would declare another era of "unusual increased interest in temple activity."

Elder Widtsoe mentioned a few new temples. He would be overwhelmed with the ambitious temple construction today. Yet this construction is an expression of renewed temple desire and understanding of the Saints. President Hinckley's announcement of the smaller "stake" temples during the October 1997 general conference[6] as well as the plans to build many more of these temples announced in subsequent general conferences, is fulfillment of prophecy: "For it is ordained that in Zion, *and in her stakes*, and in Jerusalem, those places which I have appointed for refuge, shall be the places for your baptisms for your dead" (D&C 124:36).

Perhaps with prescience, Samuel Francis Smith wrote the phrase: "I love thy rocks and rills, Thy woods *and templed hills*" in his famous anthem, *My Country, 'Tis of Thee.*[7] While the description of *his* country was the eastern United States, we are literally seeing hills templed not only in the entire United States but throughout the world.

The expansion of temple construction and worship throughout the world is also a significant part of the fulfillment of the supplication of Joseph Smith in his Kirtland temple dedicatory prayer "That the kingdom, which thou hast set up without hands, may *become a great mountain and fill the whole earth*" (D&C 109:72).

Last January, I decided to attend the Bountiful temple one Friday evening. I traveled the few miles from Salt Lake City and climbed the gently winding streets of the foothills of Bountiful. My eyes and thoughts were naturally lifted above to the elegant white house of the Lord.

As I entered the parking lot, it was evident that either there was a very large wedding or many other members had decided to visit the Bountiful temple this particular Friday. I could not find a parking place either in the parking lot above or under cover. I had to park on the street. I intended to go on the six o'clock session, but I became concerned about this start time when I couldn't find a vacant locker. Before entering the chapel, I was directed to an overflow area, already full of waiting people. It was obvious that I was in for a long evening.

The six o'clock session did not start until eight o'clock. The temple workers had never seen such attendance at the temple. Explanations could have been the cleaning closure of the Salt Lake Temple or simply the fulfillment of New Year's resolutions. Regardless of the reason, it was an impressive experience to be in a temple so full of worshippers that it could scarcely accommodate them. How wonderful if every weekend could draw such crowds to the temple as we all look with great anticipation for the work week to end.

Truly, the time has come "for more temple work to be done," not only in construction, but in understanding, worship, and practice in our daily lives. It is time for the temple to become the center of our lives to teach us the way of salvation. It is time we hear Moroni atop the temple as he calls us to come to the mountain of the Lord.

President Thomas S. Monson once said that "the Moroni statue which appears on the top of several of our temples is a reminder to us all that God is concerned for all His people throughout the world, and communicates with them wherever they may be.[8]

In response to *Moroni's heralding call to commune with God and to the increased desire to understand temple worship,* I would like to take a journey through the *scriptural temple.* Throughout the scriptures the Lord weaves a clear temple message. The word of God teaches us how and why we should center our lives in the temple. It beckons us to climb Mount Zion, the spiritual mountain of the Lord's house, to see the great view of God's kingdom. Moroni's calling trump reaches us not in musical notes, but in the words of the scriptural temple message of the everlasting gospel:

And I saw another angel fly in the midst of heaven, *having the ever-lasting gospel to preach unto them that dwell on the earth,* and to *every nation, and kindred, and tongue, and people,*

Saying with a loud voice, *Fear God, and give glory to him; for the hour of his judgment is come: and worship him that made heaven, and earth, and the sea, and the fountains of waters.* (Revelation 14:6-7)

2

Seeking the Source of Temple Worship in the Holy Land

One event that greatly changed my understanding of the importance of the temple was a visit to the Holy Land. In preparation for this trip, I read history and religious books about the Near East. One of these was *Jerusalem, the Eternal City*, by David Galbraith, Kelly Ogden, and Andrew Skinner. A statement in this book impressed me not only as particularly significant for my developing temple paradigm, but also as a testimony for the religion to which I belong:

> Though the land certainly was holy, this transfer of sanctity to sites and buildings within Jerusalem reveals, in the words of Hugh Nibley "Christian envy of the Temple." *In every ancient culture, temples represented the meeting place of heaven and earth. The destruction of the Temple in Jerusalem left a gaping hole in the life of the Christian movement after the first century, especially in theology.* Thus, "many Christian writers have expressed the conviction that the church possesses no adequate substitute for the Temple." After the first century, *Christianity seems always to have been looking for a surrogate to replace the rituals as well as the physical structure of the Temple.*[1]

After reading this, I again realized that the temple was not as central in my life as it had been in the lives and cultures of those in Jerusalem. I began to see a "gaping hole" in my own religious life. I *then* appreciated the great blessing in the restoration of true temple worship through the restored gospel. *We, as Latter-day Saints, have something extraordinarily marvelous that distinguishes us from all other religions—a true understanding of temples and the practice of true temple worship.* This understanding and practice is great evidence of the principle of revelation from God on which our beliefs are based. We could not build a temple structure and perform covenants and ordinances acceptable to God unless they were revealed from God (*see* Psalms 127:1).

True temple worship is as great an evidence of the truthfulness of our religion as the Book of Mormon. Therefore, it should be as important in our lives as the Book of Mormon.

Granite and Gossamer Veils

The day I visited the Western Wall, and contemplated the scene of men divided from women as they worshiped, I immediately thought that this is the veil of the Jewish temple today. Its Herodian stone is as thick as the disbelief of those who worship before it. Their rejection of the One who saves brought ruin to their temple, with only a stony veil as its remnant memorial. Even the veils that separated the Holy of Holies from the Holy Place in the Aaronic Priesthood temples on Mount Moriah were heavy and thick compared to the veil in Melchizedek Priesthood temples today. This thick Aaronic Priesthood veil was consequent to the rejection of the fullness of the priesthood and the "rest" the Lord offered to the children of Israel in the Sinai (*see* 2 Corinthians 3:13-16).

In the Doctrine and Covenants, we learn that *the Lord's temple is covered with a veil,* hiding the whole earth from the presence or celestial temple of the Lord (*see* D&C 101:23). This is a result of our fall from His realm. This scripture also teaches us that the veil will be removed at the Second Coming, but only those who are purified enough to see through the "veil of darkness" will endure the event (*see* D&C 38:8).

In preparation for this event, if we keep ourselves as a temple (*see* 1 Corinthians 6:19), a veil of darkness which Moroni called the "*veil of unbelief*" (Ether 4:15) can be lifted from our mortal eyes so that we see with the "eyes of our understanding" (*see* D&C 110:1).

However, before we see with the "eyes of our understanding," we must first see with "an eye of faith" (Ether 12:19). If this faith is strong enough, the "veil of unbelief" and even the veil separating us from the presence of the Lord will be rent.

In learning how to penetrate the veil and abide the presence of the Lord we become purified. This occurs in mortality through temples and temple worship. The Lord expects us to seek after Him and penetrate the veil even in this life. This is what Paul taught the Athenians on Mars Hill:

That they should *seek the Lord,* if haply they might *feel after him,* and *find him,* though he be not far from every one of us;

For in him we live, and move, and have our being; as certain also of your own poets have said, For *we are also his offspring.* (Acts 17:27-28)

This scripture stirs in me the impression of an orphan striving to find a true parent. Would we not earnestly and persistently seek our natural parents? Yet are we not all spiritual orphans?

Some mistakenly feel that they can penetrate the veil and find the Lord by communing with nature, but avoiding worship in His temple. While appreciating nature brings us closer to the Lord, the scriptural temple teaches that there is more to finding Him:

And this greater priesthood administereth the gospel and holdeth the key of the mysteries of the kingdom, even *the key of the knowledge of God.*

Therefore, *in the ordinances thereof, the power of godliness is manifest.* (D&C 84:19-20)

The "greater priesthood" is the fullness of the Melchizedek Priesthood found in the ordinances and covenants of the temple. Abraham is a prime example of one who diligently sought after the Lord and found Him through the ordinances of the "greater priesthood." Through this priesthood, he possessed "great knowledge" and held "the right belonging to the fathers" (*see* Abraham 1:2). With this right, Abraham could declare, "Thy servant has sought thee earnestly; now I have found thee" (Abraham 2:12).

Linking the priesthood with the temple, President Ezra Taft Benson said, "*To enter in the Order of the Son of God is the equivalent today of entering into the fullness of the Melchizedek Priesthood, which is only received in the house of the Lord.*"[2]

This is exactly what Abraham did, receiving the great and last promise of the temple. This promise is that the "right belonging to the fathers," the Second (other) Comforter or presence of the Lord, can be obtained in this life. As explained by Joseph Smith:

Now *what is the other comforter? It is no more nor less than the lord Jesus Christ himself . . .* this is the state and place the ancient Saints arrived at when they had such glorious visions—Isaiah, Ezekiel, John upon the Isle of Patmos, St. Paul in the three heavens, and all the Saints who held communion with the general assembly and Church of the Firstborn—*the Lord taught them face to face and gave them a perfect knowledge of the mysteries of the Kingdom of God.*[3]

Moroni told of the power of faith, referring to this great and last promise of the temple:

> For it was *by faith that Christ showed himself unto our fathers, . . .* and he showed not himself unto them until after they had faith in him; . . .
> Wherefore, ye may also have hope, and *be partakers of the gift,* if ye will but have faith.
> Behold *it was by faith that they of old were called after the holy order of God.* (Ether 12:7, 9-10)

The more we develop faith in Christ, His life and salvation, the more we become obedient to the ordinances and covenants of His Holy Order, the fullness of the Melchizedek Priesthood. With this faith and obedience, the more gossamer the veil becomes, and the easier it is to find the presence of the Lord. We learn this obedience, and we experience the thinning of the veil through the ordinances and covenants of the temple.

Topographical Temples in Israel

Topographical settings of the land of Israel provide a marvelous symbol of the importance of the temple. In every region of Israel are natural temples, reminding the people of the land that no matter their place in life, be it in the desert or the fertile valleys, they have need of a temple.

Located in the Sinai Desert is *Mount Horeb,* where Moses and Elijah had great temple experiences.

In the Judean hills rising from the Dead Sea we find the *Mount of Temptations,* where the Savior dwelt 40 days, like Moses, facing Satan's temptations and preparing for His ministry.

From the fertile Jezreel Valley rises *Mount Tabor,* called "the holy mount" by Peter (*see* 2 Peter 1:18). Many feel that on this holy mount the marvelous temple experience of the Transfiguration occurred.

On the Mediterranean coast near Haifa is *Mount Carmel,* whose dews are likened unto the knowledge of God distilling upon us, as in the temple (*see* D&C 128:19).

At the northern end of Israel, in the Golan Heights, *Mount Hermon,* the highest mountain of Israel, becomes a major source of Israel's water supply as it captures snow and stores the melted crystal in its aquifers. At the southern end of Mount Hermon is a massive rock wall from which flows the river Jor, emptying the subterranean aquifers. It is here that the Savior taught His apostles the importance of revelation and of living waters flowing from the presence of God when He asked them, "Whom do men say that I the Son of Man am?" (*see* Matthew 16:13-19). Mount Hermon is symbolic of the celestial temple, the source of the spiritual water that quenches our spiritual thirst.

In the center of these natural temple mounts of the land Israel is *Mount Zion,* including *Mount Moriah,* "the mountain of [the Lord's] holiness" (Psalms 48:1).

Just east from Mount Zion, across the Kidron Valley is the *Mount of Olives.* On both of these mounts (Mt. Zion and the Mt. of Olives or Golgotha and Gethsemane), the great atoning sacrifice of the Savior occurred. Here the Savior rent the thick veil of the Jewish temple and opened the way as the "forerunner" to *"that within the veil," meaning the celestial presence of God* (*see* Hebrews 6:19-20). *Christ is the forerunner and High Priest for all those willing to follow Him up the holy mountain of the Lord through His Holy Order.*

The man-made temple became an architectural expression of the natural or mountain temple.[4] Its construction of natural materials; its separation from the world as sacred space representing holiness and the presence of the Lord; its beauty, peace, and order as representation of the creation of cosmos out of chaos; its orientation as a climb to a higher order and celestial state—all these represent an extension of the natural mountain temple.

As a mountain is a vertical elevation on the horizon, so also is *the man-made temple, elevating one's thoughts and actions toward God.* Even within the temple, the altar is a vertical elevation on the horizon, where our covenants and sacrifices are made with God.

The mountain of the house of the Lord, *Mount Moriah,* is like a natural altar, where sacrifices and offerings to the Lord have been made for centuries. True to the Mosaic Law, on the northern end of this natural altar, the greatest sacrifice of all and for all, the crucifixion of our Lord and Savior, occurred in the meridian of time, thus lifting our thoughts and devotion to Christ.

The Concept of a Holy Nation—Then and Now

The temple was the center of many ancient Near Eastern civilizations where kings were crowned, laws codified, civil and religious authority established, and God revealed to man. John Lundquist has shown that a temple was the central organizing, unifying institution of ancient Near Eastern nations.[5] The reality that *a nation could come out of a temple experience* was given to Moses and the children of Israel in the Sinai:

> Now therefore, if ye will obey my voice indeed, and keep my covenant, then ye shall be a peculiar treasure unto me above all people: . . .
> And *ye shall be unto me a kingdom of priests, and an holy nation.*
> (Exodus 19:5-6)

The king of this holy nation was to be Jehovah. This holy nation could only function as a kingdom of righteous priests and priestesses because only they would have access to the presence of their holy king, in His holy temple. However, the formation of a holy nation did not occur in the Sinai because of the "provocation" (*see* D&C 84:23-25). A Mosaic holy nation, a level below the intended holy nation of the Lord, yet above secular government, was the result.

The nation-state of Israel did not really solidify until a mortal king was chosen and a central temple constructed. This occurred when Saul became king and Solomon's temple was constructed. Until these events, the "state" of Israel did not exist: "In those days there was no king in Israel, but every man did that which was right in his own eyes" (Judges 17:6).

However, the Israelites desired a mortal king in order to become like other nations instead of a holy nation:

> Nevertheless the people refused to obey the voice of Samuel; and they said, Nay; but we will have a king over us;
> That we also may be like all the nations; and that our king may judge us, and go out before us, and fight our battles.
> (1 Samuel 8:19-20)

The choice of a mortal king over Jehovah was a sign of rejection to the Lord, similar to the rejection of the fullness of the Lord in the Sinai: "And the Lord said unto Samuel, Hearken unto the voice of the people in all that they say unto thee: for they have not rejected thee, but they have rejected me, that I should not reign over them" (1 Samuel 8:7).

The dedicatory prayer of Solomon's temple emphasized the central role of the temple in establishing a nation-state (*see* 1 Kings 8:22-54). If the temple in ancient Near Eastern society was the very venue of universal order establishing conditions under which civil law was possible, our concept of separation of church and state would have been quite foreign to these civilizations. Yet we need to remember that the founding fathers of the United States stood on higher laws than the laws of men when they declared, "We hold these truths to be self evident." *In our zeal to protect religious freedom, have we cut the umbilical cord to the greatest lawgiver of all? (see D&C 38:22).* The best we can say about the nations of the world today is that they represent the precepts of men mingled with the laws of heaven to a greater or lesser degree. The idea of the higher laws of the cosmos revealed through the temple to guide our societies in both religious and civil needs is appealing if, in fact, "in God we trust."

Is a "holy nation" possible? The scriptures answer this question with an emphatic "yes," illustrating with examples of holy nations in past dispensations and prophecies of Zion, the New Jerusalem, the holy nation of the dispensation of the fullness of times, and the millennial dispensation. The King of this holy nation will be Jehovah (*see* D&C 38:21), and the place from which He will reign will be the temple. As in past dispensations, this is where those who seek Him will find Him, for the Lord whom we seek will "suddenly come to his temple" (*see* Malachi 3:1-2, D&C 36:8).

God: The "Primordial Source" of Temple Worship in All Civilizations

True temple worship in its purity was revealed to Adam and Eve. Joseph Smith taught that this truth was perverted and adapted to the worldly desires and cultures of man in every dispensation until true messengers from God returned some believing listeners to true temple worship:

> It is reasonable to suppose that man departed from the first teachings, or instructions which he received from heaven in the first age, and refused by his disobedience to be governed by them. But that man was not able himself to erect a system or plan with power sufficient to free him from a destruction which awaited him is evident from the fact that

God . . . prepared a sacrifice in the gift of *His own Son who should be sent in due time, to prepare the way, or open the door through which man might enter into the Lord's presence, whence he had been cast out for disobedience. From time to time these glad tidings were sounded in the ears of men in different ages of the world.*[6]

In spite of the cultural and religious differences in ancient societies, the similarities in temple worship speak for a primordial source. This source is clearly revealed in the establishment of temple worship in ancient Egypt, which was established after "the government of Ham, which was patriarchal" but without "the right of the Priesthood" (*see* Abraham 1:25-27).

The source of this Holy Order and Priesthood received by the patriarchs was God Himself (*see* Moses 5:58-59). This was also the source of Noah's ordination to this Holy Order (*see* Moses 8:19). As Joseph Smith learned, *the form of godliness without the power (the priesthood) is desecration in the eyes of God* (*see* JSH 1:19). This is why the Lord had to "proceed to do a marvellous work . . . and a wonder" (Isaiah 29:13-14) in restoring the gospel and its holy order in our dispensation.

The Holy Order of God, with its holy ordinances practiced in righteousness under the direction of the King of Righteousness and those appointed by Him, is what makes a nation a holy nation and a temple a holy temple (*see* D&C 84:19-21). This is why the doors of the temple are shut when the Lord and His true messengers are rejected (*see* Acts 21:30).

The remnants of past civilizations reveal a connection to God and the cosmos that is little understood in modern times. The loss of the temple truly left a gaping hole for the lands of the Near East and its cultures of today. For me, the inescapable comparison after this revealing travel through the Near East was between the central role the temple played in this land and the esoteric annex the temple was in my personal religious life. Once again I faced the same question: Why wasn't the temple of central importance to me?

After my trip to Israel and the Near East, I marveled at the pervading influence of the temple on this land and its cultures. My overwhelming impression was that the temple and temple worship is a fundamental and primordial necessity for the salvation of man. *The temple is God's gift to man, to remind us of the higher order from which we fell and to teach us how to return to that order.*

I will be forever grateful for the assignment to teach a temple preparation class on the stake level. I now know that this assignment was given to me as the consolidation of my developing temple paradigm. When I was given the assignment, I certainly wasn't an expert on the temple. I had never taught a class about the temple. I still considered it something associated with marriage and genealogy and a place to be visited when one had the time. However, my Holy Land experience had given me a strong desire to make the temple central in my life. Now I had to know all about it because I had to convince others to make it central in their lives.

The Mountain of Holiness

The Image of a Holy Mountain

A dominant theme of the *scriptural temple* is the representation of God's temple as a holy mountain. Mount Sinai was called "the mountain of God" (Exodus 3:1), and the portable Tabernacle built in Moses' day was a horizontal representation of this vertical mountain. In Isaiah we learn that those who are adopted into the House of Israel by keeping covenants with the Lord will be brought to the holy mountain of God through the holy temple of God (*see* Isaiah 56:6-7). *The image of a holy mountain is important in symbolizing our fall and the need to climb back to the elevated level of God. It is in climbing this mountain that our nature changes in preparation to meet God.* As we climb, we gain glimpses of the great view to be seen at the summit.

After Adam and Eve fell from the holy mountain of God, they learned how to climb back to the garden presence of God and even to a greater presence called "eternal life." This climb back was through their Guide and Savior, Jesus Christ. Sacrifice of all worldly distractions and possessions, in strict obedience to the commandments, covenants, and ordinances of the Holy Order of the Son of God, was the technique or "pattern" taught to them:

> And Adam and Eve, his wife, called upon the name of the Lord, and they heard the voice of the Lord from the way toward the Garden of Eden, speaking unto them, and they saw him not; for they were shut out from his presence.
>
> And he gave unto them commandments, that they should worship the Lord their God, and should offer the firstlings of their flocks, for an offering unto the Lord. And Adam was obedient unto the commandments of the Lord.

Once Adam demonstrated obedience to the Lord, he received a heavenly gift in the form of a heavenly messenger with more instructions about the climb back to the presence of God. From this messenger, Adam learned that the only way "all mankind" could return to God's presence would be through the grace of the sacrifice of the Son of God, "even as many as will" repent and remain obedient to the truths of His holy order:

> And after many days an angel of the Lord appeared unto Adam saying: *Why dost thou offer sacrifices unto the Lord?* And Adam said unto him: I know not, save the Lord commanded me.
>
> And then the angel spake, saying: *This thing is a similitude of the sacrifice of the Only Begotten of the Father, which is full of grace and truth.*
>
> *Wherefore, thou shalt do all that thou doest in the name of the Son, and thou shalt repent and call upon God in the name of the Son forevermore.*
>
> . . . I am the Only Begotten of the Father from the beginning, henceforth and forever, that as thou hast fallen *thou mayest be redeemed, and all mankind, even as many as will.*
>
> And Eve, his wife, heard all these things and was glad, saying: *Were it not for our transgression we never should have had seed, and never should have known good and evil, and the joy of our redemption, and the eternal life which God giveth unto all the obedient.* (Moses 5:6-9, 11)

The reason that Adam then "blessed God" (Moses 5:10) was because of his joy in receiving the Gospel, from the beginning of his mortal existence, which provided the way back to the presence of God. Adam began to return to God through "an holy ordinance": the first four principles of the Gospel (*see* Moses 5:8-9; 6:50-52, 64-66), then the higher, "temple" ordinances of the fullness of the Order of the Son of God. And thus may all become one in God, His sons and daughters (*see* Moses 6:68-69).

> And thus the Gospel began to be preached, from the beginning, being declared by holy angels sent forth from the presence of God, and by his own voice, and by the gift of the Holy Ghost.
>
> And thus *all things were confirmed unto Adam, by an holy ordinance,* and the Gospel preached, and a decree sent forth, that it should

be in the world, until the end thereof; and thus it was. Amen. (Moses 5:58-59)

The Tower of Babel: An Apostate Temple

The story of an apostate temple, the Tower of Babel, opens to us one of the great temple events in all of scripture. In this amazing scriptural story the true and false paths to the presence of God are closely contrasted. This contrast teaches us a fundamental gospel truth: that *anything built or done under the name of man or his precepts will never reach God. Only those who follow the plan of redemption in the name of the Son will reach heaven* (*see* Alma 12:34-35).

Nimrod, the great-grandson of Noah, esteemed himself more powerful than God and influenced his followers to build a tower to reach heaven. The tower Babel, which means "gate of God," was a man-made counterfeit of a true temple, built in rebellious mocking of God.[1] The comparison of this temple with the one seen by Jacob also reveals a striking contrast (*see* Genesis 28:17).

Jared and his family rejected the apostasy of those building the Tower of Babel and sought to maintain a oneness with the true God. This Jaredite community was led away to a promised land by God himself, such as he led Lehi's family and Moses with the children of Israel.

When the Jaredites came to Moriancumer, near the sea that separated them from the land of promise, the brother of Jared inquired of the Lord about the problem of air and light in crossing the sea. *The answer to the question of light occurred on a temple mountain, a mountain of holiness, where the brother of Jared demonstrated a fullness of faith that became a perfect knowledge when he saw and knew with "eyes of understanding" beyond his "eyes of faith:"*

> And it came to pass that the brother of Jared, . . . went forth unto the mount, which they called the *mount Shelem,* because of its exceeding height, and did molten out of a rock sixteen small stones; and they were white and clear, even as transparent glass; and *he did carry them in his hands upon the top of the mount, and cried again unto the Lord,* saying:
>
> O Lord, thou hast said that we must be encompassed about by the floods . . . for we know that thou art holy and dwellest in the heavens, and that we are unworthy before thee; because of the fall our natures have become evil continually; nevertheless, *O Lord, thou hast given us*

a commandment that we must call upon thee, that from thee we may receive according to our desires.

. . . I know, O Lord, that thou hast all power, and can do whatsoever thou wilt for the benefit of man; therefore touch these stones, O Lord, with thy finger, and prepare them that they may shine forth in darkness. (Ether 3:2, 4)

Because of the faith of the brother of Jared he literally received the promised blessing of Adam (*see* Moses 5:10). To be brought back into the presence of the Lord is the great and last promise of the temple. Similar to Adam, the brother of Jared learned that becoming a spiritually begotten son or daughter of Christ is necessary in becoming an exalted son or daughter of God the Father:

The Lord stretched forth his hand and touched the stones one by one with his finger. And *the veil was taken from off the eyes of the brother of Jared,* and he saw the finger of the Lord; and it was as the finger of a man, like unto flesh and blood; . . .

And the Lord said unto him: Because of thy faith thou hast seen that I shall take upon me flesh and blood; and never has man come before me with such exceeding faith as thou hast; for were it not so ye could not have seen my finger. Sawest thou more than this?

And he answered: Nay; Lord, *show thyself unto me. . . .*

And when he had said these words, behold, the Lord showed himself unto him, and said: *Because thou knowest these things ye are redeemed from the fall; therefore ye are brought back into my presence; therefore I show myself unto you.*

Behold, I am he who was prepared from the foundation of the world to redeem my people. Behold, I am Jesus Christ. I am the Father and the Son. *In me shall all mankind have life, and that eternally, even they who shall believe on my name; and they shall become my sons and my daughters.* (Ether 3:6, 9-10, 13-14)

Moroni recalled the account of the brother of Jared and encouraged the Gentiles and the House of Israel to be like the brother of Jared in rending the veil of unbelief and calling upon the Father in the name of Christ with a broken heart and a contrite spirit. Then God will remember His covenant and reveal "great things" which have been laid up from the foundation of the world (*see* Ether 4:4, 13-15).

With the teachings of the Fall and the covering veil of this life, and with the need for faith in the Lord Jesus Christ through a change in heart and covenants with Him, this marvelous mountain temple endowment of the brother of Jared again defined the way back to the presence of the Lord. Like Adam, the brother of Jared described the steps of the ascension:

- rejecting apostasy and following true messengers of God,
- having enough faith in Christ to sacrifice all worldliness in strict obedience to His covenants, and
- rending the veil of disbelief by a change of heart, from unbelief to exceeding faith, in order to receive the Second Comforter.

The brother of Jared received the gift of the patriarchs or *the Second Comforter, the great and last promise of the temple. This gift is the face-to-face ministry of the Savior, with one's calling and election made sure. With this gift, we are assured a full knowledge of the Lord and His realm of existence called eternal life.*

Eden's Temple: The Holy Mountain of God

It is notable that the scriptural account of man on this earth began in a temple setting. The presence of the Lord in the Garden of Eden, *a place of beauty, cleanliness, and innocence, defines a temple setting.*

One might wonder how Satan could be present in such a place. *The agency of man was introduced in the Garden of Eden as it is in all temple settings. Therefore we must confront Satan's temptations and make choices using our own free will in order to learn how to abide the presence of the Lord.* However, as we learn in the temple, God has the power to cast Satan out of our lives. Conversely, the choice to follow Satan's temptations removes us from the presence of the Lord, as Adam and Eve discovered.

The tabernacle of Moses and the temples of Solomon and Herod alluded to the Eden temple, with such symbols as eastward orientation, cherubim on the curtain divisions protecting the holy places, the menorah representing the tree of life, and water flowing from the temple like the river flowed out of Eden.

The pervading idea in these temples was that *a return to the Garden of Eden is a return to the presence of the Lord.* Likewise, one could say that leaving the celestial room in today's temples, and exiting the temple, is like leaving the presence of the Lord and going to the lone and dreary world. *Significantly we learn in the endowment that the Savior led Adam and Eve, and thus their posterity, into the Garden of Eden.*

The Savior leads us in the temple, and therefore to the presence of the Father.

The Eden temple was probably an elevated or mountain dwelling. The river of Eden flowed outward (downward), becoming four rivers that proceeded to the four corners of the earth.[2] The *fall* of man can easily be visualized as falling from an elevated or mountain height. Ezekiel made reference to the Garden of Eden as *"the holy mountain of God"* in his warnings to the King of Tyre, who became a fallen Adam when iniquity was found in him (*see* Ezekiel 28:13-15).

The Temples of Adam-Ondi-Ahman

Three years before Adam died, he gathered his righteous posterity in the valley of Adam-ondi-Ahman, which most likely means "Adam in the presence of God."[3]

Joseph Smith had a vision of this gathering. He said, "I saw Adam in the valley of Adam-ondi-Ahman. He called together his children and blessed them with a patriarchal blessing. *The Lord appeared in their midst. . . . This is why Adam blessed his posterity; he wanted to bring them into the Presence of God.*[4] D&C 107 gives us additional detail about this family gathering when "the Lord appeared unto them" (*see* verses 53-56).

This gathering, precursor to a future assembly at Adam-ondi-Ahman in fulfillment of the events told by the Prophet Daniel (*see* Daniel 7:9-22; also D&C 116:1), is a temple gathering because of the presence of the Lord.

It is interesting that the altar built by Adam to call on God and to offer sacrifice, as implied in Moses 5:4-6, was probably built on a hill described as the "mountains of Adam-ondi-Ahman," overlooking Adam-ondi-Ahman, "the land of my people even Zion" (*see* D&C 117:8-9).

Joseph Smith identified the remains of this altar, which still existed in his day.[5] The altar of Adam and the temple site, marked by the Saints in 1831, lie in the center of a future city near Adam-ondi-Ahman.[6] This city is the land of the Lord's people, even Zion, the New Jerusalem. Thus *the temple site at the beginning of man on this earth (the Garden of Eden) will become the temple site at the beginning of the earth's millennial existence (the New Jerusalem). The city of the New Jerusalem will be the new Mount Zion (see D&C 84:2),* and therefore the Holy Mountain of God that Adam knew as the Garden of Eden. Brigham

Young declared this truth when he said, *"Right where the Prophet Joseph laid the foundation of the Temple was where God commenced the Garden of Eden, and there he will end or consummate his work."*[7]

Literally, worthy Saints from past and present will be gathered in the presence of the Lord in the Garden of Eden of the New Jerusalem (*see* D&C 133:56). This gathering will start at the temple (*see* D&C 84:4, 32), suggesting that *in preparation for this gathering we must climb, through the temple endowment, the spiritual Mount Zion.*

Men to Match His Mountains

One of my favorite books is Irving Stone's *Men to Match My Mountains*. I even have an autographed copy of this book, dated May 8, 1961. It is a captivating book, written in the grand Irving Stone style, about the courageous men and women who explored and settled the mountains and plains of the West. It's about men such as John Fremont, Jim Bridger, and others, who met the challenge of the mountains.

While reading their stories, I could envision myself with them because I live in the land they explored. My orientation is with mountains, and my horizon is defined as the next range of mountains. When I lived in Michigan, I missed the defined mountain horizons of the West. In this flat land of the Great Lakes, visual horizons fade to a vanishing point. Orientation is not by mountain ranges but rather by shopping centers.

On the title page of this book is a quatrain from Samuel Foss's poem "The Coming American":

> *Bring me men to match my mountains,*
> *Bring me men to match my plains,*
> *Men with empires in their purpose*
> *And new eras in their brains.*[8]

In the temple paradigm, the men who match the mountains are the men and women worthy to stand in the Lord's presence on His mountain or in His temple. Men who match the plains are those obedient servants who are true messengers of the Lord, acting as "savor" and "saviors" in the plains of humanity.

These men and women have great views ("empires") in their purpose, and anticipation of a new celestial order ("new era"), because they understand the magnificent promises in store for those who are obedient to the Lord (*see* 1 Corinthians 2:9). They, like the patriarchs and prophets of old, would sacrifice anything to follow the straight and narrow path to the presence of the Lord. With this sacrifice, they obediently seek the path and make the climb of Mount Zion to the summit of the mountain of the Lord, thus becoming men and women who match His mountain.

Men Who Matched His Exceedingly High Mountains

On the mountain top one is nearer to God, and the veil between man and God, like the air, is thinner. *It is God who calls man to the mountain, symbolic of the requirement that man elevate himself to the level of God as best he can before God descends to the level of man.* Perhaps the scriptural term "exceedingly high mountain" does not mean elevation from sea level as much as it does spiritual height of the realm of God or the place of encounter as a holy place. It is our faith in Christ and our righteousness through His Holy Order that takes us to the summit of an "exceedingly high mountain." *The presence of God makes a mountain an "exceedingly high mountain."*

Joseph Smith once said, *"The rich can only get [blessings] in the temple—the poor may get them on the mountain top as did Moses."*[9]

The rich are those blessed by the Lord with the means and money to construct a temple mountain wherever they gather and are instructed by the Lord to build a temple. Often they were not rich in material possessions, but by collective sacrifice *they produced a richness in sacrifice acceptable to the Lord.* "The poor," who certainly were rich in spirit, have left us inspiring accounts of "exceedingly high mountains" or sacred-place encounters with the Lord.

After **Adam** and **Eve** fell from the holy mountain of God, they learned how to climb back to the garden presence of God, and even beyond, to a greater presence called "eternal life."

Following Adam's example, other great patriarchs and prophets had temple experiences and endowments on mountain tops or secluded sacred places as they returned to the presence of the Lord. **Enoch,** who had known Father Adam (*see* D&C 107:53), testified about Adam and the Plan of Salvation and then opened a window to his temple experience on Mount Simeon:

> As I was journeying, and stood upon the place Mahujah, and cried unto the Lord, there come a voice out of heaven, saying—Turn ye, and get ye upon the *mount Simeon.*

And it came to pass that *I turned and went up on the mount; and as I stood upon the mount, I beheld the heavens open, and I was clothed upon with glory;*

And I saw the Lord; and he stood before my face, and he talked with me, even as a man talketh one with another, face to face; and he said unto me: Look, and I will show unto thee the world for the space of many generations. (Moses 7:2-4)

Moses on Mount Sinai is the dramatic and classic example of the ascension of the mountain of the Lord:

Now Moses kept the flock of Jethro his father in law, the priest of Midian: and he led the flock to the backside of the desert, and came to the *mountain of God*, even to Horeb. . . .

And he said; Certainly I will be with thee; and this shall be a token unto thee, that I have sent thee: When thou hast brought forth the people out of Egypt, *ye shall serve God upon this mountain.* (Exodus 3:1, 12)

The words of God, which he spake unto Moses at a time when Moses was caught up into an exceedingly high mountain,

And *he saw God face to face, and he talked with him, and the glory of God was upon Moses; therefore Moses could endure his presence.* (Moses 1:1-2)

Similarly, the Prophet **Nephi** was carried away to a high mountain where he had a great vision:

For it came to pass after I had desired to know the things that my father had seen, and *believing* that the Lord was able to make them known unto me, as I sat pondering in mine heart I *was caught away in the Spirit of the Lord, yea, into an exceedingly high mountain,* which I never had before seen, and upon which I never had before set my foot. (1 Nephi 11:1)

Ezekiel's vision of a future temple to be built on the mountain of the house of the Lord in Jerusalem occurred on a high mountain: "In the visions of God brought he me into the land of Israel, and set me upon a *very high mountain*, by which was as the frame of a city on the south" (Ezekiel 40:2).

John the Revelator also had a high mountain experience: "And he carried me away in the spirit to *a great and high mountain*, and shewed me that great city, the holy Jerusalem, descending out of heaven from God" (Revelation 21:10).

Isaiah, who had seen the Lord (Isaiah 6:1-10), was vivid in temple mountain imagery:

> And it shall come to pass in the last days, that the *mountain of the Lord's house* shall be established in the top of the mountains, and shall be exalted above the hills; and all nations shall flow unto it.
> And many people shall go and say, Come ye, and let us go up to the *mountain of the Lord*, the *house of the God of Jacob*; and he will teach us of his ways, and we will walk in his paths: for out of Zion shall go forth the law, and the word of the Lord from Jerusalem. (Isaiah 2:2-3)

> Even them will I bring to *my holy mountain*, and make them joyful in my *house of prayer:* their burnt offerings and their sacrifices shall be accepted upon *mine altar;* for mine house shall be called an house of prayer for all people. (Isaiah 56:7)

> But he that putteth his trust in me shall possess the land, and shall *inherit my holy mountain.* (Isaiah 57:13)

During His mortal ministry the **Savior** returned to the mountains for solitude, prayer, and holy mountain temple events:

> And when he had sent the multitudes away, *he went up into a mountain apart to pray:* and when the evening was come, he was there alone. (Matthew 14:23)

> And after six days Jesus taketh **Peter, James,** and **John** his brother and bringeth them up into an *high mountain apart,*
> And was transfigured before them. (Matthew 17:1-2)

Does the Lord call us to match His mountain today? If so, how can we have these sacred mountaintop experiences? Consider these callings of old and liken them to us, for truly the modern-day temple of the Lord is the holy mountain of the Lord.

While warning Lot, who lived in Sodom, angels urged him to "Escape for thy life; look not behind thee, neither stay thou in all the plain; *escape to the mountain,* lest thou be consumed" (Genesis 19:17).

Having arrived in the Arabian Bountiful, *Nephi* received instruction on a mountain to build a ship to carry his people to the promised land: "And it came to pass that after I, Nephi, had been in the land of Bountiful for the space of many days, the voice of the Lord came unto me saying: Arise, and *get thee into the mountain.* And it came to pass that I arose and went up into the mountain, and cried unto the Lord" (1 Nephi 17:7).

A few verses later, Nephi notes that he "did *go into the mount oft,* and I did pray oft unto the Lord; wherefore the Lord showed unto me great things" (1 Nephi 18:3).

The admonitions to "escape to the mountain" and "arise, and get thee into the mountain" are equivalent to "escape to the temple" and "arise and get thee into the temple." This was the commandment of the Lord to our patriarch fathers and saints of old. They were men and women of faith who could match His "exceedingly high" mountains.

The Lord is making the same call to us, both through His living prophets and His prophets of old, whose admonition centuries ago is still valid today: "*O Zion, that bringest good tidings, get thee up into the high mountain*" (Isaiah 40:9).

Are we of such faith to hear and obey the command to "arise, and get thee into the temple"? *This is what Moroni's trumpet is sounding: "Come unto Christ, Arise and get thee into the temple."* Do we hear Moroni's call?

Do we have enough faith in Christ to leave the precepts of men and follow a more excellent way through the Holy Order of God in the temple? If so, *we may be partakers of the gift which is a knowledge of God and the "rest" of the Savior (see* Ether 12:9-11). Joseph Smith taught this more excellent way:

> How do men obtain a knowledge of the glory of God, his perfections and attributes? *By devoting themselves to his service, through prayer and supplication incessantly strengthening their faith in him,* until like Enoch, the brother of Jared and Moses, *they obtain a manifestation of God to themselves.*[10]

Are we so desirous to know "great things" that we will cry and pray unto the Lord in His temple and go often as did Nephi? Are we men and women to match His holy, exceedingly high mountain?

> *Who shall ascend into the hill of the Lord?* or *who shall stand in his holy place?*
> He that hath clean hands, and a pure heart; who hath not lifted up his soul unto vanity, nor sworn deceitfully.
> *He shall receive the blessing from the Lord, and righteousness* from the God of his salvation.

This is the generation of them that seek him, that seek thy face O Jacob. (Psalm 24:3-6)

Mount Zion: The Cosmic Mountain

A central idea in most Near Eastern philosophies is the primordial mound or hillock as the *first solid ground to emerge from the chaotic waters of creation.* This can be vividly imagined in the Hebrew designation of Mount Moriah as the primordial hillock, the most holy ground in all the earth. It is the center of the earth to which is attached the umbilical (*omphalos*) from heaven which sustains the earth.[11] The concept of a cosmic Mount Zion, a holy mount from which the Lord reigns (*see* Isaiah 24:23) and from which His knowledge and laws of the cosmos are revealed to man, centered on the concept of a primordial hillock[12] and "omphalos."

The Old Testament temples were architectural representations of the cosmic mountain experience in the Sinai. *Moses on Mount Sinai in the presence of the Lord is the classic cosmic experience. It is the pivotal event of the exodus of the children of Israel,* one of the most often-referenced episodes in all of scripture.

Climbing the Spiritual Mountain Is Embodied in Physical Temples

The cosmic mountain before us today—as at the time of Paul—is not a physical mountain like Mount Sinai, which our fathers in the desert refused to ascend. It is not the physical Mount Zion of Jerusalem which our fathers ascended to worship in the house of the Lord. Rather, *it is a spiritual mountain embodied in our physical temples. It is what Paul called Mount Zion,* and the view at the summit is worth the climb.

> *Ye are come unto Mount Zion, and unto the city of the living God, the heavenly Jerusalem, and to an innumerable company of angels,*
> *To the general assembly and church of the Firstborn, . . .* and to God the Judge of all, and to the spirits of just men made perfect,
> And to Jesus the mediator of the new covenant. (Hebrews 12:22-24)

Joseph Smith explained the process of climbing Mount Zion, observing that "*Men have to suffer that they may come upon Mount Zion and be exalted above the heavens.*"[13]

Suffering is synonymous with sacrifice in the context of obedience. The sacrifices acceptable to the Lord are those made in obedience to His commandments and covenants. *Suffering on our part is the internal struggle to change our nature to one of pure righteousness through obedience, until we learn to emulate the Savior, who suffered all to be obedient to His Father (see* Hebrews 5:8). This *obedience* may require externally imposed suffering and sacrifice. As Christ's suffering and sacrifice were for the benefit of others, so should ours become.

The spiritual Mount Zion is the holy mountain of the Lord before us today. It is the mountain whose summit is Zion, the heavenly kingdom of God (see D&C 105:32). We learn how to climb Mount Zion through the temple endowment at the temple altar by sacrifice. We must climb the spiritual Mount Zion of the temple to see and be part of the great view of eternal life.

4

Ascending the Mountain of Holiness

The Small and Large Steps of Spiritual Growth

A memorable event in my tour of Old Jerusalem was a visit to the Temple Mount. Much of the recent excavation has occurred along the Western Wall and the southwestern corner of the Mount. The remainder of Robinson's Arch and the stairs to the southern gates of Herod's temple have been excavated. These gates obviously were a principal entrance to the temple, requiring the worshippers to ascend as they approached the courts of the temple.

In this ascent, they climbed what are known as the Ophel steps, which in Hebrew means "ascend." The Ophel steps are unusual in that they do not accommodate quick ascent. This is because the steps have alternating deep and shallow cuts. One cannot simply run up these steps. This type of stair may have been for crowd control, but I favor the explanation of our tour guide, Wayne Brickey. As I sat on these stairs in the late afternoon, with long and short shadows cast obliquely across them, this is what I recorded in my diary based on his comments:

> *These stairs symbolize the need for a steady slow pace in our spiritual progress.* Spiritual things are cut out of rock. In Psalm 122, we read *one of the psalms of ascent, recited as worshippers climbed the stairs,* symbolizing the progressive climb in their journey to become like God:
>
> I was glad when they said unto me,
> Let us go into the house of the Lord.
> Our feet shall stand within thy gates, O Jerusalem.

Whither the tribes go up, the tribes of the Lord, unto the testimony of Israel, to give thanks unto the name of the Lord.

Pray for the peace of Jerusalem: they shall prosper that love thee.

Because of the house of the Lord our God I will seek thy good. (Psalms 122:1-2, 4, 6, 9)

"A prevalent theme of the writings of Isaiah," my diary continues, "is that our life should continually integrate great and small steps of repentance as we ever refine ourselves to become like God." *It is not good intentions that make us Godlike, but rather climbing the steps of repentance to the house of the Lord where the powers of righteousness are released by the ordinances and covenants of the temple.* The foundation of these ordinances and covenants is unselfishness and service to others, with a true love of God and man. In other words, righteousness and holiness are closely connected to unselfishness in one's love of both God and man. This is especially true in marriage.

The Admission Requirement: A Defined Level of Spiritual Maturity and Obedience

As I climbed the ramp and entered the temple courtyard, I remember being overcome with a feeling of reverence and peace, even though I saw no temple and was surrounded by Moslem shrines protected by somber Arab guards. The aged, noble trees, with sacred memory etched in their bark, were the reverent sentinels. I was standing on the ancient court of the Gentiles, where Jesus had taught and healed and cast out the irreverent.

Looking to where Herod's temple probably stood, I had to look up. It was on an elevated plane above the court of the Gentiles. I pictured the Balustrade or Soreg with its strict warning in Greek and Latin: "No Gentile shall enter inward of the partition and barrier surrounding the Temple, and whosoever is caught shall be responsible to himself for his subsequent death."

This four-to-five-foot stone wall was a physical barrier between the court of the Gentiles and the courts of the inner temple. It was symbolic of the barrier the Lord created around the holy mount in the Sinai (*see* Exodus 19:12). I thought of the many Gentile visitors wondering why they were kept out of the inner temple in Jerusalem, and then recalled the barriers confronted by the many visitors to Salt Lake City's Temple Square who ask, "Why can't I go inside the temple?"

A defined level of spiritual maturity and obedience is the requirement for admission to the higher realms of the mountain of the House of the Lord. We must ascend to God's defined level of worthiness and readiness before He will descend to our level. The temple recommend is the defined level today.

Baptism is the gate through which we must pass before we begin to climb the steps to the defined level of the temple. It is interesting that at the foot of the Ophel steps there are excavated houses of ablutions (washings). Of course, in the Melchizedek Priesthood temples of today, "Jew and Gentile alike" are welcome if they will meet the standard required for admission. "Thus we see that the gate of heaven [baptism through the temple] is open unto all, even to those who will believe on the name of Jesus Christ" (Helaman 3:28).

If we could look at an aerial drawing of the temple mount at the time of the Savior's earthly ministry, the image of ascending levels would be evident from street level, up the Ophel steps, into the court of the Gentiles, to the Holy of Holies. A description of these ascending levels is found in the book *Jerusalem, the Eternal City:*

> Overall, *the Temple area consisted of a series of rising platforms.* From the Court of the Gentiles one ascended stairs to the Court of the Women; from there, one ascended fifteen curved stairs (possibly singing fifteen Psalms of Ascent; *see* Psalms 120-134) to the Court of the Men of Israel and the Court of the Priests; and a final ascent was required to enter the Holy Place itself. Thus the phrase 'Jesus went up into the temple' (John 7:14) is literal. *The three courtyards surrounding the holiest place where the Divine Presence could be manifest may appropriately be compared to three degrees of glory and three settings for instruction in modern Temples: telestial, terrestrial, and celestial.* It is not enough to progress into the third courtyard or heaven; it is incumbent upon each worshipper, now that the Great High Priest has made it possible, for all to actually enter into the highest degree of that realm, to symbolically enter into the Presence of God and be exalted.[1]

Pressing Forward with a Steadfastness in Christ

When we enter the temple, we must press forward with a steadfastness in Christ having, as Paul said, "a full assurance of hope" (Hebrews 6:11), or "a perfect brightness of hope," as Nephi said, until we pass the final gate and enter the Holy of Holies, standing in the presence of the Father:

And then are ye in this strait and narrow path which leads to eternal life; yea, ye have entered in by the gate [baptism]; . . .

And now, my beloved brethren, after ye have gotten into this strait and narrow path, I would ask if all is done? Behold, I say unto you, Nay; for *ye have not come thus far save it were by the word of Christ with unshaken faith in him, relying wholly upon the merits of him who is mighty to save.*

Wherefore, *ye must press forward with a steadfastness in Christ,* having a perfect brightness of hope, and a love of God and of all men. Wherefore, if ye shall *press forward, feasting upon the word of Christ, and endure to the end,* behold, thus saith the Father: ye shall have eternal life. (2 Nephi 31:18-20)

This scriptural statement written by Nephi beautifully describes the climb to the highest level of the temple, which represents eternal life.

The Jerusalem Temple Falls, But the Concept of Ascending to the Temple Remains

Many writings, which draw a variety of conclusions, try to explain the destruction of the house of the Lord in Jerusalem and the expulsion of the Jews in A.D. 70 and again in A.D. 135. The fall of this people and their temple, as in all of the "falls" of man from the presence of God, can be due only to the rejection of the Savior through disobedience to His laws.

What did the Jewish faithful do when they no longer had the temple? This loss definitely left a hole in their manner of religious worship. *The practice of the law of Moses was centered in the temple as the way to ascend to the Lord.*

The Pharisaic leaders, such as Rabbi Zakkai and Gamaliel II, established a Jewish religious and governmental center at Jabneh.[2] They developed a modified Mosaic law through the techniques of the *Mishnah* and *Midrash,* which excluded temple worship but *anticipated the return of the temple and a religious Jerusalem.*

These exiled rabbis and Jewish sages *created a New Jerusalem in their minds based on their remembrance of the destroyed Jerusalem temple.* The rituals of this remembrance have been passed on from generation to generation. An example of such a ritual is the well-known breaking of a glass under foot at a Jewish wedding.[3]

For the Orthodox Christians, the temple destruction was the fulfillment of Christ's prophecy (*see* Matthew 24:1-2). They reason that Christ and the Atonement eliminated the need for the Mosaic temple.

The Ascent from an Aaronic Priesthood Temple to a Melchizedek Priesthood Temple in Jerusalem

Evangelical creeds today speak of a spiritual temple, a temple without walls, defined as a collective body of true believers. "It is this community of true believers from various denominations who are a 'spiritual temple' that replaced the temple building of the Old Testament," wrote Luke P. Wilson.[4]

Unfortunately, these creeds show no understanding of nor need for physical temple worship. They misinterpret Paul's writings about the individual human body, a unified group of believing Saints, and a physical place with covenants and ordinances as being necessary temple concepts, but not being mutually exclusive. They fail to recognize that Paul and the other apostles continued to worship at the Jerusalem temple long after the Savior's ascension. These apostles gave us scriptural hints that they made the transformation from an Aaronic Priesthood temple to a Melchizedek Priesthood temple, which truly led them to the presence of the Lord. For instance, the Epistle to the Hebrews says,

> If therefore perfection were by the Levitical priesthood, (for under it the people received the law,) *what further need was there that another priest should rise after the order of Melchisedec, and not be called after the order of Aaron?*
>
> For *the priesthood being changed,* there is made of necessity a change also of the law. . . .
>
> And it is yet far more evident: for that *after the similitude of Melchisedec there ariseth another priest,*
>
> *Who is made,* not after the law of a carnal commandment, but *after the power of an endless life.* (Hebrews 7:11-12, 15-16)

Before his ascension, Jesus had promised his disciples, "I send the promise of my Father upon you: but tarry ye in the city of Jerusalem, until ye be *endued with power from on high*" (Luke 24:49).

The events in the upper room at Pentecost and the 40-day ministry of the Savior after His resurrection give us further insight of this ascent to the covenants, ordinances, and endowments of an "endless life."

The Ancient Concept of the Celestial Ascent

Some Jewish scholars reasoned that if they could not worship God on the mountain of the house of the Lord in Jerusalem, then they would ascend to Him in their minds. This concept evolved into an even more physical transformation to the celestial temple of God. The personal ascension to God in His celestial temple certainly had scriptural foundation, as seen in the verses concerning the ascensions of Enoch, Moses, Isaiah, Ezekiel, John the Revelator, and even the Savior.

The idea of personal ascension to the presence of God is known in Jewish theological literature as *Merkavah* (chariot), *Hekhalot* (temple palace) and *Be-reshit* (creation) mysticism.[5] These Jewish ascension themes became more mystical in the Jewish creed called *Kabalism.* This creed developed mainly in medieval Spain.[6] Safed, the geographically highest city in Israel, located at the northwestern end of the Sea of Galilee, became the center of this Jewish mysticism.[7]

Along with the social importance of the temple, *the concept of celestial ascent is one of the most persisting and prevalent religious concepts in history.*[8] Writing about ascension texts, William Hamblin said:

> *The parallels between Jewish, early Christian, Hellenistic Gnostic, and Egyptian ascension texts and rituals are too numerous and exact to be explained by random chance. . . .*
>
> It is remarkable that nearly all of these *visionary ascents to the celestial temple*—whether from Jewish, pagan, or Christian sources exhibit many parallels, indicating that all of these ideas and documents were somehow conceptually and historically linked together.[9]

One of the more remarkable ascension texts in the Bible is Jacob's staircase vision. Jacob had been given the birthright by his father, Isaac. He was warned by his mother, Rebekah, to flee from Esau and choose a wife from the daughters of her brother Laban, who lived in Haran. While traveling northward from Beer-sheba to Haran, Jacob had a descriptive temple vision (*see* Genesis 28:11-22).

It is interesting to compare this staircase erected by God with the Tower of Babel, which means "gate of God."[10] The staircase experienced by Jacob was "set up on the earth" by God, unlike the Tower of Babel, because "the top of it reached heaven." Truly, the staircase seen by Jacob was the "gate of heaven" because "the Lord stood above it." *The building of an altar, the ordinance of anointing and making covenants with the Lord who stood above it established the place Bethel as "the house of God."*

The free descending of angels established that Jacob's staircase was connected to the celestial realm of God, as true heavenly messengers descend from God. *The ascending of angels implies the possibility of ascent to the presence of God if one becomes angelic.*

Jacob learned that by making a covenant with the Lord ("Jacob vowed a vow") and through the blessings ("I am with thee and will keep thee in all places") of the God of Abraham (Christ), he could become angelic and come again to his father's house in peace (which ultimately meant the house of his Father in Heaven). In this covenant, Jacob promised to be obedient to God ("then shall the Lord be my God") and offer sacrifice acceptable to the Lord in this obedience ("I will surely give the tenth unto thee"). Jacob received the same covenant and blessings that his grandfather, Abraham, had received. Indeed, Jacob received the Abrahamic covenant, which comprises the greatest blessings of the temple.

The teachings of Jacob's vision are the Fall; the path of return to our Father's house through the gate of God, which ultimately is the temple; and the ascent up its staircase by the power and blessings of Christ. We receive these blessing by ascending through the ordinances, covenants, and endowments of the temple. The technique of the ascent is faith in Christ and obedience through sacrifice to His commandments.

These same temple teachings for ascending the mountain of the Lord have been passed down from Adam, who received them from God. Therefore, God is the source and conceptual link of all the celestial ascension themes. The glory of true temple ascension is that we not only climb it ourselves, being helped and led by Christ, but we lead and help our friends and ancestors in their ascent as well. This help did not occur on the Tower of Babel.

Ascending to the Great View

While in high school, I was introduced to the techniques of mountain climbing through my experiences at *Outward Bound* in Colorado and the *National Outdoor Leadership School* in Wyoming. I have had the chance to climb some of the grand mountains of Colorado and Wyoming. Out of concern, many have asked, "Why do you do something so dangerous?"

I didn't answer with George Mallory's famous statement, "Because it is there." Rather, my answer was, "Because of the view,"—*not only the glorious, panoramic view that rewarded me for reaching the summit, but the new view of me within.* I found a totally difference perspective of myself on the summit.

In his great temple sermon, King Benjamin apparently spoke about this concept of views, for his listeners responded to him by saying, *"We, . . . through the infinite goodness of God, and the manifestations of his Spirit, have great views of that which is to come"* (Mosiah 5:3).

King Benjamin defined this great view as an understanding of "the mysteries of God" (Mosiah 2:9), and he even contrasted the "great view" with an "awful view" (Mosiah 3:25).

Since being on the stake high council and having occasion to sit on the stand in sacrament meeting, I have seen a different perspective, and have enjoyed great views of those coming to hear the word of God. It reminds me of my boyhood fascination with a magnet and iron filings, as though there were some kind of polarity with the pulpit affecting the response of the congregation. For example, the concentration of the congregation is often directly proportional to the distance from the pulpit. I know that the distribution of the congregation is similar in most wards and has nothing to do with faith and intent. It has more to do with the location of entry, the tendency to be a spectator in the chapel, or the fear of being on the other side of the pulpit giving a talk.

From his great view on the tower, King Benjamin saw, as I did on the stand, the effect of the power of the word of God on the hearts of those who heard it. The soul overcome by the Spirit shedding tears; the wayward soul finding the miracle of forgiveness; a child radiating the love of God; a servant of God speaking with the power of the Spirit: all these uncover the private corners of the chapel, lifting eyes and hearts in unison to the pulpit as though its polarity were irresistibly drawing all to it. This is a great and glorious view, and it comes by the power of the Spirit when the word of God penetrates the heart.

This *image of the polarity of the pulpit* is symbolic of our understanding of the temple and our relation to it. Like the children of Israel in the Sinai who feared the Holy Mount, some of us distance ourselves from the temple, not understanding its power to change lives. Similarly, we distance ourselves from the pulpit, not understanding how bearing testimony of the gospel from behind it can give us a great view of ourselves. Yet we are drawn to the pulpit as listeners, and thus to God when the power of His word penetrates our hearts. Likewise, God beckons us to draw near and climb His holy mountain.

The temple is a powerful, positive magnet that penetrates and cleanses the negatives in our hearts, propelling us into the presence of God. If our hearts are charged with false-positive pride of the world, we are repelled from the true-positive power of the temple. *As a chapel pulpit and the sacrament table are the focal points of resolve to remove the negatives in our lives, so should the altars of the temple be the focal points of positive spiritual rebirth.* There we will begin to see the great view of that which is to come as the word of God penetrates our hearts.

The Lead Climber and His Rope

When I lived in Durham, North Carolina, I lived in a region called the Piedmont, which translated from French means "foothill." It was pleasant to live there, but nothing like going up to the Smoky Mountains of North Carolina and Tennessee.

In his epistle to the Hebrews, Paul admonished the Jewish Saints to no longer tarry in the foothills of spiritual experience. In essence he said, "get to the mountain of perfection." Paul's words even give the impression of climbing a mountain with a rope:

> Therefore not leaving the principles of the doctrine of Christ, *let us go on unto perfection:* . . .
>
> That ye be not slothful, but followers of them who through faith and patience inherit the promises.
>
> . . . lay hold upon the hope set before us:
>
> *Which hope we have as an anchor of the soul, both sure and steadfast,* and which entereth into that within the veil." (JST Hebrews 6:1, 12, 18, 19)

Picture this hope as a rope that we grasp. This rope, anchored to Christ, is an anchor of the soul. The rope is the Atonement in which we have hope. Where do Christ and His rope lead? They lead—"by a new and living way" (Hebrews 10:20)—to the summit of Mount Zion, to that within the veil. The summit is the presence of God.

Paul's descriptive phrases imply the promises: obtaining a good report, entering into the Lord's rest, going on to perfection, entering into the holiest, being made a high priest forever, knowing the Lord, pleasing God, obtaining a witness of being righteous, and having the law written in the heart.[11] Clearly Paul is talking about the promises obtained during and after the climb to the summit of the temple. The view and realization of these promises is worth the climb.

In climbing, it is important that the rope is securely fixed to the mountain by a nail or piton. I love the image of this piton in Isaiah:

> And *I will fasten him as a nail in a sure place;* and he shall be for a glorious throne to his father's house.
> And *they shall hang upon him* all the glory of his father's house, the offspring and the issue, all vessels of small quantity, from the vessels of cups, even to all the vessels of flagons. (Isaiah 22:23-24)

This Messianic prophecy refers to the Savior as the nail (*see* Zechariah 10:3-4) in a sure place, which is the temple. We all hang on Him, holding fast to His hope, whether we are a small cup or a flagon.

Ezra identified the sure place of escape, confession, and recommitment as the temple because there we have a *"nail in his holy place"* (Ezra 9:8). The image of the nail in this verse refers to the surety of escape from iniquity because of the grace of the Savior.

In mountain climbing, both literally and figuratively, the lead climber is most important because the followers hang their lives on his abilities. Who is the lead, the guide in our ascension of the mountain of the Lord? The Lord tells us with certainty that "I am Messiah, the King of Zion, the Rock of Heaven. . . . Whoso cometh in at the gate and *climbeth up by me* shall never fall" (Moses 7:53).

The Psalms beautifully describe the Savior guiding us ever upward to higher levels, line upon line, precept upon precept, rock upon rock, until we reach the summit: "From the end of the earth will I cry unto thee, when my heart is overwhelmed: *lead me to the rock that is higher than I*" (Psalm 61:2).

It is His words, in laws and covenants, that refresh us and lead us like a light and refresh us on the ascending path of holiness (*see* Psalm 119:103, 105).

As we climb to higher levels of spirituality and are secured by our Guide upon His rock, we can feel safe against the blast of storms:

> That when the devil shall send forth his mighty winds, yea, his shafts in the whirlwind, yea, when all his hail and his mighty storm shall beat upon you, it shall have no power over you to drag you down to the gulf of misery and endless wo, *because of the rock upon which ye are built,*

which is a sure foundation, a foundation whereon if men build they cannot fall. (Helaman 5:12; *see also* D&C 6:34 and Matthew 7:24.)

When we climb to a higher rock and discover our true spiritual nature, and the spirit within us resonates with the words of Christ, *we become a light to those climbing below.* "The spirit of man is the candle of the Lord," explains Proverbs 20:27. As the Savior is drink to our thirsting soul, *so we become drink to those thirsting below,* because "out of [our] belly shall flow rivers of living water" (John 7:37-38) when we speak the spiritual words of truth.

Those thirsting below are also those who are waiting in the world of spirits for us to give them the chance to grasp the rope. As we climb the temple with an ancestor, one by one, the thirst in both of our souls is quenched with the love of the Savior.

What a wonderful image of the ascent the scriptural temple gives us: We are all roped together with hope in our lead climber, Jesus Christ. We all hang on Him, and He is secure in a sure place, the celestial temple of His Father. As He holds the rope for us until we reach a higher and more secure level, then we in turn must belay for those below us until they reach the same secure level. The sure place in which we learn how to belay and elevate others, both living and dead, and how to continue our own climb, is in the temples of the Lord. This is where we should drive our pitons—through covenants with Christ, and hang our hope on him.

The Great View of Ourselves

What if we do wander and fall? Does our Guide let us fall to our death? Ammon, one of the sons of Mosiah, while recalling the fall of himself, his brothers, and Alma the Younger, said they were "snatched" by the Lord while falling into an everlasting gulf of death and misery.

> Who could have supposed that our God would have been so merciful as to have snatched us from our awful, sinful, and polluted state? . . .
> Oh, my soul, almost as it were, fleeth at the thought. Behold, he did not exercise his justice upon us, but in his great mercy hath brought us over that everlasting gulf of death and misery, even to the salvation of our souls. (Alma 26:17, 20)

When I was a young boy about six years old, my family went to a favorite vacation site, a quiet bay near Balboa Beach. I was limited to the beach and shore line under the watch of my parents since I didn't know how to swim. In the middle of the bay was a bridge supported by wooden columns. Fastened to the wood were a variety of sea creatures such as star fish and shellfish.

I was fascinated by these columns and was determined to touch them. Early one morning, without telling my parents, I got up before anyone else and went to the beach. There was no one to watch me paddle out to the bridge, but I felt confident that I could make it. I paddled an inflated raft slowly toward the wooden columns. As I approached them a speed boat made a sharp turn on the opposite side of the bridge. Its wake quickly capsized me. I saw my raft floating away as I began to sink to the bottom.

I have a vivid memory of pushing from the bottom three times and frantically trying to find surface air. As I started to descend the fourth time, I remember thinking I wouldn't have the strength to surface again. Then suddenly, I was snatched by the anxious hands of four girls who had come to the beach just in time. I was not only snatched but severely scratched in their excitement. As I sat shivering with foolishness and fear on the beach, I was very grateful to be snatched and even scratched.

Recalling this fortuitous event in my life, I remember the Prophet Jonah who was snatched from the depths of the sea by the Lord. The Lord will go to any depth, even to the belly of hell, to deliver us if we will believe on His name. When the Lord snatches and delivers us, we, with faith, grab hold of His rope (His hope) secured in a sure place (the rock of His holy mountain or temple). We then go from the awful view spoken of by King Benjamin to the great view of the mysteries of God he also described.

The 76th section of the Doctrine and Covenants fills me with the grandeur of this view and explains how to see it:

> Great and marvelous are the works of the Lord, and *the mysteries of his kingdom which he showed unto us,* which surpass all understanding . . .
>
> Neither is man capable to make them known, for *they are only to be seen and understood by the power of the Holy Spirit, which God bestows on those who love him, and purify themselves before him;*
>
> *To whom he grants this privilege of seeing and knowing* for themselves;

That through the power and manifestation of the Spirit, while in the flesh, they may be able to bear his presence in the world of glory. (D&C 76:114, 116-118)

We must learn to be taught by the Spirit to see the "great view." When we do, *we will also see the great view of ourselves as holy like the Savior.* He said, "I am the Lord that bringeth you up out of the land of Egypt, to be your God: ye shall therefore be holy, for I am holy" (Leviticus 11:45).

Can we see that it is in ascending the staircase of the gospel (which climbs the mountain of holiness, the temple) with our Guide and Savior, Jesus Christ, that we become holy? For He is able to make us holy (*see* D&C 60:7).

Therefore, *to see this great view we must center our lives in worshiping the Lord in "the beauty of holiness"* (Psalm 29:2) *in His beautiful and holy temple,* for there we are taught by the Spirit and led by our Savior. By worshiping in the temple, we can have a "godly walk and conversation, . . . walking in holiness before the Lord" (D&C 20:69). Then we will exclaim as Jeremiah, "The Lord bless thee, O habitation of justice, and mountain of holiness" (Jeremiah 31:23).

The mountain of holiness that we climb in the temple is the spiritual Mount Zion. But before we ascend this mountain we must come to base camp and prepare for the climb.

5

The Camp of Israel: Base Camp of Mount Zion

At Winter Quarters, on the banks of the Missouri River, Brigham Young, the latter-day Moses, received the "Word and Will of the Lord" in January 1847. This word, revealed on the threshold of the great trek through the unknown West to a promised land, is recorded in the 136th section of the Doctrine and Covenants.

This revelation was part of the "Exodus to Greatness,"[1] which started in Nauvoo. There are many striking similarities between this exodus and the exodus of the children of Israel from Egypt, including the fact that *both journeys began with expulsion, then refuge in a base camp at the foot of a mountain ascent.*

In January 1847, Winter Quarters was a base camp, a "Camp of Israel" preparing the pioneer Saints "in their journeying to the West" (D&C 136:1) to become men and women who would match His mountains. In base camp, these Saints were organized into groups of multiples of tens, with "captains" and presiding men. They were led by a man like unto Moses (*see* D&C 103:16) and by the Lord, "the Lord your God, even the God of your fathers," whose "arm is stretched out in the last days, to save my people Israel" (D&C 136:21-22). The camp of Israel was prepared and would be saved with "a covenant and promise" to "walk in all the ordinances of the Lord" (D&C 136:2-4). But the revelation said that the Lord's people "must be tried in all things" and must be prepared for "the glory of Zion" (D&C 136:31).

This base camp at Winter Quarters was similar to the camps of Israel in the Sinai. The base camp at the foot of the Holy Mountain in the Sinai was a place of preparation for the children of Israel to match God's mountain. It is where "Israel camped before the mount" (Exodus 19:1-2) and received the "ordinances and laws" to teach them "the way where-in they must walk" and "the work that they must do." The camp of Israel was organized into groups of multiples of ten and led by "men of truth" (Exodus 18:20-21).

Moses said to the camp of Israel: "The Lord God of your fathers" (Exodus 3:15) has delivered you "with a mighty hand, and with an out-stretched arm" (Deuteronomy 26:8), so "fear not: for God is come to prove you . . . that ye sin not" (Exodus 20:20). With those willing to be proved, the Lord made a covenant witnessed by the "blood of the covenant" (Exodus 24:7-8). By this covenant and ordinance, the camp of Israel would know that "I am the Lord that doth sanctify you" (Exodus 31:13), therefore, "ye shall be holy men unto me" (Exodus 22:31).

Israel Lost the Melchizedek Priesthood Ordinance and the Lord's Rest

Unfortunately, the people of the camp of Israel in the Sinai were not sanctified enough to bear the presence of the Lord. Therefore, the Lord said to them: "I will send an angel before thee . . . for *I will not go up in the midst of thee;* for thou art a stiffnecked people: lest I consume thee in the way" (Exodus 33:2-3).

Joseph Smith clarified why the presence of the Lord would not "go up in the midst of them," and what the consequences were when he recorded the Lord saying,

> For *I will take away the priesthood out of their midst; therefore my Holy Order, and the ordinances thereof, shall not go before them;* for my presence shall not go up in their midst." (JST Exodus 34:1)

Now this [the ordinances of the higher priesthood, meaning temple ordinances] Moses plainly taught to the children of Israel in the wilder-ness, and sought diligently to sanctify his people that they might behold the face of God;

> But *they hardened their hearts and could not endure his presence;* therefore, the Lord in his wrath, for his anger was kindled against them, swore that they should not enter into his rest while in the wilderness, which rest is the fullness of his glory.
>
> Therefore, *he took Moses out of their midst, and the Holy Priesthood also;*

And *the lesser priesthood continued,* which priesthood holdeth the key of the ministering of angels and *the preparatory gospel.* (D&C 84:23-26; JST Exodus 34:2)

The Lord's chastisement of the Israelites in the Sinai continued 40 years in a prolonged base camp, until they were finally led into the promised land. Nephi reminded his brothers Laman and Lemuel of the recalcitrant Israelites, declaring, "He did straiten them in the wilderness with his rod; for they hardened their hearts, even as ye have" (*see* 1 Nephi 17:41-42).

It was nearly 1500 years before Israel as a people would again be offered the fullness of the priesthood and the Lord's rest. Then, only a small number of faithful Saints understood the Savior's earthly ministry as the ultimate preparation to receive the fullness of the priesthood and the promise of His rest. This is because they let the words of the Savior penetrate their hearts till they gained an understanding of His Atonement and how this final great sacrifice would open the way to that within the veil.

The Apostle Paul understood this ultimate preparation and taught the Hebrew Saints about a perfection—a sanctification far greater than they or their ancestors had known for centuries under the Levitical law. He taught them about *"the Order of the Son of God"* at the time of Melchizedek, emphasizing that *all those ordained to this order are "made like unto the Son of God"* (JST Hebrews 7:3). He reasoned that if another high priest (Jesus Christ), "after the similitude of Melchisedec," was necessary, then *"perfection" could not come by the Levitical order, but could only come through the order that has "the power of an endless life"* (*see* Hebrews 7:11, 15-16).

Too often we fail to appreciate the incredible offer, this same offer of a perfected knowledge of God, that the Lord made to the camp of Israel in the Sinai. The God of the Old Testament was going to "come down in the sight of all the people" (Exodus 19:11). Jehovah, the God of the Old Testament and the Messiah of the New Testament, was going to reveal Himself in His glory to an estimated one-and-a-half million people. After all this great camp of Israel had witnessed as the power of the Lord delivered them from bondage in Egypt, it is incredible that most of these people rejected the "rest" of the Lord (*see* D&C 84:24).

Receiving the Lord's Rest: A Preparation of the Heart

It is interesting to compare this potential event with the humble, mortal advent of the Savior in the meridian of time. Thousands of Jews saw Him, but only a few recognized Him. The Jews at that time were looking for their God to come in might and glory, as He would have appeared to their fathers in the Sinai. In both "Sinai Israel" and "Meridian Israel," the Savior of mankind came and went, with only a few recognizing their God and receiving a witness of His rest. In both cases, it required an unerring heart to really recognize Him and behold His glory.

When the Lord appears to a future camp of Israel, again in might and glory, to deliver them from their enemies, the Jews will finally recognize Him for what He is. However, this appearance will be less than a sublime encounter. It will be a time of profound sorrow, when the Jews see again the wounds in the hands and feet of their Savior, and He says to them: "These wounds are the wounds with which I was wounded in the House of my friends. . . . I am Jesus that was crucified, I am the Son of God" (D&C 45:51-52; *see also* Zechariah 13:6).

The Savior's crucifixion wounds, witnessing His declaration that He was the crucified Son of God, is recorded in a glorious temple event that occurred in the Book of Mormon. At the temple in the city Bountiful, a large group of 2,500 faithful Nephites heard the heart-piercing voice of God the Father and then saw His crucified and resurrected Son. They even had the unforgettable privilege of feeling His crucifixion wounds:

> And it came to pass, as they understood they cast their eyes up again towards heaven; and behold, they saw a Man descending out of heaven; and he was clothed in a white robe; and he came down and stood in the midst of them; . . .
>
> And it came to pass that he stretched forth his hand and spake unto the people, saying:
>
> Behold, I am Jesus Christ whom the prophets testified shall come into the world.
>
> And it came to pass that when Jesus had spoken these words the whole multitude fell to the earth; . . .
>
> And it came to pass that the Lord spake unto them saying:
>
> Arise and *come forth unto me, that ye may thrust your hands into my side, and also that ye may feel the prints of the nails in my*

hands and in my feet, that ye may know that I am the God of Israel, and the God of the whole earth, and have been slain for the sins of the world.

And when they had all gone forth and had witnessed for themselves, they did cry out with one accord, saying: Hosanna! Blessed be the name of the Most High God! And they did fall down at the feet of Jesus, and did worship him. (3 Nephi 11:8-10, 12-14, 16-17)

The personal privilege to feel the Savior's wounds by these Nephites was not just a tangible witness but also a spiritual witness of His divinity. They knew by feeling, both in their minds and in their hearts, that the Savior had been slain for the sins of the world. This is why they cried out "Hosanna! Blessed be the name of the Most High God!" and fell at the feet of Jesus.

One of the most tender, sublime moments in all of scripture occurs in chapter 17 of this great temple event with the Savior:

For I perceive that ye desire that I should show unto you what I have done unto your brethren at Jerusalem, . . .

And it came to pass that when he had thus spoken, all the multitude, with one accord, did go forth with their sick and their afflicted, . . . and *He did heal them every one as they were brought forth unto him.*

And they did all, both they who had been healed and they who were whole, *bow down at his feet, and did worship him; and as many as could come for the multitude did kiss his feet, insomuch that they did bathe his feet with their tears.*

And it came to pass that when they had knelt upon the ground, Jesus groaned within himself, and said: Father, I am troubled because of the wickedness of the people of the house of Israel.

And when he had said these words, he himself also knelt upon the earth; and behold *he prayed unto the Father,* and the things which he prayed cannot be written, . . . (3 Nephi 17:8-10, 14-15)

So great and marvelous were the words that Jesus spoke to the Father that the multitude was overcome with joy (*see* 3 Nephi 17:18-19). Because of the faith of this multitude the Savior's joy was so full that he wept:

And it came to pass that Jesus spake unto them, and bade them arise.

And they arose from the earth, and he said unto them; Blessed are ye because of your faith. And now behold my joy is full.

And when he had said these words, he wept, and the multitude bare record of it, and *he took their little children, one by one, and blessed them, and prayed unto the Father for them.*

And when he had done this he wept again. (3 Nephi 17: 8-10, 14-22)

Another tender temple encounter with the Savior occurred the week before His Crucifixion in Jerusalem:

And in the day time he was teaching in the temple: and at night he went out, and abode in the mount that is called the mount of Olives.

And *all the people came early in the morning to him in the temple,* for to hear him. (Luke 21:37-38)

These brief verses evoke a multitude of meaningful questions: Was the night time "abode in the mount" a harbinger of the dark hours of the Atonement? Who were "all the people"? Why did they go "early in the morning"? What words did they "hear" from the Savior? I can imagine an intimate, sacred gathering during these early hours on the threshold of the great Atonement. I can imagine the Savior also wept with those He taught at the temple in Jerusalem.

Can you imagine more than a million people seeing the fullness of the glory of the Lord who brought them out of Egypt, worshiping Him at His feet? What might the wonderful words of scripture have been, had the camp of Israel in the Sinai not rejected such a glorious moment with their God? This pivotal event, this rejection of the Lord in the account of the Exodus from Egypt, is known throughout scripture as the provocation. Paul reminded the Hebrew Saints to

Harden not your hearts, as in the provocation, in the day of temptation in the wilderness:

When your fathers tempted me, proved me, and saw my works forty years.

Wherefore I was grieved with that generation, and said, they do alway err in their heart; and they have not known my ways.

So I sware in my wrath, They shall not enter into my rest. (Hebrews 3:8-11)

Jacob, the brother of Nephi, recalled the provocation in the beginning of his writings when he wrote,

We labored diligently among our people, that we might persuade them to come unto Christ, and partake of the goodness of God, that they might enter into his rest, *lest by any means he should swear in his wrath they should not enter in, as in the provocation in the days of temptation while the children of Israel were in the wilderness* (Jacob 1:7).

The "rest" of the Lord is the great and last promise made in the temple. It comprises the exaltation of eternal life, but *in this life it is also the great blessing of the Second Comforter, the personal ministry of the Savior Himself, in His glory.* This "rest" occurred at the temple in the Book of Mormon and perhaps to some early Christian Saints who believed and entered into "rest" (*see* Hebrews 4:1-3) unlike their fathers in the Sinai. It is a promise that occurs by repentance to a change of heart:

> Therefore, *whosoever repenteth, and hardeneth not his heart, he shall have claim on mercy through mine Only Begotten Son, unto a remission of his sins; and these shall enter into my rest.* (Alma 12:34)

This promised rest is only possible through the cleansing power and mercy of the Atonement:

> Therefore nothing entereth into his rest save it be those who have *washed their garments in my blood.* (3 Nephi 27:19)

The Preparatory Redemption

In these last days, the Missouri Saints' failure to establish a "Zion" community in Missouri is compared to the ancient failure of the Camp of Israel in the Sinai to establish a "holy nation." The Saints in Missouri did not climb Mount Zion, like the Israelites in the Sinai, because they did not obey the Lord's commandment to be unified and then to build a temple and receive its protection. Therefore, they were chastened by the Lord "for a little season with a sore and grievous chastisement" (D&C 103:4).

The sore and grievous chastisement came through tribulation with a promise of redemption. "For after much tribulation . . . cometh the blessing," the Lord promised.

Behold, *this is the blessing which I have promised after your tribulations,* and the tribulations of your brethren—your redemption and the redemption of your brethren, even their *restoration to the land of Zion, . . .*

Behold I say unto you, *the redemption of Zion must needs come by power.* (D&C 103:12-13, 15)

Before the redemption of Zion, the Saints must be prepared by wandering through the Sinai of chastisement and tribulation, and then receive a "preparatory redemption" (Alma 13:3) by power.

Therefore, in consequence of the transgressions of my people, it is expedient in me that mine elders should *wait for a little season for the redemption of Zion.*

That they themselves may be prepared, and that my people may be *taught more perfectly, and have experience,* and know more perfectly concerning their duty, and the things which I require at their hands.

And *this cannot be brought to pass until mine elders are endowed with power from on high.*

For behold, *I have prepared a great endowment and blessing to be poured out upon them,* inasmuch as they are faithful and continue in humility before me. (D&C 105:9-12)

The preparation and perfection spoken of in this revelation will come to pass *when the Saints are chastened to obedience, then endowed with power through the temple endowment. This will prepare us for the redemption of Zion.*

This preparation of chastisement, tribulation, and power continued into Nauvoo and to the banks of the Missouri River with the Camp of Israel. It continues today as we camp in the tops of the mountains near the House of the Lord, or wherever there is a House of the Lord, awaiting the day of redemption.

Base camp, or the camp of Israel, is a place of preparation to climb Mount Zion, the mountain of the Lord's house. This climb will prepare us for the redemption of Zion and "the great day of the Lord" (*see* D&C 133:10, 12-13).

Base camp is where we begin to learn to be separate from the world and "touch not the unclean thing," turning completely to our Father in Heaven that "[He] will receive [us]" (*see* 2 Corinthians 6:17-18). It is where we practice what we learn. By so doing, we begin to develop an unerring broken heart in preparation to climb His holy mountain. There we receive a pure heart for His rest. Base camp is where we submit our-selves to the chastisement of our real Father "until [we] learn obedi-ence" to Him, even by "the things which [we] suffer" (D&C 105:6). It is where *we are straitened by His rod but comforted by His outstretched arms.*

Separating Covenant People from the World to Become the Lord's Jewels

The Lord calls us to be separate, and separates us from the world to His base camps in order to prepare us to become His jewels. This He did with the children of Israel living in bondage along the Nile. He sep-arated them from the world of the Nile to make of them His jewels because of the covenants he made with Moses and their fathers: "Now therefore, if ye will obey my voice indeed, and keep my covenant, then *ye shall be a peculiar treasure unto me above all people:* . . . And ye shall be unto me *a kingdom of priests, and an holy nation*" (Exodus 19:5-6).

The term "peculiar treasure" comes from the Hebrew word *segullah,* which means precious possession like a jewel.[2]

In spite of their transgression, the Lord still numbered the Saints in Missouri as His potential jewels because of His love and mercy for them. However, like the children of Israel, they had to be chastened (polished) to become his jewels:

> Yet I will own them, and *they shall be mine in that day when I shall come to make up my jewels.*
>
> Therefore, they must needs be chastened and tried, even as Abraham, who was commanded to offer up his only son. (D&C 101:3-4)

This scripture reminds me of the jewels worn in the temple vest-ments of Aaron and his successor (*see* Exodus 28:9, 12, 15, 17). These jewels represent the House of Israel. They were worn both on the shoul-ders and near the heart of the high priest who represented the Lord. Therefore *the Lord carries His saints, those who covenant with Him, on His shoulders and in His heart,[3] even through tribulation.*

Why are those who leave from the world and covenant with the Lord, His jewels? Moses' farewell speech to the children of Israel pro-vides perspective:

> For thou art an holy people unto the Lord thy God; *the Lord thy God hath chosen thee to be a special people unto himself. . . .*
>
> The Lord did not set his love upon you, nor choose you because ye were more in number than any people; for ye were the fewest of all people:
>
> But *because the Lord loved you, and because he would keep the oath which he had sworn unto your fathers.*
>
> *Know therefore that the Lord thy God, he is God, the faithful God, which keepeth covenant and mercy with them that love him and keep his commandments to a thousand generations.* (Deuteronomy 7:6-9. *See also* 3 Nephi 20:25-27)

Nephi summarized Moses's speech when he said, "Behold, the Lord esteemeth all flesh in one; *he that is righteous is favored of God*" (1 Nephi 17:35).

The righteous are favored of God because they keep the covenant He made with the fathers. *The righteous are His jewels because they "are bought with a price"* (1 Corinthians 6:20). *The price is the "precious blood" of His Only Begotten Son* (*see* 1 Peter 1:18-19). *This price the Father and the Son paid because of their love for their children, expecting they would become righteous jewels reflecting the price paid.*

When the Lord gathers us from the banks of the Nile (the world), He leads us to His base camps in preparation to climb His temple. In climbing the temple, He will make us His righteous jewels. For this reason, Joseph Smith declared:

> The *main object of gathering the people of God* in any age of the world *is to build unto the Lord a house whereby He could reveal unto His people the ordinances of His house and the glories of His kingdom,* and teach people the way of salvation.[4]

Therefore, the Lord commanded the Latter-day Saints to "gather together" and build a temple in Far West "that they may worship me" (D&C 115:8; *see also* D&C 101:64-65).

In keeping the covenants He made with the fathers, *the Lord makes righteous jewels by first gathering uncut, unpolished gems from the plains of the world.* He does this through true messengers, such as missionaries, parents, and prophets, who bear testimony to the souls of these gems. Then He gathers these gems as potential jewels, for "the worth of souls is great" (D&C 18:10), to His base camps, His stakes of

Zion, where He prepares them to match His mountain and climb His holy temple. *It is in climbing His temple (Mount Zion) that He polishes and purifies the gems to make them His jewels* so they can enter within the veil and abide His rest.

Put Away Strange Gods, Be Clean, and Change Your Garments

There is an important lesson to be learned from an incident in the life of Jacob, the grandson of Abraham. When Jacob returned from Haran, he lived among the Canaanites. A conflict arose when Shechem the Hivite violated Dinah, the daughter of Jacob. Sensing his peril with the Canaanites, Jacob obeyed a directive he received from the Lord to go to Beth-el where he had seen his great temple staircase vision, "and make there an altar unto God" (*see* Genesis 35:1). The Lord was telling Jacob to get out of the world, go to the temple, and worship there.

In response, Jacob "said unto his household, and to all that were with him, *"Put away the strange gods that are among you, and be clean, and change your garments"* (Genesis 35:2). *In essence, Jacob was teaching his household to prepare to be worthy to enter the temple.*

We need to follow his advice today. We need to put away strange gods by giving up our worldly idols and showing obedience to God, keeping a defined set of His commandments. This is the requirement for admission to His holy house. We give written proof of this obedience by obtaining a temple recommend, our pass to the inner courts of the temple.

However, final proof of obedience to the Lord requires a spiritual stamp on our pass. It is the stamp or certifying "seal" of the Holy Spirit of Promise (*see* D&C 76:53, Ephesians 1:13). This seal is given when we obey all the laws of the gospel and demonstrate strict obedience to the covenants of the Lord. Until then we are only anointed to be sealed.

Our obedience to the Lord cleanses us as temples so we can invite the Spirit to enter our lives and teach us the way of salvation. *To be polished and purified in the temple, we not only need the ordinances but we also need to be taught by the Spirit.* The Spirit will teach us personally about the power and grace of Christ that is necessary in our individual lives to make the mighty change in our hearts. The Spirit will show us our weaknesses and inspire us with the confident hope that we can do better, so that our weaknesses become strengths.

When we follow the personal teachings of the Spirit, we become "new creatures," desiring above all else to be sealed to our Father in Heaven.

The Spirit prompts us to be clean enough to go to the temple. There we symbolically leave the world behind by changing our worldly garments. *We change into clothing of white, symbolic of the Atonement cleansing, as if we were washed white in the blood of the Lamb.*

Before we climb Mount Zion and receive the polishing purification of the temple, we must pay the price, demonstrating a preparatory worthiness in obtaining and maintaining a temple recommend. We must keep ourselves worthy to be guided in our climb by the Holy Spirit. This preparation for the climb of Mount Zion is the ultimate goal of base camp.

6

Equipped for the First Ascent: Initiation to Mount Zion

Modern Temple Preparations Follow Ancient Scriptural Patterns

Part of the explicit instructions Moses received as the tabernacle was being prepared was the preparation of those acting as its priests:

> And this is the thing that thou shalt do unto them *to hallow them,* to minister unto me in the priest's office: . . .
>
> Aaron and his sons thou shalt bring unto the door of the tabernacle of the congregation and shalt *wash them* with water.
>
> And thou shalt *take the garments, and put upon Aaron* . . .
>
> Then shalt thou take the *anointing oil,* and pour it upon his head, and *anoint him.* (Exodus 29:1, 4-5, 7)

To be washed, anointed, and clothed in a garment are likewise preparatory or initiatory ordinances of the temples in this dispensation. "Therefore, verily I say unto you, that *your anointings, and your washings, . . . are ordained by the ordinance of my holy house*" (D&C 124:39).

Ezekiel poetically described the preparation and blessings given to Moses for temple service and endowment. Ezekiel compared Jerusalem (the Israelites) to an abandoned child at birth, orphaned with the Canaanites but loved and redeemed by the Lord. He found them, then He washed away their blood, anointed them with oil, covered their nakedness with His skirt, and clothed them with broidered work of fine linen and silk. He entered into a covenant with them, which caused the Lord to declare to them that "thou becamest mine" (*see* Ezekiel 16:8-10).

In temple initiation today, we are symbolically *washed,* then *covered* with the "garment of salvation." *Both of these ordinances represent the cleansing and covering power of the Atonement. We are also anointed with oil, symbolizing a setting apart to holiness by reception of the Holy Spirit, whose power directs us to a new covenant relationship with Christ.* The final ordinance of the initiation is to receive a new name as a token of this covenant relationship in which we take upon us the name of Christ.

In the initiatory of the temple we are equipped for the first ascent of Mount Zion. *During this ascent we will be clothed with the robes of righteousness, which represent the acquisition of a divine or holy nature.* In order to reach the summit of Mount Zion, it is important that we are equipped properly by understanding the meaning of these initiatory ordinances and blessings in our personal lives.

Covering Our Nakedness with the Power of the Atonement

The cleansing power of the Atonement is symbolically taught in the scriptural temple by a comparison between the Savior's blood (His atoning sacrifice) and our blood (our sins). Truly, the blood of Christ is "precious blood" (*see* 1 Peter 1:18-19), of great price because it does not stain our garments nor our robes. In contrast, it is *our* blood that stains our garments and His garments (*see* Alma 5:22 and Isaiah 63:2-3).

Christ's blood is precious because it can wash our bloodstained garments and robes, making them "white in the blood of the Lamb" (Revelation 7:14). The whitening of Christ's blood is so complete that it can "cleanse us all from sin" (1 John 1:7), making us "clean every whit" (John 13:10) so that our "garments be always white!" (Ecclesiastes 9:8).

In the temple, we are taught even deeper truths about the cleansing and covering power of the Atonement as we learn about the clothing of the Holy Order: the garments of salvation and the robe of righteousness, foretold by the prophet Isaiah: "My soul shall be joyful in my God; for *He hath clothed me with the garments of salvation. he hath covered me with the robe of righteousness*" (Isaiah 61:10; *see also* Psalm 132:9, 16).

In the first temple setting, a beautiful moment of hope occurred when God the Father explained the plan of salvation to Adam and Eve. Then their "nakedness" from the fall was covered, as they made a covenant of obedience to the Father, and the Son clothed them presumably with coats of skin. It is significant that this benevolent act of covering Adam and Eve occurred when the first animal sacrifice was performed by the Lamb of God! (*see* Genesis 3:21). In a similar manner today, *the nakedness of our fall is completely covered with this atonement clothing* as we make covenants with the Lord.

The garments of salvation symbolize the covering of salvation from physical death, given as a gift to all men by the power of the Atonement. To those who enter the temple, these garments become the first covering leading to exaltation, reminding them that eternal life, the greatest gift of God, comes also by the cleansing and covering power of the Atonement.

During my trip to Israel, I was taught an interesting lesson about the covering of the Atonement while visiting Galilee. In my diary, I recorded the instructions of our guide, Wayne Brickey, who explained the significance of Capernaum, the Lord's resident city:

> When Moses talked about the day of atonement he used the word *kippur* or *kfar*. It was a word that had no direct translation in English. In Near Eastern languages it means to protect, to cover, or to pay. The English word 'atonement' is the traditional substitute.
>
> The Jordanians use the word *kfar* to mean a robe that is used in ceremony to cover a candidate who is embraced or accepted into a family clan. Therefore the word *Capernaum* is very significant. *Caper* is equivalent to *kippur* or *kfar* and means a covering. *Naum* is translated to mean repentance. Thus, *Capernaum means a covering for repentance. It refers directly to the Atonement of the Savior. No wonder Capernaum was the center of His Galilean ministry.*

Perhaps there is no better example in the *scriptural temple* than the parable of the prodigal son to teach us of God's desire to cover us with His robe of acceptance. The "best robe" is a covering of acceptance for seeking our Father in Heaven and desiring His mercy:

> . . . the son said unto him, Father, I have sinned against heaven, and in thy sight, and am no more worthy to be called thy son. But the father said to his servants, *Bring forth the best robe, and put it on him.* (Luke 15:21-22)

Our Father in Heaven will forever cover us with the best robe if we repent.

The words of Nephi give the image of *kippur*, pleading to be covered with the best robe, which is the robe of righteousness: "O Lord, *wilt thou encircle me around in the robe of thy righteousness!*" (2 Nephi 4:33).

After we are anointed in the temple initiatory to become kings and queens unto God, we are symbolically clothed during the endowment with the "robes of righteousness." These regal robes, as well as the garment of salvation, are the covering of the fullness *of the priesthood. These priesthood robes symbolize the purity* (*see* 2 Nephi 9:14) *and righteousness* (*see* Revelation 19:8) *of the divine nature of a saint who emulates the divine nature of Christ. They also must be washed white by the cleansing power of the Atonement* (*see* Revelation 7:14).

Discovering Our Spiritual Nakedness

At the time of judgment, "the righteous shall have a perfect knowledge of their enjoyment, and their righteousness, *being clothed with purity, yea, even with the robe of righteousness*" (2 Nephi 9:14). Discovering our spiritual nakedness with a perfect knowledge, before the Judgment, is the challenge of this life.

When we discover our spiritual nakedness or our spiritual fall (*see* D&C 29:41, 44), *we want to be clothed with righteousness, which includes modesty, the art of deflecting attention from ourselves to the righteousness of God.* The association of righteousness and modesty is conveyed by the temple garment. This temple covering, both spiritual and physical, is contrary to the world, which is still discovering and exposing its nakedness in the literal sense.

The stark nakedness of our fall requires that we be clothed by the "garments of salvation," (the Atonement), and the "robes of righteousness," (the divine nature). Otherwise, we are forever naked and unprepared for the rest of the Lord (*see* 3 Nephi 27:19) and the redemption of Zion.

Contrast the "beautiful garments" with which the Savior covers us (*see* 3 Nephi 13:28-30) to the meager covering offered by Satan to Adam and Eve. His is the only temple clothing for which we do not initially "arise" and "put on," standing in the presence of God.

For Zion must increase in beauty, and in holiness; her borders must be enlarged; her stakes must be strengthened; yea, verily I say unto you, *Zion must arise and put on her beautiful garments.* (D&C 82:14)

Awake, awake; *put on thy strength, O Zion; put on thy beautiful garments,* O Jerusalem, the holy city: for henceforth there shall no more come into thee the uncircumcised and the unclean. (Isaiah 52:1)

The term "put on thy strength" means to put on the authority and power of the priesthood (see D&C 113:7-8), being covered by the beautiful clothing of the fullness of the Savior's Atonement and His Holy Order.

These scriptures emphatically call us to the temple, that we might be covered with the fullness of the Atonement by being clothed with righteousness. Then we "put on" the power of the Holy Order of God. This beautiful covering will prepare us and empower us for the Lord's rest and the redemption of Zion.

In the dedicatory prayer of the Kirtland Temple, the Prophet Joseph Smith called us to the temple "that our garments may be pure:"

And let these, thine anointed ones, be clothed with salvation, . . .
That our garments may be pure, that we may be clothed upon with robes of righteousness. (D&C 109:80, 76)

If we keep our garments undefiled, then we will be "clothed in white raiment," the robes of righteousness (*see* Revelation 3:4-5).

When Jesus made His triumphal entry into Jerusalem, He went to the temple. There He confounded the Pharisees and chief priests and taught several parables. *It is significant that He taught the parable of the marriage of the King's son in the temple.* This parable tells of a king who invited close neighbors and friends (those who were bidden) to the wedding feast of his son. But those who were bidden made light of this invitation and killed the king's servants who invited them. The King was angered by this rejection and sent his army to destroy the murderers. The king then sent his servants into the highways, to both the bad and good, and invited them to the wedding. But when the king came to greet his guests at the wedding, he saw one man who was not dressed in a wedding garment:

And he saith unto him, Friend, how camest thou in hither not having a wedding garment? and he was speechless.

Then said the king to the servants, Bind him hand and foot, and take him away . . .

For many are called, but few chosen; wherefore all do not have on the wedding garment (JST Matthew 22:12-14).

In this symbolic context, the wedding garment is the garment of salvation and the robes of righteousness. *It is the garment that we will wear as "chosen" for the marriage of the King's Son at the redemption of Zion,* "that we may be one" with Him (*see* D&C 29:12-13; D&C 38:24-27).

It is in the temple that we learn how this clothing symbolically prepares the temple "anointed" to one day be "chosen" (*see* D&C 95:3-6). Joseph Smith implied that we will be called up and chosen, if we remain faithful to the wedding garment, by abiding the celestial laws it symbolizes:

How many will be able to *abide a celestial law,* and go through and receive their exaltation, I am unable to say, as *many are called, but few are chosen.*[1]

All these passages combine to present a clear *scriptural temple* message: to be chosen *we must first discover our spiritual nakedness; then we must cover it with salvation and exalting righteousness by receiving the cleansing and covering power of the Atonement of Christ.* His complete power flows to us when we keep temple covenants.

Anointing with the Spirit: A Preparation to Be Taught in the Temple

The anointing of the temple sets us apart to become a kingdom of priests, a royal priesthood, a holy nation, a chosen generation, a peculiar people (*see* 1 Peter 2:9). Therefore, the anointing symbolically introduces candidates for the endowment into the Holy Order of God, anointing them to become kings and queens, priests and priestesses (*see* Revelation 1:5-6).[2] The anointing not only sets us apart for this royalty, but also, like King David's anointing (*see* 1 Samuel 16:13), *it is symbolic of receiving the Holy Spirit with His powers to teach, reveal, and seal.*

The oil in the lamps of the ten virgins was symbolic of the light provided by the Holy Spirit as a guide that they be not deceived (see D&C 45:56-47). After baptism in water, we are baptized with the fire of this symbolic oil to light our way when we receive the gift of the Holy Ghost. However, it is in the temple that we are anointed to receive a fullness of this gift (*see* D&C 109:15).

Our text for learning in the temple is the scriptures. A symbolic witness for this truth is the temple altar upon which the scriptures rest. *Our most important teacher in the temple is the Holy Spirit,* because to understand the great view in the text of the scriptural temple we need His teaching and revealing powers.

The Apostle John said the "anointing teacheth:"

> But the anointing which ye have received . . . ye need not that any man teach you: but as the *same anointing teacheth you of all things, and is truth,* and is no lie (1 John 2:27).

Jacob described the teaching and revealing power of the Holy Spirit in similar terms. "For *the spirit speaketh the truth* and lieth not . . . it speaketh of things as they really are and *of things as they really will be*" (Jacob 4:13).

How refreshing, in this world of deceit and half truths, it is to have someone teach us the truth and speak of things as they really are, even things not seen by the natural eye! No wonder we need not that any man teach us.

To Be Taught by the Holy Spirit
Our Bodies Must Become as Temples

Christ declared that His body is a temple (*see* John 2:19-21). The *scriptural temple* teaches that our bodies also are temples (*see* D&C 93:35; 1 Corinthians 6:19). *Our body as a temple, and Christ's body as a temple, come together in His holy house. There we are taught His words by the power of the Holy Spirit.*

The Holy Spirit can teach us in the temple if we become temples in which He can teach (*see* Ephesians 2:19-22; Mosiah 2:37). In the *scriptural temple,* there is a beautiful expression of the potential for each of us to become a temple in which the Holy Spirit can teach. "If your eye be single to my glory, *your whole bodies shall be filled with light,* and there shall be no darkness in you; and *that body which is filled with light comprehendeth all things*" (D&C 88:67). This verse gives the image of the light of constructed temples that are glowing beacons in the dark night.

Other scriptures speak of the light of the body as the eye, stating that "when thine eye is single, *thy whole body is full of light*" (Luke 11:33-34, 36; 3 Nephi 13:22). Like a magnifying glass, the eye single to the light of God concentrates all the rays of truth from the Son into a single powerful beam. This beam, the powerful light of God, can penetrate our blind eyes and hard hearts with understanding of spiritual knowledge (*see* John 12:35-40). Then our whole body, spirit and element connected, is filled with light and joy (*see* D&C 93:32-33).

Elder John A. Widtsoe taught that the process of being filled with the light of God is what happens to us in the temple when we are taught by the Holy Spirit. He said, "Spiritual power is generated within temple walls, and sent out to bless the world. *Light from the house of the Lord illumines every home within the Church fitted for its reception by participation in temple privileges.*"[3]

When our eyes become single to the light of God, we become "children of light" (John 12:36) with the "light of life" (John 8:12). As such, we learn a great truth: *the light of Christ is more powerful than the darkness of Satan* (*see* D&C 14:9; 6:21; 21:6; 50:25, John 12:35). Those who abide in the light of Christ receive more light, and "*that light groweth brighter and brighter until the perfect day*" (D&C 50:24) of "perfect knowledge" (2 Nephi 9:14).

The *scriptural temple* message is clear: *To become temples in which the Holy Spirit can teach, and thus become the "children of light," we must have faith, hope, and charity, as a beam of light through an eye single to the glory of God* (*see* D&C 4:5). That is, we must seek God only for His glory and not divide our devotion by serving "two masters" (3 Nephi 13:24). We seek God in total devotion when we believe in Him and His word. Then we will seek God as our only master because He can provide the power to free us from the master of our own wills. When God is our only master, His light will be the light in our eyes, filling our whole body with light and joy.

We want the Holy Spirit to teach us in the temple, not only because the Spirit "speaketh the truth and lieth not," but because He "knoweth all things" and can reveal all things to us (*see* D&C 35:19).

Joseph Smith declared that "*no man can receive the Holy Ghost without receiving revelations. The Holy Ghost is a revelator.*"[4] To know all things, to have this great view of all things, can be our gift if we seek the Lord and become holy like a temple. As we continue to obey the commandments of the Lord and follow His true messengers, we become more like a temple, filled with "truth and light" until we "know all things" (*see* D&C 93:28).

On the first ascent of Mount Zion, we are anointed and set apart to be holy like a temple. To help us in the quest to one day reach the summit, being called up and chosen as part of the great view, we are anointed with our Guide and Teacher, the Holy Spirit. *It is paramount that we learn of the power of the Holy Spirit and how He must teach us in the temple if we are to reach the summit of Mount Zion.*

Understanding the Scriptural Concept of the Heart

But the Lord said unto Samuel, Look not on his countenance, or on the height of his stature; because I have refused him: for the Lord seeth not as man seeth; for man looketh on the outward appearance, but *the Lord looketh on the heart.* (1 Samuel 16:7)

What is this heart that the Lord looks upon and knows (*see* D&C 6:16)? Can we call it the center of our deepest feelings, the interpreter of our thoughts, our intuitive and therefore *"feeling" nature?*

Is not the heart the individual spiritual self? There are scriptures that imply close association between the heart and the spirit such as Ezekiel 18:31 and 3 Nephi 9:20. A deductive reasoning for their equivalence could come from associating Romans 10:8-10 with Romans 8:16 and 2 Corinthians 2:14 concerning where we should place the word of God and how we come to know of its truthfulness. This reasoning could be applied in combining the words of Abinadi to the priest of Noah when he said, "Ye have not applied your hearts to understanding" (Mosiah 12:27), with the words of Elihu when he said, "But there is a spirit in man: and the inspiration of the Almighty giveth them understanding" (Job 32:8). Paul said there is a natural body and a spiritual body (*see* 1 Corinthians 15:44). Man is spirit and flesh just as God is spirit and flesh (*see* D&C 93:33; John 4:24; D&C 130:22). If a gift or power of the Holy Spirit is to quicken our spirits and "bring all things to our remembrance" (John 14:26), is not the heart, the spiritual self, laden with spiritual memory? *The feelings of our hearts are spiritual memories from matter more refined* (*see* D&C 131:7), that is native to spiritual truth and understanding. The prophet Joseph F. Smith taught that:

All those salient truths which come home so forcibly to the *head and heart* seem but the *awakening of the memories of the spirit* . . . But in order to tap into that knowledge we must struggle to get past "the prison-house of mortality."[5]

The difficulty we have in the prison-house of mortality is getting beyond our physical and mental impressions to the enlightenment of our spiritual impressions. It is the Holy Spirit that helps us get past the prison-house or veil of mortality that blinds our minds and hardens our hearts.

Concerning the Israelites from Moses through his time, Paul described their prison-house of mortality as the "vail upon their heart" (*see* 2 Corinthians 3:13-15). Paul said that when their hearts "shall turn to the Lord, the vail shall be taken away" because "where the Spirit of the Lord is, there is liberty" from disbelief (*see* 2 Corinthians 3:16-17). While our spirit does not usually speak to us in audible tones, it *feels* to us. We can come to recognize these feelings as *peace, assurance,* and even *burning in our hearts* from righteousness (*see* 3 Nephi 11:3) or sin.

Women have been telling men for a long time that there is a level of understanding beyond logic. Women are motivated as much by understood feelings as by logical thinking. They have a gift of this spiritual sense of feeling, to know when *something feels right.* The endowment implies that Eve had this feeling of assurance, that partaking of the forbidden fruit was the better choice for her and Adam. Abraham was advised by the Lord to listen to Sarah's feelings (*see* Genesis 21:12). If this sense of feeling in our hearts is by the power of the Holy Spirit, it will be the logical truth.

To deny these feelings, whether they feel right or wrong, especially when they come from the witness and teaching of the Holy Ghost, can bring great condemnation:

> Behold, here is the agency of man, and here is the condemnation of man; because that which was from the beginning is plainly manifest unto them, and *they receive not the light.*
>
> And every man whose spirit receiveth not the light is under condemnation. (D&C 93:31-32)

Because the spiritual body is at the heart of feeling spiritual truth, *we will be judged by the Lord according to how we receive this feeling of truth in our hearts,* and how well we respond to it:

> For I, the Lord, will judge all men according to *their works,* according to the desires [feelings] of *their hearts.* (D&C 137:9)

The Lord will judge us according to works that come from the desires and feelings of our hearts.

The Holy Spirit intimately knows our hearts because He has been dwelling and striving with our personal spirits during our mortal probation. He is a *"discerner of the thoughts and intents of the heart"* (D&C 33:1). The Lord and the Holy Spirit looketh upon and knoweth the heart. No man or woman can deceive the Holy Spirit. Perhaps this is why all acts, covenants and ordinances that have eternal consequences are only valid if sealed (certified) by the Holy Spirit of promise (*see* D&C 132:7). Before his conversion, Amulek experienced a mind unreceptive to spiritual knowledge because he did not respond to the feelings of his heart:

> Nevertheless, I did *harden my heart,* for I was called many times and I would not hear; Therefore, *I knew* concerning these things, *yet I would not know.* (Alma 10:6)

To harden one's heart like Amulek is to stifle the feelings of spiritual truth within. When we deny or stifle the feelings of our spirits, hardening our hearts with a wall of unrighteousness and worldliness like Amulek, the Holy Ghost will have difficulty in teaching us and activating our spiritual recall to bring all things to our remembrance. Then our hearts will become even more subordinate to the misconceptions of the creeds of men and the lies of Satan. This is why we are instructed to *"trust in the Lord with all thine heart:* and lean not unto thine own understanding" (Proverbs 3:5).

When we trust too much in the arm of flesh, leaning unto our own understanding, we learn only in our natural mind. We become like the pre-converted Amulek, whose type Paul described as "ever learning, and never able to come to the knowledge of the truth" (2 Timothy 3:7).

We may receive the words of spiritual knowledge in our minds through our eyes and ears, but until we feel those words in our hearts with the power of the Holy Spirit, we cannot elevate ourselves from the physical world into a spiritual perspective. It is only in feeling with our hearts that a true relationship to the Father of our spirits is remembered (*see* Romans 15:16; 2 Chronicles 16:9). *Without this feeling of the heart, we cannot see the great view of the spiritual world because we cannot fully comprehend the things of God,* for "the things of God knoweth no man but the Spirit of God" (1 Corinthians 2:11).

By living in and experiencing mortality, we see the view of the world and understand the "spirit of man" (1 Corinthians 2:11). Yet, within each of us there is a spirit that feels for a "better world" (*see* Ether 12:4).

The *scriptural temple* teaches us that

> We have received, not the spirit of the world, but *the spirit which is of God;* that we might know the things that are freely given to us of God.
>
> Which things also we speak, not in the words which man's wisdom teacheth, but which *the Holy Ghost teacheth.* (1 Corinthians 2:12-13)

In order to fully understand the imperative necessity for each of us to be influenced and taught by the Holy Spirit, it is necessary to understand our natural condition and potential state if the Holy Spirit does not influence and teach us.

The State of the Natural Mind and Potential State of the Hardened Heart

If the word of God is not illuminated by the power of the Holy Spirit in our hearts, it deteriorates to misunderstanding, unimportance, or even disbelief ("foolishness") in our natural minds:

> But the *natural man* receiveth not the things of the Spirit of God; for they are *foolishness* unto him; neither can he know them, because they are *spiritually discerned.* (1 Corinthians 2:14)

The natural man is an enemy to God because he does not become meek and seek God (*see* Mosiah 3:19). Instead, he moves in ways contrary to the Plan of Salvation and happiness (*see* Alma 41:11). He may intensely guard his right to chose, but his choices increasingly lead to captivity by Satan, resulting in a loss of his freedom to choose. Even unwittingly, the natural man who is a captive of Satan is enrolled in Satan's army to "continually" fight against God (*see* Moroni 7:12). Therefore, the natural man does not receive the things of the Spirit and does not come to know of true freedom in the redeeming love of God. *Only the man who becomes meek in his mind and heart, then seeks God with his mind and his heart, can know these things* (*see* Alma 26:21-22).

Disbelief of the natural mind permits Satan to blind it to the light of the gospel (*see* 2 Corinthians 4:4). Then the door is open for Satan to "get hold upon our hearts" with "the chains of hell." Alma defined the chains of hell in relation to hardness of heart. Those who continue to harden their heart to the word of God will be "*given the lesser portion of the word until they know nothing concerning his mysteries. . . .* Now this is what is meant by the chains of hell" (*see* Alma 12:10-11).

Physically, when the heart stops, so does the mind. The heart stopping is the final cause of physical death. It is symbolic of the final cause of spiritual death.

Our hearts have great influence on how we perceive truth in our minds. Since the heart is a strong receptor of spiritual truth, it will continue "beating" to influence the spiritually weak mind. When the heart is hardened, its beat is weakened, causing the mind to risk blindness to spiritual light (*see* Alma 13:4; 2 Corinthians 4:4). *When the mind is blind to spiritual light, it no longer maintains a reciprocal connection with the heart.* Then the heart risks becoming even more hardened until it is bound with the chains of hell and becomes spiritually dead to the influence of the Holy Spirit.

Tragically, Mormon witnessed the hearts of his people bound in the "chains of hell" because they hardened their hearts against the word of God to the point that the Spirit of the Lord ceased to strive with them. When this happened, they lost their love for their fellowmen and became as "wild beasts," without order and mercy, delighting in everything save that which is good (*see* Moroni 9:4-5, 10, 18-19).

The wicked people at the time of Enoch were in a similar state: without affection, hating their own blood, with their hearts bound in the chains of hell (*see* Moses 7:33). Laman and Lemuel were also "without principle and past feeling" (Moroni 9:20), hating their own blood. Therefore, they sought the life of their brother Nephi. Other scriptural examples of hardening and binding of the heart with the chains of hell include the Pharisees and Zoramites. Their hearts were hardened and bound by pompous piety. The Zoramites' hearts were so hardened that Alma said they were totally encased with the chains of hell, or "swallowed up in their pride" (*see* Alma 31:25, 27).

The principle of "natural affection" (*see* 2 Timothy 3:1-3), or the self-evident truths of human kindness and liberty, are the qualities that are lost when the heart is bound with the chains of hell. With our hearts bound in these chains, we cannot feel the self-evident truths of "natural affection" because they are truths of the nature of godliness, known and felt only if we "open [our] hearts" (D&C 63:1).

Without the power of the Holy Spirit to ignite the feelings in our hearts, we can know but not know, like Amulek. Consequently, we will have little faith and little resolve to seek and act on a spiritual plane. Ultimately, if we continue to harden our hearts against the feelings of the Spirit, He will "not tarry with [us]" (D&C 130:23). We then risk becoming like "wild beasts"—without affection, delighting in everything save that which is good. Then "cometh speedy destruction" (2 Nephi 26:11; D&C 1:33). *When the light of the Holy Spirit leaves our hearts, so does our ability to establish order and to show love and mercy.* Our hearts are bound and locked with the chains of hell.

To Find God We Must Seek the Lord on His Terms

Seeking the Lord on His terms has been a major problem for mankind in every generation. The state of the world at the dawn of the dispensation of the fullness of times was similar to the world and Israelite nation way back in 1100 B.C. (*see* Judges 17:6). Therefore the Lord again declared in our dispensation:

> They *seek* not to establish His [the Lord's] righteousness, but every man walketh in his own way and after the image of his own god. (*See* D&C 1:15-16.)

Nephi wrote of this lack of seeking the Lord as not asking, knocking and searching in the light for great knowledge:

> Wherefore, now after I have spoken these words, if ye cannot understand them it will be because *ye ask not, neither do ye knock;* wherefore, ye are *not brought into the light,* but must perish in *the dark.*
> ... and I am left to mourn because of the unbelief, and the wickedness, and the ignorance, and the stiffneckedness of men; for they will not *search knowledge, nor understand great knowledge,* when it is given unto them in plainness, even as plain as word can be. (2 Nephi 32:4, 7)

This state of ignoring the Lord starts to occur when we yield to Satan's temptations. In this condition, we esteem the things of God as "things of naught" (2 Nephi 33:2), therefore we do not seek "great knowledge."

Remember how the Apostle Paul instructed us to seek the Lord: We must "feel" after Him (*see* Acts 17:27). Amulek did not seek the Lord because he did not respond to the feelings of his heart. Laman and Lemuel were condemned by Nephi, and stated that they were "past feeling" (1 Nephi 17:45). They were not only past the feeling of natural affection, but they "knew not the dealings of that God who had created them" (1 Nephi 2:12) because they did not inquire of the Lord (*see* 1 Nephi 15:8-11) on His terms, by feeling after Him with humility. *We begin to seek the Lord on His terms by responding to the feelings of our hearts with a broken heart and contrite spirit.* Therefore, the Lord's ancient promise to the captive Jews in Babylon is applicable to all:

> Ye shall seek me, and find me, when ye shall search for me with all your heart. (Jeremiah 29:13)

It is not from a Rameumptom, a tower of pride like the Zoramites built (*see* Alma 31:21), that we see the great view and find the Lord. Compare the pride of the Zoramites on the Rameumptom with the humility of King Benjamin, who saw great views from his tower (*see* Mosiah 2:7, 12-17). It is only through the depths of humility, with the feelings of a meek and lowly heart, that this view and knowledge come (*see* D&C 5:23-24), because "he that humbleth himself shall be exalted" (Luke 18:14).

We cannot feel God with faith and hope if our hearts are encased with worldly pride, being set upon the things of this world and the honors of men. It is only the meek and lowly heart that is acceptable before God (*see* Moroni 7:43-44), for this is the heart that the Savior has (*see* Matthew 11:29).

The Power of the Holy Ghost: Learning in Mind and Heart

When we seek the Lord with a meek and lowly heart, we are given a gift (*see* Moroni 8:26). This gift is "the power of the Holy Ghost" (1 Nephi 10:17). Notice that even Jesus of Nazareth received this gift (*see* Acts 10:38). For the fullness of the power of the Holy Ghost, we must not only seek God with a meek and lowly heart, but we must convince Him that we want this gift more than anything else in this life. We convince God by seeking Him as though we were hungering and thirsting for righteousness (*see* 3 Nephi 12:6), while keeping all of His covenants. Then we will be filled with the Holy Spirit. Then, with the fullness of the Holy spirit, "the mysteries of God" (1 Nephi 10:19) and "the truth of all things" (Moroni 10:5) are unfolded to us.

Within the word *seek* is the word *see,* which is the gift for seeking. By the power of the Holy Spirit, we see things with eyes of understanding, as they really are. If we keep "see-king" on His terms we will see the "King Immanuel" (D&C 128:22).

Oliver Cowdery learned about the power of the Holy Ghost in his request for the gift of translation:

> Yea, behold, I will tell you in your *mind* and in your *heart, by the Holy Ghost,* which shall come upon you and which shall *dwell in your heart.*
>
> Now, behold, this is *the spirit of revelation;* behold, this is the spirit by which Moses brought the children of Israel through the Red Sea on dry ground. (D&C 8:2-3)

Note in verse two that we can learn from the Holy Ghost in our minds and our hearts because He can dwell in our hearts. That is, *He can dwell with and influence our spiritual selves.* His presence in our hearts will influence not only the feeling of our hearts but the thinking of our minds. The Holy Spirit has the power to penetrate the veil of unbelief, both in our minds and our hearts, if we will seek the Lord and cleanse ourselves as a temple (*see* Ether 4:15).

The *scriptural temple* teaches that we come to know of spiritual truth and the mysteries of God not just with logic, nor just with feelings. Rather, spiritual truth is learned in both our minds and our hearts. That is, *spiritual truth must be logical and feel right.*

The ultimate goal to understand the mysteries of God, even in this life, is to have the mind and the heart "inseparably connected" (D&C 93:33), thinking and feeling as one (*see* Moses 7:18). We demonstrate this oneness of understanding in both our minds and hearts by serving God with both mind and heart (*see* D&C 4:2), because "the Lord requireth the heart and a willing mind" (D&C 64:34).

This doctrine of learning in heart and mind taught in the *scriptural temple* is what King Benjamin preached in his great sermon at the temple of Zarahemla:

> I have not commanded you to come up hither to trifle with the words which I shall speak, but that you should hearken unto me, and open your ears that ye may hear, and your *hearts* that ye may understand, and your *minds* that the *mysteries of God* may be unfolded to your *view.* (Mosiah 2:9)

It is interesting that a similar opening of ears, eyes, minds and hearts occurred at the temple of the land Bountiful when the glory of the Savior and the mysteries of God were revealed to the Nephites (*see* 3 Nephi 1 1:3, 5).

The opening of ears, eyes, minds and hearts occurs when obedience to God ceases to be a burden and becomes a blessing. Then God will endow us with powers from on high and the mysteries of God will be revealed by the power of the Holy Spirit.

The Power of the Holy Ghost Is the Spirit of Prophecy and Revelation of Jesus Christ

The Apostle John defined the spirit of prophecy as the testimony of Jesus (*see* Revelation 19:10). The Apostle Paul confirmed that this testimony is a gift of the Spirit when he wrote that "No man can say that Jesus is the Lord, but by the Holy Ghost (1 Corinthians 12:3; *see also* D&C 46:13). A revealing and prophesying testimony of Jesus Christ is exactly what Adam received when the Holy Ghost fell upon him (*see* Moses 5:9).

Concerning the blessings from the Holy Ghost, Joseph Smith said:

> The *Spirit of Revelation* is in connection with these blessings. A person may profit by noticing the first intimation of the spirit of revelation; for instance, when you *feel* pure intelligence flowing into you, it may give you sudden strokes of ideas . . . Thus by learning the Spirit of God and understanding it, you may grow into the *principle of revelation* until you *become perfect in Christ Jesus.*[6]

Therefore, another power of the Holy Spirit is to reveal Jesus Christ. By the power of the Holy Ghost we can receive, like Oliver Cowdery, the "spirit of revelation" (D&C 8:3) of Jesus Christ in our minds and our hearts.

This spirit of revelation of Christ from the Holy Ghost is powerful because:

- with this spirit we can recognize true messengers of the Lord because we can feel in our hearts that the words they speak are true. (*see* 2 Nephi 33:1)
- with this spirit we can become true messengers of the Lord and speak the words of Christ (*see* 2 Nephi 32:2; D&C 18:33-35).
- with this spirit we can speak with "the power of God unto the convincing of men" (D&C 11:21) to come unto Christ.

- with this spirit we can know God's will for us because "the words of Christ will tell [us] all things what [we] should do" (2 Nephi 32:3).
- with this spirit the Holy Ghost "will show unto us all things [we] should do" (*see* 2 Nephi 32:5) to come unto Christ.

Alma the Younger, the son of the converted priest of King Noah, described the principle of revelation in his own life, and he demonstrated the principle of prophecy by testifying of Christ:

> Do ye not suppose that I know of these things myself? Behold, I testify unto you that I do know that these things whereof I have spoken are true. And how do ye suppose that I know of their surety?
>
> Behold, I say unto you *they are made known unto me by the Holy Spirit of God.* Behold, I have *fasted and prayed* many days that I might *know these things of myself.* And now I do know of myself that they are true; for the Lord God hath made them manifest unto me by his Holy Spirit; and this is *the spirit of revelation* which is in me.
>
> And moreover, I say unto you that it has thus been revealed unto me, that the words which have been spoken by our fathers are true, even so according to *the spirit of prophecy* which is in me, which is also by the manifestation of the Spirit of God.
>
> I say unto you, that I know of myself that whatsoever I shall say unto you, concerning that which is to come, is true; and I say unto you, that *I know that Jesus Christ shall come,* yea, the Son, the Only Begotten of the Father, full of grace, and mercy, and truth. And behold, it is he that cometh to take away the sins of the world, yea, the sins of every man who steadfastly believeth on his name. (Alma 5:45-48)

When Alma reunited with the sons of Mosiah, he found that they also had the spirit of prophecy and revelation:

> Yea, and they had waxed strong in the knowledge of the truth; for they were men of a sound understanding and they had *searched the scriptures* diligently, that they might know the word of God.
>
> But this is not all; they had given themselves to much *prayer,* and *fasting;* therefore they had the *spirit of prophecy,* and the *spirit of revelation,* and when they taught, *they taught with power and authority of God.* (Alma 17:2-3)

Alma and the sons of Mosiah knew in their minds because they were men of sound understanding. But that was not all, they also knew in their hearts because they sought the Lord and His gift of the Spirit.

Like Nephi, Alma and the sons of Mosiah "diligently" (1 Nephi 10:19) sought God, not just mentally but also by striving to feel after Him with the spiritual discipline of a lowly heart, through fasting and prayer. Such spiritual discipline teaches the flesh and mind that acting independently of the spirit or feelings of the heart will not produce a fullness of knowledge and joy, for man is spirit! Therefore, fasting and prayer discipline the will of the mind to become connected to the will of the heart. Both the mind and heart are then open to the will of God, so that "Thy will be done on earth as it is in Heaven" (3 Nephi 13:10).

Since Alma and the sons of Mosiah diligently sought God, they received the power of the Holy Ghost as a gift (*see* 1 Nephi 10:17). They sought the words of Christ through scripture study. They combined their study with the spiritual disciplines of *fasting, or literally hungering and thirsting after righteousness,* and with pleading prayer. Then His power, the spirit of prophecy and revelation, unfolded the words of Christ into a deep, profound understanding in their minds and hearts. This power of the Holy Ghost was a real gift of the Spirit, which strengthened and enhanced the power and authority with which they taught and testified of Jesus Christ throughout their missionary labors.

Christ is the grand prophecy and revelation of the spirit of prophecy and revelation. Therefore, all true messengers of God talk, rejoice, teach, write and prophesy of Christ because He is the source to whom "[all] may look for a remission of their sins" (*see* 2 Nephi 25:26).

The book of Omni reveals a powerful contrast between the writings of those who wrote without the spirit of prophecy and revelation and the writings of Amaleki, who demonstrated this gift. The book of Omni is a short historical account of the succession of the plates, passed from father to son or other relative. When Abinadom received the plates, he stated:

> I know of *no revelation* save that which has been written, *neither prophecy;* wherefore, *that which is sufficient is written.* (Omni 1:11)

It wasn't until Amaleki, the son of Abinadom, that a testimony of Christ was reintroduced into the record. He knew that "that which is sufficient is written" was not sufficient. He affirmed the goodness of King Benjamin, then bore his testimony of Christ:

> And it came to pass that I began to be old; and, having no seed, and knowing King Benjamin to be a just man before the Lord, wherefore,

I shall deliver up these plates unto him, exhorting all men to come unto God, the Holy One of Israel, and *believe in prophesying, and in revelations, . . .* and *continue in fasting and praying,* and endure to the end. (Omni 1:25-26)

One of the most remarkable scriptural examples of the spirit of prophecy and revelation of Jesus Christ as a gift of the Spirit, even the gift of the great and last promise of the temple, occurred in the temple eight days after the Savior's birth. Simeon, a devout and just man, seeking for the great and last promise of the temple in his own life, came by the spirit unto the temple where "the Holy Ghost was upon him." There he held the child Jesus in his arms and bore testimony of His divinity when he said: "Mine eyes have seen thy salvation. . . . This child is set for the fall and rising again of many in Israel. . . . that the thoughts of many hearts may be revealed" (*see* Luke 2:25-35).

If, like Simeon, we come with the Spirit to the temple, and desire to be taught in the temple by the Spirit then, in the temple, we will receive the spirit of prophecy and revelation of Jesus Christ. This is how we are prepared for the great and last promise of the temple.

The Power of the Holy Ghost Is the Power of the Word of God

As a physician who understands the piercing power required to divide bone and joint asunder, yet seeing some pleasing results in healing the delicacies of the wounded hand, I marvel at the power of the word of God (*see* D&C 6:2 and Jacob 2:8).

The word of Christ, the healing word of God, is indeed, powerful and pleasing. As Alma discovered, "it has more effect on the minds of people than the sword or anything else" (Alma 31:5). Even the written word of God contains "the convincing power of God" (3 Nephi 28:29). Perhaps this is why heavenly messengers often quote scripture, and why the Savior expounded the scriptures to the Nephites (*see* 3 Nephi 23:14).

The word of God, spoken or written, has the power to illuminate the truth that we know in our hearts. "For the voice of the Lord is unto all men, and there is none to escape; . . . neither heart that shall not be penetrated" (D&C 1:2). Like beautiful poetry, the word of God focuses our thoughts to a remembrance of the truths that we already know in our hearts.

To experience the unique power of the words and voice of God in the heart as *piercing, pleasing,* and *healing,* is a profound experience witnessed in the *scriptural temple.* On Horeb, the holy mountain of God, the word of the Lord came to Elijah, but he didn't feel the power of the Lord in the wind, a strong earthquake, or fire until he felt the power of "a still small voice" (*see* 1 Kings 19:8-9, 11-12). At the temple in the land Bountiful the voice of God, again a small voice, did pierce to the very center of those who heard it, and caused their hearts to burn (*see* 3 Nephi 11:3. *See also* Luke 24:32.)

The voice of the Spirit that can pierce the heart is heard and felt in the temple. It is the confirming response to our plea that God hear our voices.

Perhaps we are told to whisper in the temple not only for the sake of reverence, but to remind us that the pleasing voice of perfect mildness is a whisper (*see* Helaman 5:30) that "whispereth through and pierceth all things" (D&C 85:6) and inspires us to do the will of the Spirit (*see* Words of Mormon 1:7).

We can read or hear the word of God in our minds, but to have the "still voice of perfect mildness" (Helaman 5:30) pierce to the center of the soul is to feel the power of the voice of the Spirit as burning in our hearts. By this profound experience, when our spirits are enlightened, we come to know for ourselves with "surety" (D&C 5:12), the spiritual truth of things as they really are. Therefore, to avoid "condemnation" (D&C 93:32), we are commanded to "give diligent heed to the words of eternal life:"

> And I now give unto you a commandment to beware concerning yourselves, to give diligent heed to *the words of eternal life.*
>
> For *you shall live by every word that proceedeth forth from the mouth of God.*
>
> For the word of the Lord is *truth,* and whatsoever is truth is *light,* and whatsoever is light is *Spirit,* even the *Spirit of Jesus Christ.*
>
> And the Spirit giveth light to every man that cometh into the world; and the Spirit enlighteneth every man through the world, that hearkeneth to *the voice of the Spirit.* (D&C 84:43-46)

This spirit, revealing and testifying of Christ, is the Holy Spirit, our teacher in the temple. It is here that we learn most about Jesus Christ and our relation to Him. It is here that the "still voice of perfect mildness" can heal us (*see* John 12:40) and perfect us. As Joseph Smith said, because of the spirit of revelation we become healed and perfected in Christ Jesus.

Symbolic Jewels: Pearls of the Spirit

The text of the temple is the scriptures, and the teacher of the text is the Holy Spirit. *The teaching technique He uses is symbolism.* A single scripture establishes the importance of this teaching technique. "The baptismal font was instituted *as a similitude of the grave, . . . that all things may have their likeness, and that they may accord one with another—that which is earthly conforming to that which is heavenly*" (D&C 128:13).

This scripture teaches that all things on earth are a reflection of a higher spiritual reality (*see also* D&C 77:2). We need the teaching of the Holy Spirit to help us make the connection to this spiritual reality and to escape the "prison-house" mindset of mortality.

With symbols, the Holy Spirit prompts us to search for the meaning of a higher spiritual reality. Then, with the spirit of revelation, He makes the unifying connection in our minds and our hearts. This means that we need to understand the dimensions of the spiritual realm in our mind with symbols of dimension (size, shape, quality, quantity, etc.). Also, we need to "feel" truth in our heart, since many spiritual truths do not have familiar earthly dimensions but only forgotten spiritual dimensions. We really begin to see the whole picture, the great view, with this teaching technique.

As we learn this technique, we need to remember two other scriptural applications pertaining to symbolism. First, "my thoughts are not your thoughts, neither are your ways my ways, saith the Lord. For as the heavens are higher than the earth, *so are my ways higher than your ways, and my thoughts than your thoughts*" (Isaiah 55:8-9), and second, "verily I say unto you that *all things unto me are spiritual*" (D&C 29:34). If we are to be taught spiritual truths by the Holy Spirit, then we must learn to think on a spiritual level.

In *The Holiness of Everyday Life*, Joan MacDonald describes the need to think spiritually:

> Discipline, evaluation, striving for excellence, and developing personal integrity—these are common experiences of the workplace that help develop character. But developing character isn't enough . . . work can develop and reveal our souls. A soul is more than character. To develop one's soul implies a deep spiritual effort, and to be spiritual

implies a connection to God. . . . We need to see, understand, and experience God. We also need to know and understand ourselves. . . . We want to know that God loves and accepts us how we are, and we want to experience Him helping us to become better. . . . We are in luck, because the revealing of God, of ourselves, and of the connection between ourselves and God occurs all around us. . . . The key to seeing it is awareness. (p. 8.)

The spirit and the body are the soul of man (*see* D&C 88:165).

The Sabbath and the workday, the sacred and the secular are the soul of our lives.

All things are spiritual to the Lord. If I am to become more like my Heavenly Father, then all things must be spiritual to me also. (p. 4.)[7]

Elder Orson F. Whitney once said that "*the universe is built on symbols, lifting our thoughts from man to God, earth to heaven and time to eternity.*"[8]

Joan MacDonald would agree with Elder Whitney, but probably would add that through symbols, the spiritual frontier that we need to probe in this life is not so much above us as it is within us.

The teaching technique of symbolism in the temple has a focal point. Two scriptures identify this point. "*All things given of God unto man, are the typifying of Him*" (2 Nephi 11:4) and "*all things are created and made to bear record of Me*" (Moses 6:63).

The focal point is the Savior, Jesus Christ. It is an incredible awakening to realize the truth of the two preceding scriptures. This awakening is still occurring to me in the temple. It is one aspect of temple worship that is repeatedly exciting. *We should understand the core doctrines of Christ then explore the multiple meanings through the symbolic teachings of the Holy Spirit. We should see in the symbols of our temple worship the doctrines of Christ,* just as the forgotten symbols of the Aaronic Priesthood temple of ancient Israel pointed to Christ.

For instance, a circle within a square, the symbolic motif of the Bountiful, Utah temple, is very dominant. It is everywhere, even on the planter boxes in the parking lot. The *square* might symbolize measured time and space, the secular or mortal man. The *circle* could symbolize eternity, the woman, the Spirit, or the immortal God. Therefore, the circle in the square might symbolize time and eternity, the spirit in man and woman, or the Holy Spirit and God striving with man and woman, or man and woman as one. The symbol in this motif that is most revealing to me, found in a few isolated places in the temple, is the octagon: a square becoming a circle or an unpolished gem becoming a jewel.

The *symbol of the circle as a reflection of the eternal* is a powerful symbol in all temples and in our daily lives. While the earth is described in the scriptures as having four corners (North, East, South, West), it is nevertheless a globe and, in one plane, a circle, suggesting the measure of its creation. In our families and in the temple, we gather in prayer circles as we petition the Eternal Father. Often, in the celestial room, friends and families gather in circles of joy, reflecting the eternal nature of their relationships. These symbols of eternity help us understand that "the course of the Lord is one eternal round" (*see* 1 Nephi 10:19; Alma 7:20; Alma 37:12; D&C 3:2).

The eternal round of the Lord is symbolic of His omniscience and omnipresence (*see* D&C 38:2), with past, present, and future continually before Him (*see* D&C 130:7). *A significant symbolic meaning of the "eternal round" is that if we strictly follow the eternal plan of the Eternal Father, we can arrive from whence we came.*

The Apostle John Widtsoe expressed the power of endowment symbols when he said: "No man or woman can come out of the temple endowed as they should be *unless they have seen beyond the symbols, the mighty realities for which they stand.*"[9]

In his book, *Endowed from on High*, John Charles made this significant observation in a more personal interpretation of Elder Widtsoe's statement: "The most meaningful insights occur when you begin to see how events and aspects of your own life function as signified [the personal meaning of symbols], to the endowment's signifiers [the symbols], i.e. *how the endowment provides a symbolic representation of your daily life.*"[10]

As a hand surgeon, I love the symbolism of the hand in the temple and in many scriptural verses (*see* Galatians 2:9; JST Genesis 24:8; Deuteronomy 5:15; Jeremiah 18:6; 1 Timothy 2:8; Acts 7:55; D&C 123:7). The scripture with a hand symbol that is most meaningful to me is in Isaiah: "Fear thou not; for I am with thee: be not dismayed; for I am thy God: I will strengthen thee; yea, I will help thee; Yea, *I will uphold thee with the right hand of my righteousness*" (Isaiah 41:10). This is the scriptural basis for the words of the well-known hymn "How Firm a Foundation," one of my favorites.

In May 1977, I began my final examinations in medical school. I already had a job in Detroit, and my family was waiting for me there. All had to go well. Therefore, I prayed for a feeling of assurance that all would go well.

The Sunday before the examinations began, I went to church and sang the opening hymn *How Firm a Foundation.* "Fear not, I am with thee; oh, be not dismayed," the third verse began. Suddenly the words stood out in bold, brazen type and penetrated me with such force that I could no longer sing. I listened, transfixed, as the remaining words were sung: "For I am thy god and will still give thee aid. I'll strengthen thee, help thee, and cause thee to stand, . . . Upheld by my righteous, upheld by my righteous, upheld by my righteous, omnipotent hand."

The experience was so powerful that I knew I had just received an answer to my prayers. I went to the exams with great confidence.

John Charles's observation, connecting the events of our own lives with the symbols and teachings of the endowment, *results in making personal covenants with the Lord* (*see* D&C 40:1). Because of my "How Firm a Foundation" experience, *the symbolism of the "omnipotent hand"* will always have deep, personal meaning for me. It draws me to the Lord to be bound to Him with covenants.

While there is repetitiveness in temple worship, it should never be banal to us. This is true because *we symbolically climb Mount Zion and personally enter the Lord's presence each time we receive the endowment.* In this climb, we are symbolically taught by the Spirit. As the layers of meaning unfold to us, *we see personal application and meaning* in our climb of Mount Zion. Then we should make personal covenants with the Lord and return and report to Him on our progress. As we keep the covenants, the climb becomes easier but more exciting because the Lord unfolds the great view and prepares us for His rest.

The Savior's advice to those who listened to his temple sermon in the Book of Mormon can aptly be applied to us as we learn the teaching technique of symbolism in the temple. "Therefore, go ye unto your homes, and *ponder upon the things which I have said, and ask of the father, in my name, that ye may understand and prepare your minds* for the morrow, and I come unto you again" (3 Nephi 17:3).

When pondering what we learn from symbols in the temple, we should correlate them to the scriptures and to our daily lives. We should ponder these things in our hearts (*see* Luke 2:19). If we do, we will be taught with the spirit of revelation by the Holy Spirit. Then we will understand the meaning and application of these symbols in order to know all things that we should do to come unto Christ.

We should prepare our minds and our hearts by study, prayer, fasting, and righteous living, then *come again to the temple often, eager to be taught by the Spirit.* When we do this, the Savior will come again and draw near to us through our teacher, the Holy Spirit, because He is eager to teach us.

A New Name for a New Birth in a New Marriage Covenant

The final act of initiation for the first ascent of Mount Zion is a very personal expression of love from the Lord before He sends us on our way. I like to think it is as personal as the privilege that I have as a father and priesthood holder to name and bless my newborn children before they ascend through life. Perhaps we received such a blessing at the hand of our Father in Heaven before descending to mortality.

The act of renaming is a sign that we personally will enter into a new covenant relationship. A married woman understands that taking upon her the name of her husband is the sign of a new relationship in her life. This custom is probably a residual practice from the renaming of Eve by Adam, and then both of them taking the name of "Adam" (*see* Genesis 5:2) because they had united as one in the covenant of marriage. The practice of taking the name of the bridegroom extends to the spiritual marriage of Jehovah and the House of Israel, when all under this marriage covenant will be called "the Lord Our Righteousness" (*see* Jeremiah 23:6; 33:16).

This covenant sign was even given to the children of Israel in the Sinai, who erred in their hearts as the Lord attempted to redeem them: "And *they shall put my name upon the children of Israel;* and I will bless them" (Numbers 6:27).

The full covenant meaning of this sign was given to our patriarch fathers such as Abraham and Jacob and the Apostle Paul. I think it is significant that Jacob had to "wrestle" (diligently seek) the Lord to get this sign. *The covenant nature of this sign expresses that God accepts us as spiritually begotten sons or daughters* as we accept Him with an eye single to His glory as our God and our Father. *We accept Him by accepting His Son as our Bridegroom in a "marriage covenant" relationship.* In his book *Our Father Abraham,* Marvin Wilson said that "to understand Biblical marriages is to understand the Biblical concept of covenant."[11]

In the temple, we symbolically enact a "marriage covenant" relationship with God, when we receive a new name, in anticipation of a future naming by the Lord Himself:

> And the Gentiles shall see thy righteousness, and all kings thy glory: and *thou shalt be called by a new name which the mouth of the Lord shall name.* (Isaiah 62:2)

> Him that overcometh will I make a pillar in the temple of my God . . . And *I will write upon him my new name.* (Revelation 3:12)

In his great temple sermon in Zarahemla, King Benjamin gave to the people gathered at the temple a new name to distinguish them as a righteous, covenant people:

> And moreover, *I shall give this people a name,* that thereby they may be distinguished above all the people which the Lord God hath brought out of the land of Jerusalem; and this I do because they have been a diligent people in keeping the commandments of the Lord.
> And *I give unto them a name that never shall be blotted out, except it be through transgression.* (Mosiah 1:11-12)

At the end of his sermon, King Benjamin revealed the name he had chosen to give his people:

> Therefore, I would that ye should take upon you *the name of Christ, all you that have entered into the covenant with God that ye should be obedient unto the end of your lives.*
> And it shall come to pass that whosoever doeth this shall be found at the right hand of God, for *he shall know the name by which he is called; for he shall be called by the name of Christ.*
> And I would that ye should remember also, that this is the name that I said I should give unto you that never should be blotted out, except it be through transgression; . . .
> I say unto you, I would that *ye should remember to retain the name written always in your hearts,* . . . that *ye hear and know the voice by which ye shall be called, and also, the name by which he shall call you.* (Mosiah 5:8-9, 11-12)

When Alma, who was asked to judge the "rising generation" (Mosiah 26:1) of those children who could not understand and then who would not believe the words of King Benjamin, he inquired of the Lord. When the Lord said to Alma "They are mine" (*see* Mosiah 26:18), he was reminded of the close "marriage covenant" relationship that those who bear the name of Christ have with Him. This is the same possessive expression the Lord used when He established and will establish a covenant relationship as "the time of love" with the House of Israel (*see* Ezekiel 16:8).

In giving our hearts to Christ by accepting his covenants, He becomes our bridegroom and we become his bride. We who keep His covenants are not only the bride of Christ, but through the travail of the Atonement (*see* Isaiah 42:14; John 16:21; John 17:1; Alma 7:11-12), we can become his spiritually begotten children.

King Benjamin taught that entering into and keeping covenants with Christ is how we become the children of Christ. "And now, *because of the covenant which ye have made ye shall be called the children of Christ, his sons and his daughters; for behold, this day he hath spiritually begotten you;* for ye say that your hearts are changed through faith on his name; therefore, ye are born of him and have become his sons and his daughters" (Mosiah 5:7. *See also* D&C 5:16).

The Meaning of Taking the Name of Christ Upon Us

When we become the new bride and the new sons and daughters of Christ, we receive a new name. It is His name. Weekly, we are reminded of this new name as we listen to the sacrament prayer: ". . . And witness unto thee, O God, the Eternal Father, that *they are willing to take upon them the name of thy Son*" (Moroni 4:3).

At the sacrament altar we make a covenant to take Christ's name upon us. The most significant word of the sacrament prayers, and thus the covenant, is "witness." This word implies action on our part, by witnessing to the world that we have taken upon us the name of Christ in the sense that we carry or "bear" His name (*see* Mosiah 26:18). *The action required is emulation of the actions of the Savior. It is to "walk in his ways"* (Deuteronomy 30:16) and *"confess (witness) Him,"* not fearing to be "put out of the synagogue" or desiring "the praise of men more than the praise of God" (John 12:42-43).

It is not sufficient to just do the expected or the customary; we must do the right thing, though it is often unexpected, regardless of environmental or social pressures. Emulation of the Savior includes being a "good Samaritan" and being so "unto the least of these my brethren"

(Matthew 25:40). It is being able to say, "If it were not so I would have told you" (John 14:2). It is to "render therefore unto Caesar the things which are Caesar's; and unto God the things that are God's" (Matthew 22:21). It is overcoming sin with both justice and mercy through repentance and forgiveness (*see* John 8:7, 10-11). It is to have such great love for others "that a man lay down his life for his friends" (John 15:13).

By these actions, performed with a broken heart and contrite spirit, we keep the sacramental covenant and thus partake of it worthily. This sacrament covenant prepares and reminds us to keep temple covenants that we "do always remember Him" by witnessing that we take His name upon us.

Bearing the Name of Christ Starts with a Seed Planted in the Heart

Before we can take the name of Christ upon us and be called "the people of the Lord," we must first "hear the word of the Lord and His will concerning [us]," listening with an "ear from afar" and with "open hearts" (*see* D&C 63:1).

It is no wonder then, that the Savior was disturbed at the dispute among the Nephites concerning the name of their church. In the great sermon on the Temple Mount, He had taught this same sacramental covenant. In addition, King Benjamin's temple sermon must have been part of the scriptures these Nephites had in their possession. Therefore, the Savior reminded them that taking His name upon them was a matter of endurance and of functioning with an eye single to His work and His glory when He said, "Have they not read the scriptures, which say *ye must take upon you the name of Christ, which is my name? For by this name shall ye be called at the last day; And whoso taketh upon him my name, and endureth to the end, the same shall be saved at the last day*" (3 Nephi 27:5-6).

In his teachings, Alma explained that taking the name of Christ upon us is not only believing in Him but also on His word, and then acting in accordance with this belief:

And now, behold, I say unto you, and I would that ye should remember, that God is merciful unto all who *believe on his name;* therefore he desireth, in the first place, that *ye should believe, yea, even on his word.*

. . . if ye will awake and arouse your faculties, even to an experiment upon my words. (Alma 32:22, 27)

The experiment will work if His words are mixed with our faith (*see* Hebrews 4:2).

Alma compared the word of Christ to a seed planted in the heart, that grows and enlightens our understanding until we can say "it beginneth to be delicious to me" (Alma 32:28). Once we experiment upon the word by keeping commandments and covenants, and feel the "swelling within our breasts," and "taste the light" (Alma 32:35), then we must "press forward, feasting upon the word of Christ" (2 Nephi 31:20).

We partake of the fruit of the tree of life by feasting upon and obeying all the words of Christ. This is how we can fully take Christ's name upon us. Then His name will be written always in our heart (*see* Mosiah 5:12) by the covenants of the heart that we keep with Him. Alma even reasoned that if we plant the seed and nourish it, it will "take root" in you and become "a tree springing up unto everlasting life" (*see* Alma 32:40-42). Therefore, we can grow a tree of life within us and ultimately become like the Savior, by taking His name upon us.

In its early growth, as we experiment upon the word, with patience, diligence and faith, demonstrating obedience to commandments, then the young tree of life within us will "bring forth therefore, fruits worthy of repentance" (*see* Luke 3:8; Alma 34:30).

The taste of the fruits of repentance makes us want to taste more of the tree of life. Therefore we take the name of Christ upon us through baptism. This covenant with Christ brings the baptism of fire by the Holy Spirit, which baptism produces in our personal tree of life fruits of the Spirit (*see* Galatians 5:18, 22-23). We then realize that the fruits "meet" or worthy of repentance and the fruits of the Spirit come from the growth we experience in keeping ordinances and covenants with the Lord (*see* Alma 13:13-16). As we continue to keep more covenants, especially temple covenants, our nature continues to change until the fruit produced by the tree of life within us truly becomes "delicious," or "fruit meet for their Father's Kingdom" (D&C 84:58).

The Temple Blessings
for Taking Christ's Name Upon Us

Taking the name of Christ upon us in the sacrament covenant prepares us to fully feast upon the tree of life and nourish our own tree of life in the temple. This occurs when we graft or bind ourselves through covenants to His tree, that we grow straight and produce much fruit. "I am the vine," the Savior said. "Ye are the branches: *He that abideth in me, and I in him, the same bringeth forth much fruit:* for without me ye can do nothing" (John 15:5).

When we are bound by covenant to Christ, we become His spiritual, covenant offspring (*see* D&C 5:14). As His spiritual "branches," we can bring forth much spiritual fruit. Through temple covenants, we will grow from branches to a "pillar [king or queen] in the temple . . . to go no more out" (Revelation 3:12).

It is in the temple that we truly learn how to take His name upon us, "that no combination of wickedness shall have power to rise up and prevail over *thy people upon whom thy name shall be put in this house*" (D&C 109:26).

In the temple we can fully take the name of the Lord upon us because there both men and women can receive the powerful blessings of the fullness of the Priesthood in His Holy Order. This is what Abraham learned when he left the Chaldeans. The Lord said to him, "Behold, I will lead thee by my hand, and *I will take thee, to put upon thee my name, even the Priesthood of thy father, and my power shall be over thee*" (Abraham 1:18).

In the temple we learn that the covenants we make with Christ will be as valid as covenants with the Father. Taking upon us the name of Christ and remaining true to His name ultimately leads to taking upon us the name of the Father with the "Father's name written" upon us (*see* Revelation 14:1; 22:4).

Elder Bruce R. McConkie exclaimed the ultimate meaning of taking upon us the name of God when he said, "*to have his name written on a person is to identify that person as a god. How can it be said more plainly? Those who gain eternal life become gods!*"[12]

As we become sealed to our Heavenly Father through our spiritual rebirth by His Son, then the Father gives us a new name as a token of this sealing because we have become new creatures (*see* Isaiah 62:2; Revelation 3:12):

> Then the white stone mentioned in Revelation 2:17, will become a Urim and Thummim to each individual who receives one, whereby things pertaining to a higher order of kingdoms will be made known;

And *a white stone is given to each of those who come into the celestial kingdom, whereon is a new name written, which no man knoweth save he that receiveth it. The new name is the key word.* (D&C 130:10-11)

Apparently, learning how to take upon us the name of Christ is the key to that key word, a new name that will unlock the knowledge of celestial glory. This is why Joseph Smith said that *"knowledge through our Lord and Savior Jesus Christ is the grand key that unlocks the glories and mysteries of the kingdom of heaven."*[13]

The New and Everlasting Covenant: A Covenant of the Heart

To be equipped to climb Mount Zion and understand the great endowment we must understand the nature of covenants with the Lord. We already learned one aspect of the nature of His covenants: they bind us to Him with a close, personal relationship like a marriage covenant.

The Lord taught that strict obedience to the commandments of God, by sacrifice of all earthly things, is how we must keep covenants and therefore obtain the keys to the knowledge of eternal life:

Verily I say unto you, all among them who know their hearts are honest, and are broken, and their spirits contrite, and are willing to *observe their covenants by sacrifice*—yea, every sacrifice which I, the Lord, shall command—they are accepted of me. (D&C 97:8)

Joseph Smith reaffirmed this scripture when he said, "If a man would obtain the keys of the kingdom of an end, *he must sacrifice all things.*"[14]

Under the law of Moses, the main covenant principle taught was making and keeping covenants by sacrifice (*see* Psalms 50:5). Animal sacrifice was not only symbolic of the sacrifice of Jesus Christ, but it also symbolized the sacrifice of the beast-like nature of each person who promised to keep the covenants.

In reference to making covenants with the Lord by taking His name upon us, it is interesting that King Benjamin stated that we *"retain the name always written in our hearts"* (Mosiah 5:12). This significant statement refers to the type of temple covenants we keep with the Lord. They are not carnal covenants written on stone, except to reflect the "everlasting" nature of the covenant. They are not stone-cold business contracts. They are spiritual covenants made with our spirit—our true heart. Therefore, *they are covenants based on love, written by "the spirit of the living God; in the fleshy tables of the heart"* (2 Corinthians 3:3) as the Holy Spirit lovingly teaches us. For "after this manner bringeth to pass the Father, the covenants which He hath made unto the children of men (Moroni 7:32).

To those under the law of Moses, the Lord prophesied "this manner" of covenants. "Behold, the days come saith the Lord, that I will make a new covenant with the House of Israel," the Prophet Jeremiah wrote. "I will put my law in their inward parts and *write it in their hearts"* (Jeremiah 31:31, 33).

The "days" came when Christ came to the earth, making possible the new and everlasting covenant through the Atonement. This new covenant is contained in the Sermon on the Mount and the Sermon on the Temple Mount. *Their core doctrine is a transformation of the heart by making covenants with Christ through His holy ordinances, that we might be prepared to meet God.*

Perhaps, as emphasized in all four Gospels and the Book of Mormon, this is why Christ consistently taught and performed at the temple, directing our attention to this holy place as the place where we will find His sanctifying power (*see* Matthew 12:6). It appears that His message at "His Father's house," that disturbed so many Jews (*see* Mark 14:58), was the fulfillment of the Mosaic temple order and the need for a change to the original "Melchizedek" temple order. This change required not only proper priesthood authority, but also ordinances of holiness and covenants of the heart, not just outward acts of the hand (*see* Hosea 6:1-2, 6-7). This new (original) temple order and covenant was based on the power and grace of the Atonement. Thus, Christ truly came to fulfill the laws of the Gospel including the law of Moses (*see* Alma 34:13-14). Paul and the early Christian saints understood this new covenant and temple order:

> Now of the things which we have spoken [the new temple order] this is the sum: *We have such an high priest, who is set on the right hand of the throne of the Majesty in the heavens;*
> A minister of the sanctuary, and of the true tabernacle, which the Lord pitched and not man.
> *But now hath he obtained a more excellent ministry, by how much also he is the mediator of a better covenant, which was established upon better promises.*

For if that first covenant had been faultless, then should no place have been sought for the second.

For finding fault with them, he saith, Behold, the days come, saith the Lord, when *I will make a new covenant with the house of Israel and with the house of Judah:*

Not according to the covenant that I made with their fathers in the day when I took them by the hand to lead them out of the land of Egypt; because they continued not in my covenant, [the first covenant] and I regarded them not, saith the Lord.

For this is the covenant [the new covenant] *that I will make with the house of Israel after those days, saith the Lord; I will put my laws into their mind, and write them in their hearts: and I will be to them a God, and they shall be to me a people.* (Hebrews 8:1-2, 6-10)

The "new covenants" that we receive in the Melchizedek Priesthood temples today are not the schoolmaster Mosaic laws that lead us to Christ. They are the spiritual covenants of Christ (see D&C 29:35) with which He leads us to the Father.

I give unto you these sayings that you may understand and *know how to worship,* and know *what you worship, that you may come unto the Father in my name, and in due time receive of his fulness.*

For if you keep my commandments you shall receive of his fulness, and *be glorified in me as I am in the Father.* (D&C 93:19-20)

I am the Lord thy God; and I give unto you this commandment— that *no man shall come unto the Father but by me or by my word,* which is my law, saith the Lord. (D&C 132:12)

As John Charles said, *the covenants of the temple "penetrate to the core of how we will live our life."*[15] They take us to the threshold of spiritual decision: *How much are we willing to sacrifice to become holy?* Therefore they are spiritual covenants to be understood by the mind and the heart.

Our relationship with the Lord is developed through covenants. Psalm 24:14 points out that *"the secret of the Lord is with them that fear Him: He will show them His covenant."*

Without covenants, God could not fulfill His promise to bless His people, because a covenant "binds (seals) God to us" (*see* D&C 82:10) and us to Him in a marriage of loving commitment, while maintaining the law of agency. *A covenant binds us together by the power of love.*

A covenant is an ultimate expression of our desire to live a command-
ment of the Lord because we love Him (see 1 John 5:3). Therefore,
Christ's name is always written in our hearts *(see* Mosiah 5:12) because
His covenants are written in our hearts. *This is how we come to the Lord*
with "full purpose of heart" (see 2 Nephi 31:13; Jacob 6:5).

To covenant with the Lord is to enter an order of solemn ordinances,
obligations, and promises, instituted from before the foundation of the
world. In the 132nd section of the Doctrine and Covenants, which introduces the "new and everlasting covenant" (the total of all gospel
covenants[16]) and specifically the Holy Order of Matrimony, the Lord
used very direct terms explaining how we are bound to Him in His order
through His everlasting covenants:

> For all who will have a blessing at my hands shall abide the law
> which was appointed for that blessing, and the conditions thereof, as
> were instituted from before the foundation of the world.
>
> And as pertaining to the new and everlasting covenant, it was insti-
> tuted for the fullness of my glory; and he that receiveth a fullness there-
> of must and shall abide the law, . . .
>
> And verily I say unto you, that the conditions of this law are these:
> *All covenants . . . that are not made and entered into and sealed by the*
> *Holy Spirit of promise, . . . by revelation and commandment through*
> *the medium of mine anointed, whom I have appointed on the earth to*
> *hold this power, are of no efficacy, virtue or force in and after the res-*
> *urrection from the dead; for all contracts that are not made unto this*
> *end have an end when men are dead.*
>
> Behold, mine house is a house of order, saith the Lord God, and not
> a house of confusion.
>
> Will I accept an offering that is not made in my name? Or will I
> receive at your hands that which I have not appointed?
>
> *And will I appoint unto you, saith the Lord, except it be by law, even*
> *as I and my Father ordained unto you, before the world was?*
>
> I am the Lord thy God; and I give unto you this commandment—
> *that no man shall come unto the Father but by me or by my word,*
> *which is my law,* saith the Lord.
>
> For whatsoever things remain are by me; and whatsoever things are
> not by me shall be shaken and destroyed. (D&C 132:5-12, 14)

The principle of order in this new and everlasting covenant was certainly applied by the Lord concerning the dead works performed before
the restoration of priesthood authority:

Behold, I say unto you that all old covenants have I caused to be done away in this thing; and *this is a new and an everlasting covenant, even that which was from the beginning.*

Wherefore, although a man should be baptized an hundred times it availeth him nothing, for you cannot enter in at the strait gate by the law of Moses, neither by your dead works.

For it is because of your dead works that I have caused this last covenant and this church to be built up unto me, even as in days of old.

Wherefore, enter ye in at the gate, as I have commanded, and seek not to counsel your God, Amen. (D&C 22:1-4)

The Holy Spirit of Promise ignites the bonding reaction of us to Christ and to each other through covenant relationships of the heart. The Holy Spirit is the catalyst of this bonding because He can reveal to us "things as they really are" and "bring all things to [our] spiritual remembrance" (*see* Jacob 4:13; John 14:26). *Perhaps one reason He is the Holy Spirit of Promise is because He can plant the promises of the Father in our heart and make them grow to understanding in our mind.* If we respond and are true to His teachings, the bond (the covenant with Christ) will be sealed (certified) by the Holy Spirit and hold forever.

Covenants for the Last Time in the Fulness of Times

The Apostle Paul had a vision of our dispensation and the great covenants and sealings with the Lord that will gather all things in Christ when he said "that in the dispensation of the fulness of times he might gather together in one all things in Christ, both which are in heaven, and which are on earth; even in him" (Ephesians 1:10).

The beginning of the gathering "together in one all things in Christ . . . all things, both which are in heaven, and which are on earth" (*see* D&C 27:13) was the restoration of the fullness of the gospel "for the last time [in the] fulness of times." This occurred when the keys, covenants. and ordinances of God's kingdom were given to Joseph Smith.

In a revelation concerning the Nauvoo Temple, the Lord made the connection between this dispensation of the fullness of times and the temple:

And verily I say unto you, let this house be built unto my name, that I may reveal mine ordinances therein unto my people;

For I deign to reveal unto my church things which have been kept hid from before the foundation of the world, things that pertain to the dispensation of the fulness of times. (D&C 124:40-41)

Brigham Young encouraged worthy Saints in Nauvoo to receive ordinances and covenants in the temple. He did this with great urgency, not only because he knew the Nauvoo Temple would be destroyed but because of the importance of temple covenants and work in this dispensation (*see* D&C 112:30-31; D&C 124:47). The dispensation of the fullness of times is the dispensation of great temple work, as defined by President Wilford Woodruff, when he said, *"this is the great work of the last dispensation—the redemption of the living and the dead."*[17]

It is the dispensation when righteous men and women understand the importance of taking upon themselves the name of Christ. In so doing they receive in the temple new names for themselves and the dead, entering into a new covenant relationship with their Redeemer and their Heavenly Father.

7

The Great Endowment—
The Purifying Power of Mount Zion

An Endowment Is Given
When We Serve God upon His Mountain

In spite of procrastination by the Saints, the Lord persisted in endow-
ing His people with temple ordinances and covenants hid from the foundation of the world. Even in the midst of the afflictions of Zion's Camp,
the Lord declared a great blessing, a "great endowment": "For behold,
*I have prepared a great endowment and blessing to be poured out upon
them, inasmuch as they are faithful and continue in humility before me*"
(D&C 105:12).

Joseph Smith may have known about the endowment as early as
1823 when Moroni appeared to him and "offered many explanations"
(JHS 1:41) about the restoration of the gospel. The Prophet of this
restoration was certainly aware of an endowment of power from God as
early as 1831, when he received a revelation concerning the "exodus"
to the Ohio from Fayette, New York: "Wherefore, for this cause I give
you the commandment [D&C 37:1] that ye should go to the Ohio; and
there I shall give unto you my law; and *there you shall be endowed with
power from on high*" (D&C 38:32).

This scripture reflects the commandment of the Lord to Moses on
Mount Sinai concerning the exodus from Egypt, that "when thou hast
brought forth the people out of Egypt, *ye shall serve God upon this
mountain*" (Exodus 3:2).

The greatness of the blessing awaiting the Saints' exodus to Ohio
echoes the "holy nation" blessing promised in the Sinai exodus: "And
inasmuch as my people shall assemble themselves at the Ohio, *I have
kept in store a blessing such as is not known among the children of men,*

and it shall be poured forth upon their heads. And from thence men shall go forth into all nations" (D&C 39:15).

The commandment to build a holy mountain, a temple, in which the saints of the Ohio exodus would serve God was given in 1832, in the "olive leaf" revelation:

> Tarry ye, tarry ye in this place, and call a solemn assembly, even of those who are the first laborers in this last kingdom.
>
> And I give unto you, who are the first laborers in this last kingdom, a commandment that you assemble yourselves together, and organize yourselves, and *prepare yourselves, and sanctify yourselves; yea, purify your hearts, and cleanse your hands and your feet before me, that I may make you clean;*
>
> Organize yourselves; prepare every needful thing; and *establish a house, even a house of prayer, a house of fasting, a house of faith, a house of learning, a house of glory, a house of order, a house of God.* (D&C 88:70, 74, 119)

This commandment to build a house of God in Kirtland was not immediately obeyed. Joseph Smith was reminded of the commandment six months later in a revelation where the connection between the temple and the endowment was established:

> Yea, verily I say unto you, *I gave unto you a commandment that you should build a house, in the which house I design to endow those whom I have chosen with power from on high;*
>
> *For this is the promise of the Father unto you;* Therefore I command you to tarry, even as mine apostles at Jerusalem. (D&C 95:8-9)

What a marvelous reference to the companion scripture, for the apostles in Jerusalem also received a "great endowment," probably as they served God on holy mountains or places set apart for holiness:

> And, behold, *I send the promise of my Father upon you:* but tarry ye in the city of Jerusalem, *until ye be endued with power from on high.* (Luke 24:49)

Section 88 of the Doctrine and Covenants is particularly significant to the temple endowment because it contains important scriptures concerning the great and last promise of the temple. This promise is the same great promise given to the children of Israel after their exodus from Egypt. This great promise was the rest of the Lord once they were sanctified (*see* Exodus 19:10-11).

To Be Endowed Is to Be Covered with the Power of Christ

The Greek meaning of the word *enduo* is *a covering of raiment or virtue.*[1] Therefore a metaphorical expression in the Savior's sermon on the Temple Mount implied an endowment of glorious clothing to the chosen twelve.

> And why take ye thought for raiment? Consider the lilies of the field how they grow; they toil not, neither do they spin;
> And yet I say unto you, that even Solomon, in all his glory, was not arrayed like one of these.
> Wherefore, if God so clothe the grass of the field, which today is, and tomorrow is cast into the oven, *even so will he clothe you,* if ye are not of little faith. (3 Nephi 13:28-30)

To be "arrayed like one of these," in the context of the temple, is to be endowed with the garment of salvation and the robes of righteousness. The endowment is a great gift of power from Christ. It is the gift for which He paid with His blood to purchase us, as the Hebrew groom purchased his bride. This gift becomes *our dowry, or "en-dower-ment."*[2]

To help us understand the power of the Atonement, *the temple endowment teaches us about the realm from which we fell and the possibility of our return to this realm because of the Atonement.* The endowment gift is not only this knowledge of the Atonement, but also, where it is given. It is as though the Lord out of love sent the Garden of Eden with us in our fall, as a power to entice us to return to His presence. Truly, *the temple is the Garden of Eden in our midst.*

The great endowment is a great enrichment of knowledge about the power of Christ to make in us a mighty change so we can return to the celestial realm. *This change is symbolized in the form of holy clothing which represents the covering or endowment of the power and grace of Christ in our personal lives.* As we climb Mount Zion in making and keeping covenants with Christ, He will provide the power to guide us to the summit.

Endowed with Power
to Return to the Presence of God

Brigham Young stressed the importance of feeling or experiencing the endowment. Only a temple setting can provide this experience. He then said the purpose of the endowment is to receive everything necessary to return to the Father:

> But be assured, brethren, there are but few, very few of the Elders of Israel, now on earth, who know the meaning of the word endowment. To know, they must experience; and to experience, a Temple must be built.
>
> Let me give you the definition in brief. *Your endowment is to receive all the ordinances necessary to walk back to the presence of the Father. Passing the angels . . . being able to give them key words, the signs and tokens pertaining to the Holy Priesthood.*[3]

With similar emphasis on returning to the Father, Joseph Smith said the endowment comprises *"all those plans and principles by which anyone is enabled to secure the fullness of those blessings which have been prepared for the Church of the Firstborn, and come up and abide in the presence of the Eloheim in the eternal worlds."*[4]

The endowment is the power to return to the presence of God. Each time we go through the endowment we prepare for this reality. It is real, because during its *ceremonial drama,* we see, hear, speak, act, and feel the realization within ourselves that we can become sanctified to endure the presence of the Lord. During this becoming, *we are endowed or enriched with the power of authority, truth and light, a divine nature, pure love, key words, tokens and signs, sealings, protection, celestial law, and glory.* We are sanctified or made clean and pure before the Lord.

The actual reality of being in the presence of the Lord was given to Joseph Smith and Oliver Cowdery after He blessed them with His purifying power in the temple:

> Behold, your sins are forgiven you; you are clean before me; therefore, lift up your heads and rejoice.
>
> Yea the hearts of thousands and tens of thousands shall greatly rejoice in consequence of the blessing which shall be poured out, and *the endowment with which my servants have been endowed* in this house. (D&C 110:5, 9)

This declaration of the Lord becomes even more significant when we comprehend what the endowment will do to our heart, our true spiritual self. The endowment, according to Elder H. Burke Peterson, is not just knowledge but also a power that brings about the mighty change of heart. *"We can talk about the process, but it is a power. The endowment is a power, and it can come to us only by revelation. We must feel the endowment to know its meaning."*[5]

We can feel the power of the endowment, explained Elder Boyd K. Packer, as we feel the warmth of truth, then see the light of the sun. "In the temple we face the sunlight of truth. The light of the temple, that understanding, shines upon us as does the light of the sun. And the shadows of sin, ignorance and error, of disappointment and failure, fall behind us."[6]

The warmth of pure love and the light of pure truth from the Son is the power of the endowment that brings about the mighty change of heart.

Endowed with Holiness
Through Covenants with the Lord

The Lord requires that we become holy (see Leviticus 11:45) *during our climb back to the Father's presence.* We become holy by becoming perfect (*see* Matthew 5:48). The Jewish scriptural concept of the term "perfect" was faithful observance of covenants.[7] Therefore this power to become perfectly holy is given to us as we make and keep covenants with the Lord. By the power of the garment of salvation (the Atonement), we are clothed with the robes of righteousness (the divine or holy nature), as we keep covenants with our Savior.

The process of becoming holy is sacred for a consecrated or set apart people. Therefore, *the endowment is only secret in the sense that it is sacred for God's covenant people.* "Remember that that which cometh from above is sacred, and must be spoken with care, and by constraint of the Spirit"(D&C 63:64).

Endowed with Knowledge to Understand the Gospel

When we are taught by the power of the Holy Ghost in the temple, the endowment greatly enriches our understanding of gospel principles. This is another reason why I find the endowment exciting. I wish to share gospel principles under the titles of "Accountability," "Sweetness of the Fruit," and "True Messengers," that have been enhanced in my understanding because of the endowment.

Accountability

Once a year the bishop invites me to be fiscally accountable to the Lord. I must report and declare my status concerning the law of tithing. Throughout the year I have numerous other occasions to account my stewardship with the Lord through priesthood leaders. The most important and sacred account that I make to these priesthood leaders is during the temple recommend interview.

Giving account is a remarkable practice in our Church that distinguishes us from most other religions. It is a necessity because we are the clergy of our Church. We do not follow a professional clergy and rely on them to mediate between us and the Lord. It is interesting that the children of Israel in the Sinai wanted Moses to be the mediator between them and the Lord because they did not want to be directly accountable to the Lord. Here we see the beginning of religious intercession with mortal mediators, common in most orthodox Christian religions today, was born.

We are not only accountable to the Lord but to each other. By this accountability we learn how to edify each other because we learn that we are our brothers' keeper. Paul expressed this accountability to others and to God in his writings to the Hebrews. "Obey them that have the rule over you, and submit yourselves: for *they watch for your souls, as they that must give account, that they may do it with joy, and not with grief*" (Hebrews 13:17).

The Order and Age of Accountability

Yes, there is an order, even a priesthood order in this accountability. This priesthood order includes the Holy Order of Matrimony. Women have as important a role in the Holy Order of Matrimony as men. Both are to "bring forth" and sustain physical and spiritual life.

We cannot declare ourselves independent of those in this priesthood order and please God. Whatever we do to the least of the servants of God we do unto Him. Fathers and mothers, husbands and wives, especially in the Holy Order of Matrimony, are servants of God. "Evil speaking of the Lord's anointed," men or women, is a displeasing declaration of independence to the Lord.

This priesthood order is the order of accountability between God and man, as taught in the temple. It is the law of heavenly order which states "There are last which shall be first, and there are first which shall be last" (Luke 13:30). This law inherently implies that "first" is not necessarily better than "last." It is a matter of order according to the laws and covenants of God (*see* 3 Nephi 20:26). God taught Adam and Eve this law when Eve was the first to yield to Satan. Therefore God first instructed Adam, who then instructed Eve. A father's responsibility and accountability is not only to sustain physical life but to bring forth spiritual life to his family through the word of God (*see* Matthew 12:36). At age eight, children become accountable to their parents, for this word of God. A wife is accountable to her husband, for this word of God, as he is accountable to his priesthood leaders. These leaders are accountable to their leaders until the earthly father of the Church, the holder of the keys of authority, the prophet, seer and revelator of the word of God, is reached. He is accountable to Heavenly Father for His word being taught to the kingdom of God on earth.

By being accountable to each other, in spite of our weaknesses, we demonstrate faith in the omnipotent hand of the Lord to sustain and direct those chosen as stewards of His word (*see* D&C 20:3-4). We also demonstrate faith in the "principles of righteousness" and "love unfeigned" (*see* D&C 121:36, 41) upon which this order works. One reason we practice this order of accountability in spite of our weaknesses is to prepare to fully live the law of consecration with love unfeigned. Accountability to determine need is an integral part of this law (*see* D&C 42:32).

The Lord has fixed the starting time of "the years of accountability" (*see* D&C 18:42) to be the age of eight years during our mortal probation (*see* D&C 68:25, 27). *The age of eight years* is not an arbitrary number; it is the age at which we begin to partake of the fruit of the knowledge of good and evil with free agency. *At this age we begin to understand the good of spiritual knowledge and the evil of Satan's temptations because he is permitted to tempt us* (*see* D&C 29:46-47, 49-50), *and after baptism we receive the gift of the Holy Ghost to counter this temptation.*

Therefore, it is imperative that parents do "great things" (D&C 29:48) in planting the seeds of truth in the hearts of their children so the Holy Ghost can cause these seeds to grow, bringing all things to their remembrance. *Truly at the age of accountability it is given unto us through the temptations of Satan and the Gift of the Holy Ghost that we might know good from evil (see Helaman 14:31).*

Our Final Accountability to the Savior

Our final accountability is to the Savior. We become accountable to Him when we take His name upon us by joining His Church (see D&C 20:71). Then we "receive of God" and must "account it of God" (see D&C 50:34, also D&C 72:3).

The Savior is the one to whom we are accountable at the veil, before entering the presence of the Father. To Him we will give account as "stewards of the mysteries of God" (see 1 Corinthians 4:1). To Him we can give account in the temple of the personal covenants we make with Him.

Christ employs no servant at the veil. He is the only true mediator. He is the one who will plead our case with the Father and make the final accounting. So let us heed the instruction of the temple and return and report often to those in this priesthood order who have responsibility for us. Let us return and report to the Lord in His holy house.

Sweetness of the Fruit

While living in Detroit, we eagerly anticipated Saturday. We didn't miss our Saturday morning trip to the downtown open market. Any imaginable earth product or man-embellished variation was available. We particularly enjoyed the fresh Ohio corn and tomatoes. We would impale the ears of corn on a nail driven through a board, then the kernels were quickly harvested with a sharp blade. These golden kernels were frozen to be mixed later with a bottle of tomato preserves, heated gently, and topped with a little cheese and pepper. I can still taste this delight.

One Saturday, there seemed to be an abundance of citrus fruit. Bartering for price was fierce. All the juice oranges looked alike, but one vendor was selling a particularly sweet-tasting orange. We bought a bushel and consumed half of them the same day in a most joyous citrus feast. It wasn't the good price or the appearance. It was the exquisite sweetness of the fruit that brought the joy of this feast.

The Need for Opposition: Tasting the Bitter to Prize the Sweet

When Father Lehi instructed his sons shortly before his death, he addressed his son Jacob with the great words found in 2 Nephi 2. Here he reasoned for the need of opposition in all things. He even used the example of the two opposing fruit trees in the Garden of Eden. "And to bring about his eternal purposes in the end of man, . . . *it must needs be that there was an opposition; even the forbidden fruit in opposition to the tree of life; the one being sweet and the other bitter*" (verse 15).

It is interesting that Eve was enticed by a bitter fruit. Or was it really bitter? Eve's initial impression of the fruit attracted her. "And when the woman saw that the tree was good for food, and that it became pleasant to the eyes, and a tree to be desired to make her wise, she took of the fruit thereof, and did eat, and also gave unto her husband with her and he did eat" (Moses 4:12).

When Eve offered Adam the fruit, she described it as "delicious to the taste." How could this fruit be bitter? Certainly it had a bitter result causing mortality compared to the fruit of the tree of life, which would result in immortality. Yet the forbidden fruit had a sweetness in the form of knowledge and remembrance of good. After partaking, Eve began to "see." Then Adam partook and both began to see a difference between good and evil. They recognized the difference between God their Father and Satan their rebellious brother. Remember, Lehi compared the forbidden fruit to the fruit of the tree of life. *Both were a delicious fruit surrounding a seed of life: one mortal, the other immortal. To have knowledge of the eternal fruit of the tree of life it was necessary to partake of the mortal forbidden fruit.*

When Adam and Eve partook of this fruit, they began to see that the forbidden fruit, no matter how delicious it tastes, is ultimately bitter without the fruit of the tree of life. They also understood that the sweetness of the fruit of the tree of life could not be enjoyed in a state of sin. Therefore, God the Father revealed to them how sin could be removed from their life through the plan of redemption.

The Meaning of the Tree of Life

Father Lehi partook of a fruit from the tree in his dream and described it as "to exceed all whiteness," being "most sweet," "to make one happy" even with "exceedingly great joy." Therefore, it was "desirable above all other fruit" (*see* 1 Nephi 8:10-12).

After being asked by the Spirit of the Lord: "Knowest thou the condescension of God?", Nephi was shown the mortal birth of the Son of God. Then he was asked:

Knowest thou the meaning of the tree which thy father saw?

And I answered him, saying; Yea, it is the love of god, which shed-deth itself abroad in the hearts of the children of men; wherefore, it is the most desirable above all things.

And he spake unto me, saying; Yea, and the most joyous to the soul. (1 Nephi 11:22-23)

With the terms "most desirable," and "most joyous," similar to those of his father, Nephi understood about the tree his father reached and the fruit of which he ate. *The tree represents the love of God, which sheds forth in the hearts of men when they taste or comprehend the shedding of the blood of His Son for them.* This comprehension occurs by the power of the Holy Spirit *"because the love of God is shed abroad in our hearts by the Holy Ghost which is given unto us"* (Romans 5:5).

The love of God is clearly demonstrated in His condescension to us. "For God so loved the world, that he gave his only begotten Son, that whosoever believeth in him should not perish, but have everlasting life" (John 3:16).

This scripture is a description of the tree of life, the love of God, because when we partake of its fruit by taking Christ's name upon us and receive the fullness of His Atonement, we do not perish but become a tree of life, producing the fruit of everlasting life (*see* John 15:5). *Therefore, the tree of life represents the love of God, and the fruit of that love is His Son and our Savior.* He makes the "fruit" of everlasting life possible for all. True to Mosaic law and sacrifice, Father Lehi described Christ as the "firstfruits" (*see* 2 Nephi 2:9).

The Reality of Partaking of the Fruit of the Tree of Life

The Levitical temple symbol of the *shew bread, which means "bread of the presence of God" or the bread "set forth,"*[8] is reflected in Paul's teachings of Christ to the Roman Saints: "Whom God hath set forth to be a propitiation through faith in his blood" (Romans 3:25).

This concept of "showing Christ" set before us as sustenance to consume like fruit, the firstfruit, or bread, the bread of life, is even more directly illustrated by the sacramental instructions of the Savior to the Nephites at the temple of Bountiful. "And this shall ye do in remembrance of my body, which I have shown unto you. And it shall be testimony unto the Father that ye do always remember me. And if ye do always remember me ye shall have my Spirit to be with you" (3 Nephi 18:7).

The body of Christ shown to the Nephites was the sacrificed and resurrected body of the Savior. He was sacrificed that they might live as He lives if they would partake of His saving sustenance. In the world room of the Salt Lake Temple, on the upper back mural, is a striking scene that symbolically depicts the sacrifice of the Lamb of God that life might live more abundantly.

The shew bread was a symbol of Christ and a precursor of the sacrament symbols of the body and blood of Christ that we partake of today. Like His forerunner, the great high priest Melchizedek, Christ "brought forth bread and wine" (Genesis 14:18; *see also* Matthew 26:26-29 and 3 Nephi 18:1) for the covenant meal. *We symbolically eat of the fruit of the tree of life in the covenant meal when we physically partake of the sacrament bread and water. We partake of the "firstfruits."*

This physical gesture should direct our thoughts and actions to a spiritual feast of the fruit of the tree of life. This occurs in the temple where the *Holy Spirit feeds us the fullness of the firstfruits by teaching us about the Atonement and the graces of Christ.* This was the feast of those who listened to King Benjamin at the temple of Zarahemla. This feast is what Nephi envisioned when he said "press forward, feasting upon the word of Christ" (2 Nephi 31:20).

Growing a tree of life within us and then feasting upon its precious fruit is how we personally feast upon and are filled with the words of Christ. This is what Alma taught when he spoke about planting the word of God in our heart and nourishing it with faith, patient repentance, and diligent obedience until it become a mature tree of life within us (*see* Alma 32:41-42).

This mature tree will produce a pure fruit that will fill our spiritual hunger and thirst in this life (Alma 32: 28-43). *Partaking of the fruit of the tree of life during the sacrament and in the temple is preparation for partaking fully of the tree of life (the full blessings of the love of God) in the realm of eternal life.* This will fill our spiritual hunger and thirst everlastingly. "To him that overcometh will I give to eat of the tree of life," said the Lord, "which is in the midst of the paradise of God" (Revelation 2:7).

Heartburn from the Forbidden Fruit

Just as spiritual truth must be understood in our hearts even with joyous heartburn, so it is in our hearts that sin must be understood by producing a painful feeling in our conscience. This is how we taste (recognize) the bitter to prize the sweet. This heartburn from sin, different from the heartburn experienced at the temple of the land Bountiful (3 Nephi 11:3), and on the road to Emmaus, occurs when the Spirit withdraws or warns us of sin (*see* D&C 19:20). We all have this heartburn, for example, when we tell a lie. Even a physical reaction, which can be measured by a lie detector, occurs from this heartburn.

When we partake of the fruit of the tree of knowledge of good and evil, by being "conceived in sin" or falling into mortality, we discover our nakedness, meaning our mortal weaknesses, our vulnerability to sin, corruption, and death. This is the bitterness we taste.

Satan would have us believe that, through the arm of flesh and his satanic powers, he can cover this nakedness. However, his covering always leads to more bitterness. *If the bitterness of this nakedness (when the Spirit withdraws) is tasted in our hearts with a bitter heartburn leading to godly sorrow, we can come to know of the sweetness of good.*

The source of good is always God (*see* Ether 4:11-12; Moroni 7:12-13), and the source of every good thing to cover the nakedness of our fall is Christ (*see* Moroni 7:24). God, through His Son, will cover our nakedness everlastingly with the good fruit of the joy of redemption and eternal life.

Exceedingly Great Joy: A Cure for the Heartburn of Sin

Lehi desired to give the fruit of the tree of life to his family. Eve desired to give the fruit of the tree of knowledge of good and evil to Adam. Did Eve sense or savor a deeper sweetness in the fruit of this tree than first met her taste? When Eve partook of the fruit it was delicious, just as most temptations from Satan. They are at first delicious and enticing but ultimately lead to sorrow, bitterness, and death.

Eve tasted of the knowledge of good in the fruit of the tree of knowledge. She tasted in part the sweetness of good. This sweetness is the light of Christ and the Spirit of Christ given to all men who enter mortality (*see* D&C 93:2; Moroni 7:16). It is the sweetness of the self-evident truths of natural affection found in our conscience. The sweetness of these truths is part of the sweetness we taste when we learn how to love and edify others in this life.

When my 17-year-old daughter, Leslee, returned from a stake summer youth conference, I asked her about the event. She said her favorite part of all was sharing time and love with the handicapped youth who had been invited to participate. This is the real fruit of "good" in this mortal life. It is a reflection of the love of God. To do an altruistic, benevolent act for someone else is most desirous above all things and most delicious to the soul. It is what gives us joy.

The sweetness of good we can taste in the fruit of the tree of knowledge should cause us to desire to taste the greater sweetness of the fruit of the tree of life and "lay hold of every good thing" (Moroni 7:20) *by hearkening to the voice of the Spirit* (see D&C 84:46). The Spirit will teach us to have faith in Christ (*see* Moroni 7:25-26, 38), who is the fruit of the tree of life.

In the forbidden fruit, Eve savored in part the fruit of the tree of life. This is the taste of charity, the pure love of God. She knew she needed to bring forth children in mortality to share this love with them. Adam knew that he would not have joy without Eve. Therefore he fell to be with Eve that their children would also have joy. As Adam, Eve, and Lehi knew, *only in contrast with the taste of evil could they come to a full taste of the love of God and a fullness of joy: "Were it not for our transgression, we never should have had seed, and never could have known good and evil, and the joy of our redemption"* (Moses 5:11). Lehi taught the same concept later when he said

> wherefore they [Adam and Eve] would have remained in a state of innocence, having no joy, for they knew no misery; doing no good, for they knew no sin. . . .
> *Adam fell that men might be and men are, that they might have joy.* (2 Nephi 2:23, 25)

Eve specifically related joy to redemption. It is the joy of the redemption from the misery of the Fall. This joy is an expression of the joy in the pure redemptive love of Christ. It is this "exceedingly great joy" that Lehi tasted in the fruit of the tree of life. It is this joy we express when we sing "the song of redeeming love" (Alma 5:26) of our Savior with our fellowmen because of the power of His word (*see* Alma 26:13). It is this joy we feel when we practice charity in redemptive ways, edifying our fellowmen, even becoming saviors on Mount Zion (see Obadiah 1:21). Without a fall, there never could be a redemption. Without evil, there never could be good. *The joy of good is redemption from evil to righteousness. The fullness of this joy in mortality can be experienced in the temple.*

Those hearing the words of King Benjamin sang "the song of redeeming love" when they were born again. They expressed the exquisite joy of redemption through their mighty change of hearts because of their obedience to the commandments and faith in the Atonement of Christ.

> *O have mercy, and apply the atoning blood of Christ that we may receive forgiveness of our sins, and our hearts may be purified, for we believe in Jesus Christ . . .*
>
> And it came to pass that after they had spoken these words *the Spirit of the Lord came upon them, and they were filled with joy, having received a remission of their sins, and having peace of conscience,* because of the exceeding faith which they had in Jesus Christ" (Mosiah 4:2-3).

It was at the temple that these saints of Zarahemla partook of the fruit of the tree of life and experienced "exceedingly great joy":

> that as ye have come to the knowledge of the glory of God, [knew] his goodness, . . . tasted of his love, and . . . received a remission of [their] sins, which causeth such *exceedingly great joy* in [their] souls" (Mosiah 4:11).

While teaching his son Helaman about the joy he tasted in being "born of God," Alma, like Ammon (*see* Alma 26:13), spoke of this "exceeding joy" as the "fruit" of his labors due to the power of the word of God:

> Yea, and from that time even until now, I have labored without ceasing, that I might bring souls unto repentance; that I might bring them to *taste of the exceeding joy of which I did taste; that they might also be born of God, and be filled with the Holy Ghost.*
>
> Yea, and now behold, O my son, the Lord doth give me exceedingly great joy in the fruit of my labors;
>
> For because of the word which he has imparted unto me, behold, *many have been born of God, and have tasted as I have tasted, and have seen eye to eye* as I have seen; therefore they do know of these

things of which I have spoken, as I do know; and *the knowledge which I have is of God.* (Alma 36:24-26)

The redeeming love of Christ is a taste of exceeding joy that causes a mighty change of heart so that we are born of God. It is the focal point of the "great view," so we know and see as Alma and King Benjamin's people:

> And they all cried with one voice, saying: Yea, we believe all the words which thou hast spoken unto us; and also, we know of their sure-ty and truth, *because of the Spirit of the Lord Omnipotent, which has wrought a mighty change in us, or in our hearts, ...*
>
> And we, ourselves also, through the infinite goodness of God, and manifestations of his Spirit, *have great views.* (Mosiah 5:2-3)

It is in the temple that we can feast upon the fruit of the tree of life, see great views of the glory of God, experience the mighty change of heart, and feel exceedingly great joy. It can be in the temple that we are born of God, becoming the spiritual offspring of Christ, and thus His "firstfruits" (*see* John 15:16; Jacob 4:11).

God taught Adam a great truth when he learned that being conceived in sin, that "sin conceiveth in their hearts" implies the need for a com-plete experience in immortality to understand spiritual truth. "Inasmuch as thy children are conceived in sin, even so when they begin to grow up, sin conceiveth in their hearts, and *they taste the bitter, that they may know to prize the good*" (Moses 6:55).

When we honestly react to this type of heartburn and do not attempt to cover it up by hardening our hearts, we experience what Paul called "*Godly sorrow*" (2 Corinthians 7:10). *Godly sorrow sharply defines the difference between good and evil in our lives and helps us "prize the good."* It therefore invites the Spirit's return to comfort and teach us.

The Promptings of the Spirit: A Cure for the Heartburn of Tribulation

We also gain knowledge of the difference between good and evil by experiencing adversity or tribulation. *Tribulation can produce a fear, even a pain in our hearts, that causes us to feel after the Lord* if our hearts are not too hardened:

They were slow to hearken unto the voice of the Lord their God; therefore, the Lord their God is slow to hearken unto their prayer, to answer them in the day of their trouble.

In the day of their peace they esteemed lightly my counsel; but, in the day of their trouble, of necessity they feel after me.

. . . notwithstanding their sins, my bowels are filled with compassion towards them. (D&C 101:7-9)

Adversity and tribulation can be either a stumbling block or a stepping stone in our spiritual progress, depending on how we partake of the fruit of the tree of knowledge of good and evil. Because of tribulation, do we curse God, then continue to yield to Satan's deception, relying on the arm of flesh? Or does tribulation cause us to feel humility, then the sweet comfort of the love of God by yielding to the promptings of the Spirit? The answer depends upon the hardness of our hearts.

Paul learned how to overcome the bitter tribulations of the forbidden fruit with the sweetness of the fruit of the tree of life by yielding to the promptings of the Spirit:

But we glory in tribulations also: knowing that tribulations worketh patience;

And patience, experience; and experience, hope:

And hope maketh not ashamed; because *the love of God is shed abroad in our hearts by the Holy Ghost which is given unto us.* (Romans 5:3-5; *see also* D&C 127:2)

The more good (love of God) we taste in the forbidden fruit by letting adversity and tribulation purge us with patience, meekness, experience, and hope, the more our nakedness to the precarious nature of life is covered with the good fruits of the Holy Spirit. The sweetness of this fruit is the enticing taste of the fruit of the tree of life. It takes meekness from adversity, then a perfect brightness of hope in the love of God, to discover the sweetness of this exquisite fruit.

The fruit of the tree of life will finally grow from a tree of life within us when we are "crowned with much glory" (D&C 58:4), having a "crown of righteousness" (*see* 2 Timothy 4:8; D&C 25:15). As the beautiful rose blooms at the end of a thorny stem, or the sweet fruit grows at the end of a knarred branch that has survived the winter frosts and summer heat, so are we who are "faithful in tribulation" (D&C 58:2) crowned: "For after much tribulation come the blessings."

Even the tribulation of aging, as we accelerate with infirmities to the fixed result of partaking of the fruit of the tree of knowledge, can be covered and crowned with sweetness. *To those who die in the Lord by partaking of the fruit of the tree of life, death is sweet* because it has been swallowed up in victory (*see* D&C 42:46-47; 1 Corinthians 15:54-57).

The sweetness of the fruit of the tree of life is not immediately apparent, just as the blessings of the temple are not immediately apparent. To discover which fruit is really sweet, it takes the enticing of the Holy Spirit who teaches of things as they really are, and not the enticings of Satan, who deceives us with lies, putting "bitter for sweet and sweet for bitter" (Isaiah 5:20), making bad fruit taste sweet or good fruit taste bitter. It appears desirable but ultimately tastes bitter, or it appears undesirable but in reality tastes sweet. Moroni warned about this deception and then eloquently explained how to judge between good and evil (Moroni 7:14-17). *The key is to taste (recognize) the light by which we may judge. This light is the light of Christ (see Moroni 7:18) illuminated by the Holy Spirit. Then we may know with a perfect knowledge* as the daylight is from the dark night (Moroni 7:15).

The Holy Spirit will lead us back to where the fruit is truly sweet. It is the fruit of the tree of life and the pathway to it is found at the sacrament altar and at the altars of the temple.

The Law of Agency
Continues Through the Forbidden Fruit

When Satan said to Eve: "Partake of the forbidden fruit, and ye shall not die, but ye shall be as God, knowing good and evil" (2 Nephi 2:18), he was telling a lie (ye shall not die) and a half truth (ye shall be as God). *Adam and Eve learned after the Fall that it takes more than knowledge of good and evil to become like God. It also requires choosing to partake of the fruit of the tree of life to learn the "mysteries of God."* This was something they could not do in the Garden of Eden after they chose the forbidden fruit. They needed their days prolonged, to be given sufficient time, in a probationary state of choice between the knowledge of good and evil.

This state of choice is given to all men by the Spirit of Christ (Moroni 7:16) to see how they will act on this knowledge (D&C 19:4). With this comparative knowledge, they can judge (Moroni 1:15) between good and evil, and be "agents unto themselves," doing "many things of their own free will" (D&C 58:27-28). Then because of free agency, all men and women would hopefully respond to heartburn from sin and tribulation with godly sorrow. Then they would experience the bitter to prize (seek after and partake of) the sweet, saving fruit of the tree of life. "And it must needs be that the devil should tempt the children of men, or they could not be agents unto themselves; for if they never should have bitter they could not know the sweet" (D&C 29:39).

We Still Must Choose Between the Two Fruit Trees

As the two trees with two kinds of fruit were before Adam and Eve, so are they before us in mortality. Because of the Fall, we must partake of the fruit of the tree of knowledge of good and evil in mortality. We can partake of this fruit as freely as Adam and Eve because of our agency and its apparent attraction.

The tree of life is still before us, and still guarded as in the Garden of Eden. In this life it is guarded by solemn covenants. Unlike the Garden of Eden, we can pass the sentinels by keeping the covenants and then partake of the fruit of the tree of life in the temple. We can even partake of the fruit of our own tree of life if we develop and keep our souls as a temple.

The great question is how will we partake of the fruit of the tree of knowledge of good and evil in this life? How sensitive are we to the feelings of our hearts? Will we continue to yield to the will of the flesh under Satan's beguiling, tasting more and more the bitterness of evil? Or will we relieve bitter heartburn from sin and tribulations, yielding to the enticings of the Spirit, tasting more and more of the good, until we partake of the sweetest fruit of all, the fruit of the tree of life?

> Wherefore, men are free according to the flesh; and all things are given them which are expedient unto man. And *they are free to choose liberty and eternal life, through the great Mediator of all men or to choose captivity and death according to the captivity and power of the devil;* ...
>
> And now, my sons, I would that ye should look to the great Mediator, and hearken unto his great commandments; and be faithful unto his words, and *choose eternal life, according to the will of his Holy Spirit:*
>
> And *not choose eternal death, according to the will of the flesh and the evil which is therein, which giveth the spirit of the devil power to captivate.* (2 Nephi 2:27-29)

Lehi was telling his sons to partake of the fruit of the tree of life, the same fruit that he tasted in his great tree-of-life vision. He was teaching them that *unless they are taught by and follow the will of the Holy Spirit, they will never taste the sweetness of the fruit of the tree of life.* They may even lose their freedom to choose because forbidden fruit leads to captivity by the devil.

If we do not yield to the enticings of the Holy Spirit and are not "led by the Spirit becoming humble, meek, submissive, patient, full of love and all long-suffering" (Alma 13:28) we will never taste the exquisite atoning sweetness of the fruit of the Tree of Life. This is why Laman and Lemuel would not partake of the fruit of the tree in Lehi's dream (*see* 1 Nephi 8:17-18). Thus, they and many of their descendants would not believe in the Atoning Christ.

It is deeply significant to me that in film-assisted endowments, Satan is lurking behind dead trees without fruit (*see* Jude 1:12). These trees are the antithesis of the tree of life. Annually, most of the trees that surround us are stripped naked and appear dead as they lose their leaves. *This fall of leaves in the fall is symbolic of the Fall of man. Because of the Fall, our foliage is lost. We are stripped naked, exposed to death.* Yet, as sure as the plan of redemption, the spring always comes and the apparently dead trees respond to the light, resurrect with new leaves, and bear fruit.

If we learn to turn to the light of God and "taste the light," then the warmth of the love of God will cause the dormant seed within us (the word of God bringing all things to our spiritual remembrance), to swell and grow to a tree of life—producing precious fruit. If not, we will remain a dead tree, captive of Satan.

The parable of the sower (see Mark 4:3-20) *is a wonderful teaching about responding to light.* It teaches that we can either produce a dead tree or a living tree of fruit within us. The difference depends on the environment and soil in which the seed falls. More importantly, it depends on the soil's response to light. Our hearts are the best soil for the seed (the word of God). As we respond by experimenting upon the word with faith, even if the seed is simply planted in our minds, the light of the Holy Spirit will cause the seed to grow not only in our minds but in our hearts. The light of the Spirit penetrating the heart results in miraculous growth:

And unto you that hear shall more be given

. . . So is the kingdom of God, as if a man should cast seed into the ground;

And should sleep, and rise night and day, and the seed should spring and grow up, he knoweth not how.

For the earth bringeth forth fruit of herself; first the blade, then the ear, after that the full corn in the ear. (Mark 4:24, 26-28)

It is in the mission field that many investigators who have received the seed "spring up" overnight. We know it is by the power and light of the Holy Spirit penetrating their hearts. It is in the temples of the kingdom of God that the blade and the ear "grow up" with a miraculous growth to the "full corn in the ear," producing the fruit of the tree of life. This miraculous springing and growing up is the work of the Father showing forth "His own works" (3 Nephi 27:10) through the power of the Holy Spirit in the kingdom of God on earth built upon the gospel of Christ.

As we are taught by the Holy Spirit in the temple, we really learn about the qualities of our Savior Jesus Christ, the fruit of the tree of life. As we follow the promptings of the Holy Spirit, these qualities become part of our lives:

But if ye be led of the Spirit, ye are not under the law. . . .

But the fruit of the spirit is love, joy, peace, long suffering, gentleness, goodness, faith, meekness, temperance: against such there is no law. (Galatians 5:18, 22-23)

If we continue to seek the fruits of the Spirit, we will finally be allowed to taste the sweetest of His fruits. It is the taste of charity, the pure love of Christ. It is most delicious to the soul and most desirous above all fruit because it emulates the matchless love of the Father.

In the temple we often taste the sweetness of this fruit as a personal witness that Christ knows and loves us individually. We marvel and say "how could it be?" But we do feel and know He is concerned about our trials and desires because "all things" are numbered unto God and He knows them (*see* Moses 1:34-35).

Then we marvel as did Moses, who heard the loving words, "Moses, my son" (Moses 1:6). After feeling the love of the Lord, Moses could have expressed the words of Nephi concerning the condescension of God when he said, "*I know that he loveth his children*" (1 Nephi 11:16-17). This personal knowledge that God loves us is sweet fruit that gives us strength to overcome weakness and rise above the arm of flesh to follow His Son in a personal, loving relationship (*see* D&C 1:19-20).

The Holy Spirit can fill us with the sweetness of pure love and help us impart it to others. This is what happened to King Benjamin and his followers at the temple. They came there to give thanks to the Lord their God because of true messengers, just men, their teachers and their king who had "taught them to keep the commandments of God, that they might rejoice and *be filled with love towards God and all men*" (Mosiah 2:4).

Fruit of the Olive Tree: The Pure Oil of Charity

A different fruit tree can teach us about moving from the tree of knowledge of good and evil to the tree of life and becoming the first-fruits of Christ. This tree is not at first considered a fruit tree. It does not produce a delicious fruit spontaneously. However, with time and care, this tree produces a fruit that contains a pure oil.

This fruit tree is the olive tree, which the Savior often used to refer to the House of Israel (*see* Jacob 5). It is a perennial tree whose leaves do not change with seasons. While the tree may wither, the roots (representing the covenants of God with the House of Israel) live on, growing new, tender trees alongside the old dying tree. Therefore, the olive tree does not "abide alone; but if it die, it bringeth forth much fruit" (John 12:24).

The olive fruit is not produced until many years of cultivating the tree. When the olive is harvested, it is bitter, requiring a purging process of salt and vinegar. Slowly the bitterness is purged, then the meek and mellowed fruit is crushed under the weight of a heavy stone to force out the oil.

The multiple uses of pure olive oil in Near Eastern life testify of its ability to edify lives. *The anointing oil, symbolic of the Holy Spirit, and the oil for the lamps of the temple, symbolic of the light of Christ,* both testify of the blessings from heaven for those who seek the pure spiritual oil of the Holy Spirit and the Savior.

Pure olive oil, the universal antidote for all that ails us physically and spiritually, also represents the fruit of the tree of life. This pure oil comes from the fruit of the tree of life that we can grow within us. This oil can be pressed from each of us if we let ourselves be purified by the power of Christ. *It is in the temple that we learn how to become purified.* Here we feel the power of Christ to purge us and press us with covenants, that we might demonstrate faithfulness in sacrificing anything to be purified. Then, through the power of His atoning love, we can become His firstfruits filled with pure oil, the "oil of joy" (Isaiah 61:3), the pure love of Christ.

Our individual spirits, our true selves, our hearts, can become the olive oil. Purged in life with tribulation to be sweetened and purified, with the final press of death, our spirits return to the Father who made them. With resurrection they reunite with a perfected olive fruit to become fruit of eternal life. *The purifying process of the olive—the cultivation from grace to grace, the purging to the sweetness of meekness, the pressing weight of trials and of obedience to covenants, the sacrifice even of its own life—the Savior experienced in mortality.* He leads the way for us.

We cannot become as the olive tree, submitting to pressure and sacrificing bitterness to produce a pure oil, until we partake of the fruit of the tree of knowledge of good and evil. The purging and mellowing of the experience of adversity makes real sacrifice possible. As we sacrifice all in obedience to the Savior and sacrifice all to edify others, then the love within us becomes the fruit of the tree of life within us. This love is the pure oil of charity.

True Messengers

One of the most important, often-repeated truths of the endowment is the principle of true messengers. This is how we are "taught by God" (John 6:45).

God Calls on Men with True Messengers and Holy Works

When Adam and Eve fell from the presence of God, a most profound principle of hope was taught to them. "I, the Lord God, gave unto Adam and unto his seed, that *they should not die as to the temporal death, until I, the Lord God, should send forth angels to declare unto them repentance and redemption, through faith on the name of mine Only Begotten Son*" (D&C 29:42).

> And thus the Gospel began to be preached, from the beginning; *being declared by holy angels sent forth from the presence of God; and by his own voice; and by the gift of the Holy Ghost.* (Moses 5:58)

Alma, responding to the inquiry of Antionah, explained the plan of redemption precisely, in the manner that Adam received it:

> Now, if it had not been for the plan of redemption, which was laid from the foundation of the world, there could have been no resurrection of the dead;
>
> And now behold, if it were possible that our first parents could have gone forth and partaken of the tree of life they would have been forever miserable, having no preparatory state; and thus the plan of redemption would have been frustrated, . . .
>
> But behold, it was not so; but it was appointed unto men that they must die; and after death, they must come to judgment, . . .
>
> And after God had appointed that these things should come unto man, behold, then he saw that it was expedient that man should know concerning the things whereof he had appointed unto them; . . .
>
> God did call on men, in the name of his Son, (this being the plan of redemption which was laid) saying: If ye will repent, and harden not your hearts, then will I have mercy upon you, through mine Only Begotten Son;
>
> Therefore *he sent angels to converse with them,* who caused men to behold his glory.
>
> And they began from that time forth to call on his name; therefore *God conversed with men, and made known unto them the plan of redemption,* which had been prepared from the foundation of the world; and *this he made known unto them according to their faith and repentance and their holy works.* (Alma 12: 25-28, 33, 29-30)

The word of God, the gospel, the plan of redemption, the truth of things as they really are, spiritual truths and covenants would come to man by messengers. In "divers ways" (*see* Moroni 7:24), the true message would come from God through divers messengers, carried by His own voice, the voice as heavenly messengers, the power of the Holy Spirit in the form of prophecy and revelation and through earthly messengers. The principle of "diverse ways" is what we learn in the temple endowment as we symbolically hear the voice of God and His messengers in succession.

The importance of "holy works" or "an holy ordinance," meaning a temple ordinance (*see* D&C 84:20-22), to confirm (verify) the truthfulness and authenticity of the fullness of the gospel revealed in divers ways was taught to Adam:

And thus all things where confirmed unto Adam, *by an holy ordinance,* and the Gospel preached, and a decree sent forth; that it should be in the world, until the end thereof; and thus it was. Amen. (Moses 5:59)

God will reveal His message to man on earth through His messengers and confirm it by holy ordinances. Until the end of the world, as long as "there shall be one man upon the face thereof," this will be God's way of revealing Himself to man. Even today, "at the last day," when it is said that miracles and revelation from God have ceased (*see* Moroni 7:35-37), God calls on men in the same divers way.

These messengers mentioned in D&C 29, Moses 5, and Alma 12 aren't just any messengers. They are true messengers from the presence of God, with God's message. We learn in the temple that Peter, James, and John were some of these holy angels or true messengers. Perhaps their post-mortal calling as ministering angels is a continuation of their premortal ministry (*see* D&C 128:20; 7:5-7; 130:5).

The Importance of Seeking True Messengers

It is significant that Adam did not follow any doctrine until he was sure it came from a true messenger of God. The first inquiry he made after partaking of the forbidden fruit was about true messengers. This inquiry demonstrated that Adam, like Eve, was able to taste the good in the forbidden fruit. After partaking of the fruit, he was injured spiritually, feeling bitter heartburn and then he felt godly sorrow. Therefore he wanted to be healed by seeking a true messenger from God, avoiding "the philosophies of men mingled with scripture."

This is the same patient search for truth that Moses and Joseph Smith demonstrated. It is the same patient and persistent search, with faith and repentance, that we must demonstrate to be assured that the light of Christ within us will enlighten us to be led to a true messenger from God. This is how we must seek the Lord. As we have seen, *a gift for seeking the Lord is the Holy Spirit, a true messenger* (*see* Moses 5:58). *This gift is important because we cannot become true messengers without it* (*see* D&C 14:8; 42:14, 16-17).

True Messengers with the Word of God as Iron Rods

The opening scene of Lehi's dream is a striking contrast, illustrating the need for a true messenger to lead us through the dark and dreary waste of life:

> Methought I saw in my dream, a dark and dreary wilderness.
>
> And it came to pass that I saw a man, and he was dressed in a white robe; and he came and stood before me.
>
> And it came to pass that he spake unto me, and bade me follow him.
>
> And it came to pass that as I followed him I beheld myself that I was in a dark and dreary waste. (1 Nephi 8:4-7)

The man dressed in white, a true messenger, mortal or spiritual, led Lehi to the strait and narrow path and the rod of iron leading to the tree of life.

In surgery, an important modern technique uses the principle of a true messenger or guide in the form of an iron rod. With the use of modern imaging radiology, it is possible to deliver a surgical instrument to a precise target in the body using a guide wire. Through X-ray visualization, the guide wire is passed through bone, blood vessels, or body cavities to reach a specific site. The surgical instrument follows the guide wire until it reaches the target. This technique eliminates the need for extensive dissection.

Like a true messenger, the surgical guide wire is the "rod of iron," which leads safely through the fields of danger to the desired target. The surgical principle of the guide wire is the same as the scriptural principle of the iron rod. We need a true messenger of the word of God (a prophet, a parent, a missionary, a true friend, the Holy Spirit) who has the iron rod which is the word of God. They will lead us to understand and help us grasp hold of this rod, which will surely guide us to the tree of life.

This gift of the Holy Ghost as a true messenger is an X-ray perspective in our lives because the Holy Spirit helps us see things not seen by the natural eye. With this perspective, the Holy Spirit helps us firmly grasp and follow the iron rod. The Holy Spirit secures us to the iron rod by helping us understand and personally taste the fruit of the Tree of Life. *It is significant that the "Spirit of the Lord" in 1 Nephi 11 is the Holy Spirit.*[9] He led Nephi to an understanding of the Tree of Life and its fruit.

The iron rod leads to and through the temple. In the temple, as we covenant with God, the iron rod leads to the tree of life.

The path really becomes strait and the rod sturdy in the temple. Here we grasp hold of the word of God through His covenants, keeping solemn commitments to commandments that will secure us on the path to the tree of life. Here we see and taste the reality of this tree so we no more desire to wander in the dark and dreary waste of mortality.

The Compass as an Iron Rod and a True Messenger

Lehi and his family literally traveled through the dark and dreary waste of the desert to a promised land. As with Lehi and the children of Israel in the Sinai, so it is with us. The course to the promised land is through the flesh pots of Egypt and the Sinai desert of mortal life.

A unique true messenger guided Lehi and his family through the desert. The Liahona, a compass that worked by faith and righteousness, pointed the way through the desert to the promised land, like a magnetic compass.

As a testament of the reality of God, the magnetic compass faithfully points to the north. *The temple in Jerusalem, as God's throne, was placed on the north side of Mount Zion. This was because the Hebrew concept of the universe placed God's throne near the North Star, around which the constellations turn and where the summit of the heavenly mount is located.*[10] *This is the mount that is called "the mount of congregation" located "in the sides of the north" in the description of Lucifer's desired ascent into heaven* (*see* Isaiah 14:12-13).

In this sense, a compass is a true messenger and an iron rod. If a compass is left in our pocket unheeded, considered as "naught" (*see* 2 Nephi 33:2) or trampled upon (*see* D&C 3:15; D&C 17:1), we will not know the exact direction to follow. If we do not give heed to the words of true messengers, we will not recognize that they point the way to salvation.

Alma taught Helaman this same truth about the Liahona:

> And now, my son, I would that ye should understand that these things are not without a shadow; for as our fathers were slothful to give heed to this compass (now these things were temporal) they did not prosper; even so it is with things which are spiritual.
>
> For behold, *it is as easy to give heed to the word of Christ, which will point to you a straight course to eternal bliss, as it was for our*

fathers to give heed to this compass, which would point unto them a straight course to the promised land.

O my son, do not let us be slothful because of the easiness of the way; for so was it with our fathers; for so was it prepared for them, that if they would look they might live; even so it is with us.

The way is prepared, and if we will look we may live forever. (Alma 37:43-44, 46)

Alma was referring to the serpent raised by Moses to heal those stricken by fiery serpents in the Sinai. Therefore to look is to look up and seek the light. It is seeking the Lord in our minds and in our hearts with the eyes of faith. It is recognizing that the Lord, as a true messenger, will lead us through this world of fiery serpents. He will lead us to His holy house where He will endow us with power to "look up to God at that day [of judgment] with a pure heart and clean hands" (Alma 5:19).

A True Messenger's Mark of Authority

To look up results in seeing the light and understanding the vision that only the gifts of the spirit of prophecy and revelation can bring (see Alma 17:3). This gift is the mark of authority of a true messenger. This is why it was said of the Great True Messenger in the meridian of time, that "he taught as one having authority from God, and not as having authority from the Scribes." (JST Matthew 7:37).

Even in His youth, the Great True Messenger needed not that any man should teach Him. "And he served under his father, and he spake not as other men, neither could he be taught; for he needed not that any man should teach him" (JST Matthew 3:25).

Christ knew of His divine calling, as testified by the scriptures and confirmed by His Father in Heaven. He knew His calling for the salvation of men. His understanding was not blinded like the Jews of His day who sought the philosophies, traditions, and ambitions of men, to interpret the law and the scriptures. His was the message of a true messenger: *"Look to me and live."* Do not wander in the "forbidden paths" and "strange roads" (*see* 1 Nephi 8:28, 32) of the philosophies and traditions of men. Thus, He condemned the Pharisees for teaching "the commandments of men" (*see* Mark 7:7-9).

The Pharisees, scribes, and many Jews, with eyes blinded by pride in traditions and doctrines of men, could not look up and see the light of a true messenger:

> Then said his disciples unto him, they will say unto us, We ourselves are righteous, and need not that any man should teach us. God, we know, heard Moses and some of the prophets; but us he will not hear.
>
> And they will say, We have the law for our salvation, and that is sufficient for us. (JST Matthew 7:14-15)

The Pharisees recognized true "dead" messengers in "some of the prophets." They could not recognize the Savior, a living prophet, filled with the spirit of prophecy and revelation. He would not recognize or "hear" them as true messengers because they were not filled with this gift and authority.

Looking from the court of the Gentiles across the Kidron Valley to the whited tombs at the base of the Mount of Olives, Christ said the Pharisees where full of dead men's bones: "Woe unto you scribes and Pharisees, hypocrites! for ye are like unto whited sepulchres, which indeed appear beautiful outward, but are full of dead men's bones, and of all uncleanliness" (Matthew 23:27).

It is the spirit of prophecy and revelation within a true messenger that gives the authority of truth and the authority to teach it (see D&C 42:14, 16-17). It is not the outward appearance or even the intellectual appearance. During their ministries, Alma and the sons of Mosiah clearly demonstrated this important truth:

> And Alma went and began to declare the word of God unto the church which was established in the valley of Gideon, *according to the revelation of the truth of the word which had been spoken by his fathers, and according to the spirit of prophecy which was in him, according to the testimony of Jesus Christ, the Son of God,* who should come to redeem his people from their sins, and the holy order by which he was called. (Alma 6:8)

> Therefore *they had the spirit of prophecy, and the spirit of revelation,* and when they taught, *they taught with power and authority of God.* (Alma 17:3)

Joseph Smith taught that the key to distinguishing a true from a false messenger is the spirit of prophecy and revelation:

If any person should ask me if I were a prophet, I should not deny it, as that would give me the lie; for, according to John, the testimony of Jesus is the spirit of prophecy; therefore, if I profess to be a witness or teacher, and have not the spirit of prophecy which is the testimony of Jesus, I must be a false witness; but *if I be a true teacher and witness, I must possess the spirit of prophecy, and that constitutes a prophet; and any man who says he is a teacher or preacher of righteousness, and denies the spirit of prophecy, is a liar, and the truth is not in him; and by this key false teachers and impostors may be detected.*[11]

The spirit of prophecy and revelation is a full testimony of Jesus Christ given to men by the Holy Spirit (see Revelation 19:10; 1 Corinthians 12:3). They have this testimony both in their minds and in their hearts. Therefore, this testimony must ultimately come by revelation. This is why the Ethiopian recognized Philip as a true messenger:

And Philip ran thither to him, and heard him read the prophet Esias, and said, understandest thou what thou readest?

And he said, how can I except some man [true messenger] should guide me? and he desired Philip that he should come up and sit with him.

Then Philip opened his mouth, and began at the same scripture, and preached unto him Jesus. (Acts 8:30-31, 35)

In the meridian of time, as today, it took a messenger with the spirit of prophecy and revelation to recognize the words of Isaiah as a testimony of Christ. *"For the words of Isaiah are not plain unto you, nevertheless they are plain unto all those that are filled with the spirit of prophecy"* (2 Nephi 25:4). The message of true messengers is always truth and testimony about Jesus Christ and His gospel.

Contrast the reasoning of the Pharisees who claimed that "we need not that any man should teach us" (JST Matthew 7:14) with the reasoning of the Apostle John who said, "Ye need not that any man should teach you" (1 John 2:27). Both declared similar words but for entirely different reasons.

The Pharisees reasoned that "the law" (the written law of Moses) was sufficient for their authority and salvation. This reasoning is exactly what is heard in the religious world today: "A Bible! A Bible! We have got a Bible and there cannot be any more Bible" (*see* 2 Nephi 29:3). Or, in other words, "We have the written law as our authority in the Christian world today."

In contrast, the Apostle John reasoned that "the anointing," the Holy Spirit, a true messenger, who "teacheth you of all things and is truth" is the assurance of authority and salvation. His authority in revealing pure truth is why no man or man's interpretation of the written law can provide that assurance. This is why the Ethiopian was converted and baptized when his spirit received a witness from the Holy Spirit through the Apostle Philip, both true messengers prophesying and revealing Jesus Christ.

How clearly this contrast is present in the religious and secular world today! There are many religious messengers today who preach Christ but deny revelation. Therefore they do not have a fullness of the testimony of Christ. There also are many religious messengers today who deny both Christ and revelation. Thus the Lord gave today's world the following warning:

> And when the times of the Gentiles is come in, *a light shall break forth among them* that sit in darkness, and it shall be the fulness of my gospel;
> But they receive it not; for *they perceive not the light, and they turn their hearts from me because of the precepts of men.* (D&C 45:28-29)

They "perceive not the light" because they turn their hardened hearts from the spirit of prophecy and revelation, to the precepts of men who deny the spirit of prophecy and revelation.

The fulness of the gospel has been revealed by true messengers from God, not by the precepts of men. One true messenger, the Holy Spirit, can really show us the light and give us the vision of this true message. Filling us with the spirit of prophecy and revelation, He removes the shades of pride and tradition from our eyes so that we might look up and see the light carrying the great view of the true message. Therefore, we no longer want to follow the precepts of men.

Identifying a true messenger from God was the great issue in the meridian of time. I wonder if I would have recognized the man Christ as the Savior of the world had I lived during His ministry? As the Savior said to the scribes and Pharisees: "*Search the scriptures . . . they are they which testify of me*" (John 5:39).

How could the scribes and Pharisees have missed Christ, even in their written law? It is because they interpreted the written law with the traditions and commandments of men (*see* Mark 7:7, 9), and not with the spirit of prophecy and revelation from the Holy Spirit as did the apostles and prophets (*see* Ephesians 3:3-5).

Are we missing a true messenger today because we follow the traditions and commandments of men, even in a scholarly interpretation of the scriptures? To know the truth of God, we must know both in our minds and in our hearts, which requires not only scholarly study but the teaching of the Spirit. To be taught by the Spirit we must humbly seek Him through study, fasting, and prayer. Then we must learn to recognize His language, being present where it is spoken. Once we hear His word, we must obey it. The ultimate and motivating confirmation must come from God or His true spiritual messenger, the Holy Spirit. This is pure knowledge that gives us "unwavering conviction." If we do not have this kind of conviction then we cannot experience God's and the Holy Spirit's unique roles in our ability to recognize truth.

True Messengers on Both Sides of and Between the Veils of Birth and Death

The calling of Peter, James, and John to act as holy angels, sent to declare the gospel to Adam and Eve, portended their mortal calling as apostles of the Savior, and also portends their post-mortal calling as ministering angels (*see* D&C 128:20; 7:5-7). There have been many who have worked on both sides and between the veils as true messengers. Even Christ did this. He is the ultimate true messenger, as declared by His Father: "This is my Beloved Son; Hear Him" (JSH 1:17). On either side and between the veils, He was the "*Word . . . even the messenger of salvation*" (D&C 93:8) like no other messenger from God.

In this life, *Christ is "the messenger of covenants"* (Malachi 3:1). He has established temple covenants in every gospel dispensation. This will dramatically occur at his Second Coming to introduce the Millennium.

Christ's role as a true messenger of salvation and of the covenant continued beyond this life to the other side of the veil in the spirit world. There, He organized His true messengers, as section 138 of the Doctrine and Covenants so vividly reveals: "But behold, *from among the righteous, he organized his forces and appointed messengers, clothed with power and authority,* and commissioned them to go forth and carry the light of the gospel to them that were in darkness, even to all the spirits of men; and thus was the gospel preached to the dead" (D&C 138:30).

Melchizedek Priesthood Holders
Are Called as True Messengers

The importance of true messengers as guiding rudders, to steer us on a straight course that we be not "tossed to and fro," is emphatically stated by Paul:

> And he gave some, apostles: and some, prophets; and some, evangelists [patriarchs] and some, pastors [bishops] and teachers [home teachers];
> *For the perfecting of the saints, . . .*
> *Till we all come in the unity of the faith, and the knowledge of the Son of God, unto a perfect man . . .*
> That we henceforth be no more children, tossed to and fro, and carried about with every wind of doctrine, by the sleight of men, and cunning craftiness, whereby they lie in wait to deceive. (Ephesians 4:11-14)

Verse 11 mentions essentially Melchizedek Priesthood offices or messengers. It is a sobering fact that *all those who hold the Melchizedek Priesthood were foreordained to become true messengers of salvation for those on earth:* "And this is the manner after which they were ordained—*being called and prepared from the foundation of the world according to the foreknowledge of God,* on account of their exceeding faith and good works; in the first place being left to choose good or evil; therefore they having chosen good, and exercising exceedingly great faith, *are called with a holy calling, yea, with that holy calling which was prepared with and according to, a preparatory redemption for such*" (Alma 13:3).

The Apostle Paul taught how holders of the Melchizedek Priesthood will be true messengers of salvation for the preparatory redemption of their fellow men. "For every high priest taken from among men is ordained for men in things pertaining to God, that he may offer both gifts and sacrifices for sin" (Hebrews 5:1).

In messianic imagery, Paul defined "high priest" as one who offers spiritual gifts and makes sacrifice for others.[12] As we will see in Chapter 9, "The Great and Last Promise: Reaching the Summit of Mount Zion," which discusses the pure love of Christ, *the greatest application of this pure love is sacrifice of self for the edification of others.*

Paul's definition of *high priest* could likewise be the definition of a mother. *Love through sacrifice is the essence of the calling in this Holy Order, even the Holy Order of Matrimony.* I believe the most important calling I have in this Holy Order is that of husband and father. *I am called to sacrifice in obedience to the Lord in order to lead my wife and children in the way of salvation as a true messenger.*

We learn in the temple that it is God's will that we follow His true messengers during our mortal probation (*see* 3 Nephi). These messengers are His prophet and counselors—the current Peter, James, and John of His church. As true messengers, they point the way through this mortal desert, leading us to the iron rod and the straight path up Mount Zion.

Becoming True Messengers: Our Imperative Duty

It is not only important that we learn how to recognize true messengers, but that we as parents, gospel teachers, church leaders, missionaries, and true friends *become true messengers.*

During my tour of Israel, an enjoyable break from the sightseeing was listening to the thoughts of someone who is a true messenger. After dinner, our guide Wayne Brickey selected scriptural topics and discussed them with those interested. I particularly enjoyed his discussion of D&C 123:7-17.[13] These verses of scripture contain profound doctrine from the inspired mind of the Prophet Joseph, a true messenger who had languished in Liberty Jail for months. It is the doctrine of our "imperative duty," which is becoming a true messenger of God:

> *It is an imperative duty that we owe to God, to angels, with whom we shall be brought to stand, and also to ourselves, to our wives and children,* who have been made to bow down with grief, sorrow, and care, under the most damning hand of murder, tyranny and oppression, supported and urged on and upheld by the influence of that spirit which hath so strongly riveted the creeds of the fathers who have inherited the lies, upon the hearts of the children, and filled the world, with confusion, and has been growing stronger and stronger, and is now the very mainspring of all corruption, and the whole earth groans under the weight of its iniquity.
>
> It is an iron yoke, it is a strong band; they are the very handcuffs, and chains, and shackles, and fetters of hell.
>
> For there are many yet on the earth among all sects, parties, and denominations, who are blinded by the subtle craftiness of men, where-

by they lie in wait to deceive, and who are only kept from the truth because they know not where to find it. (D&C 123:7-8, 12)

After explaining how the creeds (traditions, philosophies, and precepts) of men, so strongly entrenched in the hearts of men by the father of lies, have become the "mainspring of corruption," the Prophet explained our imperative duty: "Therefore, that we should waste and wear out our lives in *bringing to light all the hidden things of darkness, wherein we know them; and they are truly manifest from heaven*" (D&C 123:13).

This is a passionate call for us to be true messengers of God. This is the same call that Mormon, who on the verge of seeing the destruction of his people, remarkably made to his son Moroni: "And now, my beloved son, notwithstanding their hardness, *let us labor diligently; for if we should cease to labor, we should be brought under condemnation; for we have a labor to perform whilst in this tabernacle of clay, that we may conquer the enemy of all righteousness, and rest our souls in the kingdom of God*" (Moroni 9:6).

To be a true messenger we must declare the gospel as Moroni with the voice and sound of a trump (*see* D&C 24:12; 29:4; 42:6), serving as an instrument in the Lord's hands to save and preserve all the people (*see* Alma 2:30). Yet, we must also be content with a still small voice and example of humility, suffering "all manner of afflictions" that we might be the means of "saving some souls" (Alma 26:30). *Our words and actions must be ignited and constrained by the Spirit. We must become true messengers by following the doctrine of the priesthood (see* D&C 121:41-43). *Thus, to be a true messenger we must have the true message from the True Messenger.*

While traveling in Cambridge, England, I tried "punting" on the Cam River, which saunters through the college campuses. A punt is an English-style gondola, propelled by a long pole. My wife sat in the middle of the punt as I stood on the back, pushing the pole off the muddy bottom of the Cam. Instead of steering a straight course, I followed a desultory path from bank to bank, much to the humor of the local students.

Observing the true gondoliers, I noticed that the punt would steer a straight course if the pole were left in the water as a rudder after it lifted from the bottom. The ending words of Joseph Smith, following the verses declaring the imperative duty of true messengers, remind me of my punting experience. "You know, brethren, that a very large ship is benefited very much by a very small helm in the time of a storm, by being kept workways with the wind and the waves" (D&C 123:16; *see also* James 3:4).

A very small true messenger is a great benefit to keep those who follow him on a straight course ("workways") through the confusion of the creeds of the world ("with the wind and the waves"). Reflecting the image of God holding the ark of Noah in His hand (*see* Moses 7:43), a true messenger can steady the ark.

Becoming True Messengers in the Temple

It is in the temple that we really learn how to become true messengers, because in the temple we learn the fullness of the Lord's love and the fullness of His true message. *Here we learn to submit to the will of the Lord and follow him up Mount Zion as our true messenger.*

We become true messengers of the Lord by accepting and keeping His everlasting covenant. As this covenant is a messenger preparing for Christ's return, so we who keep the covenant are prepared as true messengers for this great event:

> And even so I have sent mine *everlasting covenant* into the world, to be a light to the world, and to be a standard for my people, and for the Gentiles to seek to it and *to be a messenger* before my face to prepare the way before me. (D&C 45:9)

We who keep the everlasting covenant are the true messengers of Christ, the salt and light to the world. The gift for keeping the covenant is the light of knowledge and power from the Holy Spirit of truth (*see* D&C 6:15; 14:8). Thus, it is the true message by the spirit of prophecy and revelation. In the temple we become the messengers to match His message, in the dispensation of the fullness of times.

8

A Full View of Mount Zion

From a Glimpse to a Full View: Parting the Veil of Clouds on Mt. Zion

Moses resisted the honor of Egypt and endured the base camp of Midian to find a true messenger. He was rewarded with the great and last promise of the temple, given in an "exceedingly high" mountain.

> The words of God, which he spake unto Moses at a time when Moses was caught up in an exceedingly high mountain,
> And *he saw God face to face, and talked with him, and the glory of God was upon Moses;* therefore Moses could endure his presence. (Moses 1:1-2)

After God showed Moses "the world and the ends thereof," the glory of God withdrew, and Moses, "being left unto himself," fell to the ground. When Moses regained his natural strength he exclaimed: "Now, for this cause I know that man is nothing, which thing I never had supposed" (Moses 1:10).

This is a remarkable statement coming from Moses, who had known the wonders of Egypt and the power of Pharaoh. On this exceedingly high mountain, Moses saw the full view and experienced the "rest" of the Lord. He tasted of the fruit of the tree of life when he heard the loving, redemptive words from God: "Moses my son" (Moses 1:6). What a confirmation of love this was to a man who was unsure of his parentage and heritage. What a contrast to the declaration of Satan: "Moses, son of man, worship me" (Moses 1:12). Moses realized that being a son of God, in the similitude of his Only Begotten Son, is glorious beyond description when compared to being a son of man like Pharaoh.

Moses was presented with the tree of knowledge of good and evil when Satan appeared before him. He had heartburn from fear when

Satan exclaimed: "I am the Only Begotten, worship me" (Moses 1:19). Then he "tasted" the bitterness of the forbidden fruit: "and as he began to fear he saw the bitterness of hell" (Moses 1:20).

Moses had to use his agency and choose a messenger: God or Satan.

Moses faced Satan without the glory of God, just as Adam faced Satan immediately after the Fall. And just as Adam had done, Moses straightforwardly sought a true messenger from his Father. He recognized that Satan was not such a messenger.

Likewise, *we must face Satan in mortality.* We must partake of the tree of knowledge of good and evil. Just as Moses and Adam, *we must choose between true and false messengers* when we are "left unto ourselves," having fallen from the presence of God. It is from this condition that we must begin to part the veil of clouds covering Mount Zion in order to see the full view of this exceedingly high mountain.

All conflicts requiring choice in this life are an extension of the great war in heaven. In all of these conflicts we must ultimately answer the question: Will I follow Satan or Christ? If we listen to the promptings in our hearts from the light of Christ given to each of us, we will start to part the veil by judging correctly between good and evil to discern truth. The truth always directs us to follow Christ (*see* Moroni 7:15-16).

Because Moses and Adam tasted of the sweetness and glory of the tree of life, they could discern a true from a false messenger by comparison (*see* Moses 1:14, 18).

When we taste of the tree of knowledge of good and evil, being left unto ourselves, we learn from our own mortal experience. Then, if we seek and follow Christ, through the spirit of prophecy and revelation we will taste the sweetness and see the glory of the Tree of Life. With this comparative knowledge, we gain the ability to clearly discern like Moses. When he said, "for his glory has been upon me, wherefore I can judge between him and thee" (*see* Moses 1;14, 18), he was teaching us the important lesson that *until we experience to some degree the glory of God we cannot fully appreciate the bitterness of hell. We must taste the bitter to savor the sweet, but also we must savor the sweet to really taste the bitter.*

With clear distinction between good and evil, we learn how to separate the spiritual wheat from the mortal tares. We learn how to separate the many things that cumber and trouble us from that good part of our lives which shall not be taken away (*see* Luke 10:38-42). We learn how to distinguish a prophet clothed modestly (*see* D&C 42:40) or even strangely (*compare* 2 Kings 1:8: Mark 1:6 with Matthew 7:15), but full of the spirit of prophecy and revelation, from a whited sepulcher full of dead men's bones. As the distinction between good and evil becomes clearer to us, the cloudy veil covering Mount Zion will dissipate to reveal the full view of its glory.

To Know God: The Exceeding Height of Mount Zion

With the spirit of prophecy and revelation we begin to get a full view of Mount Zion as an "exceedingly high" mountain. There is no other mountain that compares, because *on Mount Zion the Lord reveals Himself more and more as we climb to the summit and come to understand what eternal life means.*

During his glorious encounter with God, Moses learned why God created this earth and all His other created worlds (*see* Moses 1:33). *"For behold, this is my work and my glory—to bring to pass the immortality and eternal life of man"* (Moses 1:39).

It was the Savior, during His mortal ministry, who defined "eternal life": "And this is life eternal that they might know thee the only true God, and Jesus Christ, whom thou hast sent" (John 17:3).

The Savior again defined eternal life—or in this case "eternal lives"—through a revelation to the prophet Joseph Smith, now found in th Doctrine and Covenants: *"This is eternal lives—to know the only wise and true god, and Jesus Christ, whom he hath sent. I am he. Receive ye, therefore, my law"* (D&C 132:24).

In this verse, the Savior taught that to know Him and His Father, we must receive His law. To receive His law, we must take not only His name but His word upon us, by making and keeping covenants with Him. "I am the Lord thy God; and I give unto you this commandment—that no man shall come unto the Father but by me or by my word, which is my law, saith the Lord" (D&C 132:12).

Perhaps this is why the Savior said, in His sermon on the temple mount, that

> Many will say to me in that day: Lord, Lord, have we not prophesied in thy name, and in thy name have cast out devils, and in thy name done many wonderful works?
>
> And then will I profess unto them: I never knew you; depart from me ye that work iniquity." (3 Nephi 14:22-23)

Christ will not know us unless *we know Him by taking His name upon us, becoming His spiritually begotten sons and daughters through the covenants and ordinances of His Holy Order.*

Eternal life is to know God in the sense of being like God. It is to be a son or daughter of God in the similitude of His only Begotten Son. A son really "knows" his father when he grows to maturity and emulates his father. It is only then that the son comes to know himself. This is why Joseph Smith said, *"If men do not comprehend the character of God, they do not comprehend themselves."*[1]

To know God is the challenge of climbing the exceeding height of Mount Zion. If we are men and women to match the challenge of this climb, we will see a full view of ourselves as God sees us.

The Full View of Mount Zion Is the Full View of Christ upon Mount Zion

While teaching investigators as a missionary in France and Belgium, I constructed on a flannel board the foundation of the church of Christ with an adhesive strip that read "apostles and prophets." The remaining structure of the church was built on this foundation. When I taught the apostasy lesson, I removed the foundation strip of apostles and prophets. Simultaneously, my companion disengaged the spring that supported the flannel board, and the whole church flew apart. I read the words of Paul to the investigators as I reconstructed the church of Christ on the flannel board:

> Now therefore ye are no more strangers and foreigners, but fellow-citizens with the saints, and of the household of God;
> And are *built upon the foundation of the apostles and prophets, Jesus Christ himself being the chief corner stone.* (Ephesians 2:19-20)

Then I explained the need for apostles and prophets and other offices in the church by again reading from Paul:

> And he gave some, apostles; and some, prophets; and some, evangelists [patriarchs]; and some, pastors [bishops] and teachers;
> Till we all come in the unity of the faith, and of the knowledge of the Son of God, unto a perfect man, unto the measure of the stature of the fulness of Christ. (Ephesians 4:11-13)

I did not realize at that time the importance of true messengers as I do now. In verse 11, Paul was saying that God provided us with the

Melchizedek Priesthood, even the fulness of the Melchizedek Priesthood declared by true messengers, until we all come to a knowledge of the fulness of Christ. Only then can we come to a full knowledge of the Father. As Christ said, this knowledge is "eternal life."

I did not recognize this scripture as a great verse of the *scriptural temple,* even though I read it many times as a missionary. It was not until I pondered a verse from the dedicatory prayer of the Kirtland Temple that I understood the full meaning of Paul's words: "For thou knowest that we have done this work through great tribulation; And out of our poverty we have given of our substance to build a house to thy name, *that the Son of Man might have a place to manifest Himself to His people"* (D&C 109:5).

This verse is reminiscent of the declaration of the Lord to the Israelites in the Sinai. "And let them make me a sanctuary; *that I may dwell among them"* (Exodus 25:8).

It is in the temple, His holy sanctuary, that Christ manifests Himself to us as we learn of the fulness of His stature unto a perfect man. Here we see the great view of the stature that He promises us if we receive His law and follow Him. To get a full view of Mount Zion, we must get a full view of the Savior on Mount Zion. It is in the temple that the Lord promises to "reveal" Himself today, even as literally as He promised the children of Israel on the temple mount of Sinai:

> And as your fathers [in the Sinai] were led at first, even so shall the redemption of Zion be.
>
> I say unto you: *mine angels shall go up before you, and also my presence, and in time ye shall possess the goodly land.* (D&C 103:18, 20)

The promise of "the Son of Man revealing Himself" in the temple of our dispensation was first given to Joseph Smith in 1833. This revelation is concerning "the beginning and foundation of the city of the stake of Zion, here in the land of Kirtland, beginning at *my house"* (D&C 94:1), when the Lord said *"my glory shall be there, and my presence shall be there"* (D&C 94:8). This promise was fulfilled the Sunday after the dedication of the Kirtland Temple when the Lord appeared to Joseph Smith and Oliver Cowdery:

For behold, I have accepted this house, and my name shall be here; . . . Yea, *I will appear unto my servants,* and speak unto them with mine own voice, if my people will keep my commandments, and do not pollute this holy house. (D&C 110:7-8)

This promise continues today. It should draw us to the temple and fill us with great anticipation and desire to know the fullness of Christ, so we can receive "eternal life" in this life and the life to come.

A Full Order: Receiving the Fullness of the Melchizedek Priesthood

If we are to understand the fulness of Christ and become like Him, we must understand the fulness of His Order. Therefore we must learn the fulness of the Melchizedek Priesthood. The Apostle Paul understood this truth:

For this Melchizedek was ordained a priest *after the Order of the Son of God,* which order was without father, without mother, without descent, having neither beginning of days, nor end of life.

And all those who are ordained unto this priesthood are made like unto the Son of God, abiding a priest continually. If therefore perfection were by the Levitical priesthood, what further need was there that another priest should rise after the order of Melchizedek, and not be called after the order of Aaron?

And it is yet far more evident: for that after the similitude of Melchizedek there ariseth another priest,

Who is made, not after the law of a carnal commandment, but after *the power of an endless life.* (JST Hebrews 7:3, 11, 15-16)

The truths of the "revelation on the priesthood" (D&C 84) clearly state the connection between the fulness of Christ ("the power of godliness"), the promise of His rest ("see the face of God"), and the fulness of the Melchizedek Priesthood ("the key of the knowledge of God" and "the ordinances thereof"):

And *this greater priesthood* administereth the gospel and holdeth the *key of the mysteries of the kingdom,* even *the key of the knowledge of God.*

And *without the ordinances thereof, and the authority of the priesthood, the power of godliness is not manifest unto men in the flesh.*

For without this no man can see the face of God, even the Father and live. (D&C 84:19, 21-22)

In D&C 124, the Lord informed Joseph Smith that we learn about and receive the fulness of the Melchizedek Priesthood in the temple: "*For there is not a place found on the earth that He may come to and restore again that which was lost unto you, or which He hath taken away, even the fulness of the priesthood*" (D&C 124:28).

In an epistle to the Church in Nauvoo concerning baptism for the dead and alluding to all the keys, powers, and glories of temples, Joseph Smith again stressed the importance of obtaining the keys and powers of the Holy Priesthood in the temple: "Now the great and grand secret of the whole matter, and the *summum bonum* of the whole subject that is lying before us, consists in obtaining the powers of the Holy Priesthood. *For to whom these keys are given there is no difficulty in obtaining a knowledge of facts in relation to the salvation of the children of men, both as well for the dead as for the living*" (D&C 128:11).

The meaning of the "whole matter" is the whole subject of temple work, as implied by the statement "both as well for the dead as for the living." The keys, powers, and knowledge for this work of salvation are obtained *in the temple where the fulness of the Holy Priesthood is obtained.*

In this same epistle, an offering in righteousness, as required by the Lord (*see* Malachi 3:3; D&C 13:1) was proposed (*see* D&C 128:24). *This offering, in the form of a book of temple work done for the dead,* was offered in the Nauvoo Temple. This was *the beginning of this "acceptable offering,"* which will be completed when the "whole work on Mount Zion" (temple work of the dispensation of the fulness of times, through the Millennium) is completed (*see* 2 Nephi 20:12). Through this great temple work for the living and the dead, and with the fulness of the priesthood, the sons of Levi, that is both the Aaronic (sons of Aaron) and Melchizedek (sons of Moses) priesthood holders will be purified:

> Therefore, as I said concerning the sons of Moses—for the sons of Moses and also the sons of Aaron *shall offer an acceptable offering and sacrifice in the house of the Lord,* . . .
>
> And the sons of Moses and of Aaron *shall be filled with the glory of the Lord, upon Mount Zion in the Lord's house,* whose sons are ye and also many whom I have called and sent forth to build up my church.

> For whoso is faithful unto the obtaining these two priesthoods of which I have spoken, and the *magnifying their calling, are sanctified by the Spirit unto the renewing of their bodies.* (D&C 84:31-33)

Verse 32 notes that "also many," all those, both men and women, who magnify their calling to build the Church will be sanctified through the fulness of the priesthood in temple ordinances and covenants.

When we are sanctified by the fulness of the priesthood and become one in Christ, we become the "seed of Abraham" (*see* Galatians 3:28-29; D&C 84:34) *and receive, as did Abraham, "all that the Father hath,"* (D&C 84:38). *This is the promise of the oath and covenant of the priesthood (see* D&C 84:39), *which applies to receiving the fullness of the priesthood.* This is why Abraham sought to become the "seed" of his patriarch fathers (Adam, Enoch, Noah, Melchizedek, etc.), who held the fulness of the priesthood (*see* Abraham 1:4).

Priesthood Power Is Given to Those Who Climb Mount Zion

Joseph Smith provided further enlightening insight into the fulness of the Melchizedek Priesthood when he said, "*If a man gets a fulness of the priesthood of God he has to get it in the same way that Jesus Christ obtained it, and that was by keeping all the commandments and obeying all the ordinances of the House of the Lord.*"[2]

Brigham Young continued the teachings of the prophet Joseph Smith when he stated that "*for any person to have the fulness of that [Melchizedek] priesthood, he must be a king and priest.*"[3]

On another occasion, President Young also explained that "*those holding the fulness of the Melchizedek Priesthood are kings and priests of the most high God, holding the keys of power and blessings*"[4] (*see also* D&C 76:56; Revelation 1:6, 5:10, 20:6, 22:5).

The association of the terms *king* and *priest* implies that the authority of a king over a kingdom or a patriarch over his family in the Holy Order of God derives from the power of the priesthood.[5] This truth we clearly learn at the veil.

In opening a window on Enoch and his seed, we get a full view of the great power of the fulness of the Melchizedek Priesthood:

> For God having sworn unto Enoch and unto his seed with an oath by Himself; that every one being ordained after this order and calling should have power

. . . to stand in the presence of God; to do all things according to his will, according to his command; . . . and this by the will of the Son of God which was before the foundation of the world.

And *men having this faith, coming up unto this Order of God, were translated and taken up into heaven.* (JST Genesis 14:30-32)

As declared in a revelation on the doctrines of this Order of God, we can have the heavens opened to us and even experience a change of state in communion and relationship through priesthood power:

The power and authority of the higher, or Melchizedek Priesthood is to hold the keys of all the spiritual blessings of the church—

To have the privilege of receiving the mysteries of the kingdom of heaven, to have the heavens opened unto them, to commune with the general assembly and church of the Firstborn, and to enjoy the communion and presence of God the Father and Jesus the mediator of the new covenant. (D&C 107:18-19)

However, the mighty power of the priesthood is wrapped in a soft shell because priesthood power only works through the power of love (*see* D&C 107:30-31; 121:41-43, 45).

The endowment teaches that receiving the fulness of the Holy Priesthood leads men and women from the telestial realm to the terrestrial realm and, finally, to a celestial existence.

When do we enter the terrestrial realm in this mortal, telestial existence? It occurs when we live under the loving power of oneness in the Holy Order of the Son of God. It occurs when we truly live the Holy Order of Matrimony. It occurs when we truly worship in the temple. It can occur in our Church assemblies, homes, and individual lives if we live the laws of the fulness of the priesthood. *By regularly experiencing a change of state from telestial to terrestrial through the power of the priesthood, we prepare for the rest of the Lord.*

Those who receive and magnify a fulness of the priesthood receive an aura of light as a token of its power. It changes their countenance to behold, as in a mirror, the glory of the Lord (*see* 2 Corinthians 3:18). It is the countenance of a perfect brightness of hope. It is the light of the power of love. By this countenance, we literally become a light unto the world because we reflect the light of the Savior. "And now behold, I ask of you, my brethren of the church, have ye spiritually been born of God? *Have ye received his image in your countenances:* Have ye experienced this mighty change in your hearts?" (Alma 5:14).

The fulness of the Melchizedek Priesthood is synonymous with temple worship. The two cannot be separated. *"You cannot receive the fulness of the priesthood,"* declared President Joseph Fielding Smith, *"unless you go into the temple of the Lord and receive these ordinances of which the prophet speaks. No man can get the fulness of the priesthood outside of the temple of the Lord.*[6]

Therefore, to receive a full view of Mount Zion we need to receive the fulness of the priesthood.

The Fullness of Priesthood Power Is for Both Men and Women

A pearl of temple worship is that men and women participate equally in its ordinances and endowment. They are endowed to become kings and queens in God's Holy Order. When they are sealed as one in celestial marriage, they enjoy equally the greatest blessings of the fulness of the priesthood. *Men and women cannot have the fulness of the Melchizedek Priesthood without each other.* The altars of the temple require both a man and a woman to kneel in covenant. *The altar is symbolic of the sacrifice of the Savior, who sacrificed all in obedience (see* Hebrews 5:8) *to His Father to become one with Him.* Both the man and the woman become one with the Savior as they covenant to sacrifice all in obedience to Him. We must kneel, sacrificing our independence to our spouse and to our Savior, before we can stand in God's presence (*see* JST Genesis 14:31).

The full measure of the fulness of the Holy Order of the Son of God is the Holy Order of Matrimony. *It is an "Holy Order," not just a marriage ceremony.* As we learn in the temple, *this Holy Order has laws, rights, and ordinances.* I do not think that all of the laws, rights, and ordinances of this Holy Order of Matrimony have yet been revealed. However, it is the order in which men and women learn to become one with each other and with God. This principle of oneness of a man and woman with God, so beautifully taught and enacted in the temple, is the meaning of Paul's declaration to the Corinthian saints: *"Neither is the man without the woman, neither the woman without the man, in the Lord"* (1 Corinthians 11:11).

With this union, men and women learn that the whole is greater than the sum of its parts. Therefore, as the endowment implies, the Holy Order of Matrimony in this life should be at least a terrestrial or paradisiacal relationship. Adam and Eve were united by God in the Garden of Eden, and the endowment law of this union is given in the terrestrial world.

Even more than the official titles of the Melchizedek Priesthood, *the titles key to eternal progression are that of husband and father, wife and mother.* A mother is to bring spirit children into mortality. A father is to bring the word of God to his family. A righteous holder of the titles of husband and father can only function in unison with a righteous wife and mother. Adam clearly understood this truth when he gave Eve the title of "the mother of all living" before she even experienced the travail of motherhood. It was as though he understood the divine nature of a mother in this Holy Order. The importance of women and motherhood in God's Holy Order is witnessed in the temple when all men stand in the presence of this "elect lady" (D&C 25:3). Polite men continue, in a similar gesture, to show respect when a woman enters.

In the Holy Order of Matrimony, the fulness of the Melchizedek Priesthood becomes the Patriarchal Priesthood. At the head of the fulness of any priesthood of God is always a father figure who, with perfect love, brings the words and blessings of eternal truth to his children. These children are "born under the covenant," inheriting the blessings and rights of the Abrahamic covenant in the Patriarchal Order of the Priesthood.

The fulness of the Melchizedek Priesthood, in the dispensation of the fulness of times, directs its holders to the Patriarchal Priesthood through the Holy Order of Matrimony. *The great blessings of the Patriarchal Priesthood are given at the veil and at the altar of celestial marriage.* Now we understand the declaration of our patriarchal fathers in Adam's book of remembrance: "Now this same Priesthood which was in the beginning, shall be in the end of the world also" (Moses 6:7).

The Spirit of Elijah: The Fullness of the Priesthood Restored on Mount Zion

The restoration of the priesthood to Joseph Smith and Oliver Cowdery through true messengers is the sequence prophesied by Malachi when he said, "Behold, I will send my messenger, and he will prepare the way before me *and the Lord, whom ye seek, shall suddenly come to his temple*" (Malachi 3:1).

First an Elias, John the Baptist, then Peter, James, and John, then other heavenly messengers restored the fulness of the keys of the priesthood. As Joseph Smith taught, this was in preparation for the return of the ultimate Elias, who would truly restore all things (*see* JST John 1:21-28):

> The spirit of Elias is first, Elijah second, and Messiah last. Elias is a forerunner to prepare the way, and the spirit and power of Elijah is to come next, holding the keys of power, building the temple to the capstone, placing the seals of the Melchisedec Priesthood upon the house of Israel, and making all things ready; *then Messiah comes to His temple, which is last of all.*[7]

It was in the Kirtland Temple, a temple in which the full endowment was not practiced, that the keys of the fulness of the Melchizedek Priesthood were restored for the first time in this dispensation of the fulness of times. This restoration was foretold by Moroni when he appeared to the boy Joseph in his room and recited the words of Malachi. "And again, he quoted the fifth verse thus: Behold, *I will reveal unto you the Priesthood, by the hand of Elijah the prophet,* before the coming of the great and dreadful day of the Lord" (JSH 1:38).

It was in the Kirtland Temple on April 3, 1836, that *Elijah the Prophet returned to give his keys, which comprise the keys of the fulness of the Melchizedek Priesthood, the keys of sealing power,* to Joseph Smith:

> After this vision had closed another great and glorious vision burst upon us; for *Elijah the prophet,* who was taken to heaven without tasting death, stood before us, and said:
>
> Behold, the time has fully come, which was spoken of by the mouth of Malachi—testifying that he (Elijah) should be sent, before the great and dreadful day of the Lord come—
>
> To turn the hearts of the fathers to the children, and the children to the fathers, lest the whole earth be smitten with a curse—
>
> *Therefore, the keys of this dispensation are committed into your hands;* and by this ye may know that the great and dreadful day of the Lord is near, even at the doors. (D&C 110:13-16)

Joseph Smith later said that *"the spirit, power and calling of Elijah is that ye have power to hold the keys of the revelations, ordinance, oracles, powers and endowments of the fulness of the Melchizedek Priesthood and of the Kingdom of God on the earth.*[8]

The Fullness of the Priesthood Leads to Eternal Life, a Full View of Mount Zion

The fulness of the Melchizedek Priesthood is the power and authority to ascend to the presence of God through the temple. How could the temple be considered an esoteric annex? It is the gate of heaven through which we must pass to ascend the strait staircase of Mount Zion and stand in the presence of God. *To stand in His presence is the great and last promise of the temple. Therefore, the temple should be the center of our lives, to teach us "the way of salvation."*

Can we comprehend and embrace this "full order?" Are we men and women who have enough desire to see the full view of Mount Zion to match the fulness of this spiritual mountain? The Lord warns us, if we do not: "And there are none that doeth good except those who are ready to receive the fulness of my gospel, which I have sent forth unto this generation" (D&C 35:12; *see also* D&C 49:2).

To see and match the fulness of the Lord's mountain, we must receive the fulness of the gospel, and to receive the fulness of the gospel is to receive the fulness of the new and everlasting covenant. This occurs when we receive the fulness of Christ (*see* Ephesians 4:13) through the fulness of His priesthood order, keeping the fulness of temple covenants in the dispensation of the fulness of times (*see* Ephesians 1:10).

Receiving the fulness of the gospel brings great rewards: "Verily I say unto you, *blessed are you for receiving mine everlasting covenant, even the fulness of my gospel,* sent forth unto the children of men, that they might have life and *be made partakers of the glories which are to be revealed in the last days,* as it was written by the prophets and apostles in days of old" (D&C 66:2).

Receiving the fulness of Christ leads to the fulness of the Father:

> I give unto you these sayings *that you may understand and know how to worship, and know what you worship, that you may come unto the Father in my name, and in due time receive of his fulness.*
>
> For if you keep my commandments you shall receive of his fulness and *be glorified in me as I am in the Father.* (D&C 93:19-20)

The path up Mount Zion to know and become like God the Father is clearly established in the scriptures: we must discern true messengers of God who have the spirit of prophecy and revelation, which is the testimony and knowledge of Christ. Then we must take Christ's name and words upon us through His covenants and keep these covenants by emulating Him in our thoughts and actions, which will then lead us to know the Father.

As we covenant in the temple with Christ, His atoning power can make us "new creatures," His spiritually begotten sons and daughters in His similitude. Since the Father and Son are one in likeness, we then become one with the Father, sealed to Him as a son or daughter, with a new name and *a new nature called "eternal life."* It is only in God's presence, with eternal life, that we get a full view of Mt. Zion.

9

The Great and Last Promise: Reaching the Summit of Mount Zion

To climb Mount Zion is to seek after the mysteries or richness of God. As the Savior explained, if we seek the riches of the Father, we will be "the richest of all people" (D&C 38:39). Eternal life is the full view of Mount Zion. It is the view at the summit. It is the richest and greatest gift of God.

> *And, if you keep my commandments and endure to the end you shall have eternal life, which gift is the greatest of all the gifts of God.* (D&C 14:7)

> Seek not for riches but for wisdom; and, behold, *the mysteries of God shall be unfolded unto you, and then shall you be made rich. Behold, he that hath eternal life is rich.* (D&C 6:7; 11:7)

A Glimpse of the Great and Last Promise

A glimpse of the summit, a momentary view of this great gift—this richness—is possible in mortal life. This blessing is known by several names: it is the "promise of the fathers," the "rest of the Lord," the "Second Comforter," the "great and last promise":

> Therefore, sanctify yourselves that your minds become single to God, and the days will come that you shall see Him; for He will unveil His face unto you, and it shall be in His own time, and in His own way, and according to His own will.
> *Remember the great and last promise which I have made unto you.* (D&C 88:68-69)

If eternal life is to know God, then to see His face is a great view of this knowledge. Many of the patriarch fathers, such as the Brother of Jared, had this view:

And there were many whose faith was so exceedingly strong, even before Christ came, *who could not be kept from within the veil, but truly saw with their eyes the things which they had beheld with an eye of faith,* and they were glad.

And behold, we have seen in this record that one of these was the brother of Jared. (Ether 12:19-20)

The children of Israel in the Sinai were offered this view "with their eyes," but declined to be sanctified for the privilege because they did not have "eyes of faith" and erred in their hearts. Today we are offered this view as a "great and last promise."

The reality of this great and last promise should instill within us enough faith to be men and women to match His mountain. We should have faith enough to sacrifice anything, if necessary, to climb to the summit and find His presence. Even during our climb, a glimpse of this promise is possible. However, I wonder if many of us consider this promise beyond our view? If so, we walk like the blind men in the Sinai with eyes of faith in Moses, their "seeing-eye dog," but not in the power of the Lord to sanctify our fallen nature and cure our blindness so as to be in His presence with eyes of understanding. It is in the temple that we can make the great paradigm shift, becoming purified and sanctified to bear His presence. If we keep the new covenants of the temple, we are endowed with a heart that will bear His presence. Notice the connection between the great and last promise of the temple (vs. 11) and the new covenant (vs. 10) in Paul's writings to the Hebrews:

For *this is the covenant* that I will make with the House of Israel after those days, saith the Lord; *I will put my laws into their mind, and write them in their hearts: and I will be to them a God, and they shall be to me a people;*

And they [all those who keep the new covenant] shall not teach every man his neighbour, and every man his brother, saying, Know the Lord: for *all shall know me,* from the least to the greatest. (Hebrews 8:10-11)

The Other, or Second Comforter

In June of 1978, my wife called me at work. "You will never believe what has happened," she reported excitedly. "The blacks have been given the priesthood."

This was a particularly significant announcement for us while living in Detroit because we associated with wonderful black families in our Southfield Ward. It was a joyous occasion to ordain these worthy fathers as holders of the priesthood.

The Sunday following this historic announcement, our stake conference was held. Elder David Haight was the visiting authority. There was great anticipation and standing room only at this conference. The witness of Elder Haight was so powerful that we were all frozen in spiritual rapture. As though he were an angel, a true messenger bearing witness of a profound truth, he testified of the doctrine taught by Joseph Smith that the knowledge of God and his attributes is the foundation of our faith and the greatest knowledge that we can acquire.

As he peered upward, he said that he knew better than ever before the reality of God. The only other time I have seen such a look of assurance is when I was a deacon sitting on the front row of the chapel, looking up at Elder Hugh B. Brown as he looked into the heavens and testified of the reality of Christ during a Christmas Eve address. This is the look of unwavering assurance of the spirit of prophecy and revelation. Elder Haight did not say that he had seen Christ, but there was no doubt in my mind that he and those present in the temple who received this priesthood declaration from the Lord had experienced the Second Comforter.

This Other Comforter, the Second Comforter, was promised to the apostles in the meridian of time by the Savior:

> And I will pray the Father, and *he shall give you another Comforter, that he may abide with you for ever;*
>
> Even *the Spirit of truth;* whom the world cannot receive, because it seeth him not, neither knoweth him: but ye know him; for he dwelleth with you, and shall be in you.
>
> I will not leave you comfortless: *I will come to you.* (John 14:16-18)

Joseph Smith gave precise insight to this scripture:

> [When a man joins the church and receives the Holy Ghost] . . . then let him continue to humble himself before God, and the Lord will soon say unto him: "son, thou shalt be exalted." *When the Lord has thoroughly proved him, and finds that the man is determined to serve Him at all hazards, then the man will find his calling and election made sure, then it will be his privilege to receive the other comforter . . .* as is recorded in the testimony of St. John in the 14th chapter . . . *Now*

what is the other comforter? It is no more nor less than the Lord Jesus Christ Himself. When any man obtains this last comforter, he will have the personage of Jesus Christ to attend to him from time to time and even He will manifest the Father unto him, and they will take up their abode with him, and the Lord will teach him face to face, and he may have a perfect knowledge of the mysteries of the Kingdom of God."[1]

The Great and Last Promise of the Temple

When the Lord explained the plan of salvation to Adam, before he was baptized, the Lord concluded by saying

... That ye might be sanctified from all sin, and enjoy the words of eternal life in this world, and eternal life in the world to come, even immortal glory; ...

Therefore it is given to abide in you; the record of heaven; the Comforter; the peaceable things of immortal glory; the truth of all things; that which quickeneth all things, which maketh alive all things; that which knoweth all things, and hath all power according to wisdom, mercy, truth, justice, and judgment.

And now, behold, I say unto you: This is the plan of salvation unto all men, through the blood of mine Only Begotten, who shall come in the meridian of time. (Moses 6:59, 61-62)

The great and last promise of the temple is that we may have the fulness of the first Comforter (the Holy Ghost) (*see* D&C 109:15), and also the visitations of the Second Comforter even "in this world." By this great and last promise, we may receive "revelation upon revelation, knowledge upon knowledge ... the mysteries and peaceable things— that which bringeth joy, that which bringeth life eternal," (D&C 42:61). The joy from these words can be as great as the joy felt by the 2,500 Nephites at the temple of Bountiful, and by the apostles gathered in the Salt Lake Temple in June of 1978.

This great and last promise is the promise that Adam left as a blessing to his posterity in Adam-ondi-Ahman, and thus as a blessing to all of us: "And in that day Adam ... began to prophesy concerning all the families of the earth, saying: Blessed be the name of God, for because of my transgression my eyes are opened, and *in this life I shall have joy, and again in the flesh I shall see God*" (Moses 5:10).

Referring to the Resurrection, Job again pronounced Adam's blessing, which can occur before physical death: "And though after my skin worms destroy this body, yet in my flesh shall I see God" (Job 19:26).

In a centennial address at the Logan Temple, President Ezra Taft Benson asked: *"How did Adam bring his descendants into the presence of the Lord? The answer: Adam and his descendants entered into the priesthood order of God. Today we would say they went to the House of the Lord and received their blessings."*[2]

The Apostle John A. Widtsoe taught that for most of us the great and last promise of the temple comes by the spirit of revelation through a "wonderfully rich communion with God" in the temple that will prepare us for a face-to-face meeting.[3] Yet, we should not consider the great and last promise of the temple beyond our view, even in mortality. We should be encouraged by the enticing nearness of the Savior:

> But behold, verily, verily, I say unto you that *mine eyes are upon you, I am in your midst and ye cannot see me;*
> But the day soon cometh that *ye shall see me, and know that I am.*
> (D&C 38:7-8)

Emphasizing the mortal reality of the great and last promise, Elder Bruce R. McConkie once said that *"we must not wrest the scriptures and suppose that the promises of seeing the Lord refer to some future day,* either a Millennial or a celestial day, days in which, as we all know, the Lord will be present. *The promises apply to this mortal sphere in which we now live."*[4]

The principles of perfection and purification, preparing us for the great and last promise of the temple, can be learned only by the power of the Holy Spirit. These mysteries of God are "not the wisdom of this world," but rather *"the wisdom of God in a mystery, even the hidden wisdom, which God ordained before the world unto our glory"* (1 Corinthians 2:6-7). When we learn this wisdom in the temple, we feel Christ's power to purify us in preparation for His rest.

The Great and Last Promise Comes by Patiently Seeking the Lord

While the promise is to "see the Lord's face," we may have to patiently progress through the implied meanings of the word "see," such as understand with the "eyes of faith," "having not seen," yet loving and believing (*see* 1 Peter 1:8) before we visually see. Thus Joseph Smith exhorted us: "Let us here observe, that after any portion of the human family are made acquainted with the important fact that there is a God, who has created and does uphold all things, *the extent of their knowledge respecting his character and glory will depend upon their diligence and faithfulness in seeking after him, until like Enoch, the brother of Jared, and Moses, they shall obtain faith in God, and power with him to behold him face to face.*"[5]

The Prophet also encouraged the Saints "to go on and *continue to call upon God until you make your calling and election sure for yourselves,* by obtaining this more sure word of prophecy, and wait patiently for the promise until you obtain it."[6]

The scriptures teach that it is with patient and diligent seeking that this promise comes: "*Ye are not able to abide the presence of God now,* neither the ministering of angels; wherefore, continue in patience until ye are perfected" (D&C 67:13). And in D&C 101:38, we are instructed to "*seek the face of the Lord always, that in patience ye may possess your souls, and ye shall have eternal life*" (D&C 101:38). Finally, in Nephi, we learn that "*he that diligently seeketh shall find; and the mysteries of God shall be unfolded unto them, by the power of the Holy Ghost*" (1 Nephi 10:19).

A Comforting Assurance as a Great and Last Promise of the Temple

If we diligently seek the Lord, doing "the works of righteousness" (D&C 59:23), we can receive the great and last promise of the temple as a promise from "the Holy Spirit of Promise" (D&C 88:3). As part of the great and last promise, He promises to provide us with a comforting assurance, even a peace in this world, leading to the more sure word of the spirit of prophecy and revelation (*see* 2 Peter 1:19). It is a calling and election made sure to the reality of eternal life (*see* 2 Peter 1:10).

In this comforting assurance, Christ abides with us as a comforter so the Holy Spirit teaches us of His perfect stature. We see great possibilities for ourselves as we take hold of the hand of our Guide, who will edify us to His level. With this comforting assurance, there is no tribulation or temptation of life too great to overcome. This is the communion and comfort expressed by a beautiful aphorism of the scriptural temple: "Be still, and know that I am God" (D&C 101:16; Psalms 46:10). When we are still in the Lord's house, we can know the peace that He gives unto us (*see* John 14:27) in His holy house (*see* Haggai 2:9).

This is the comforting assurance and peaceful communion that will purify and prepare us for the consummation when the veil is rent (*see*

D&C 38:8; 101:23). This is the communion that will prepare us and let our hearts be comforted (*see* D&C 101:16) for the redemption of Zion:

> Behold, now are we the sons of God, and it doth not yet appear what we shall be; But we know that, when He shall appear, we shall be like Him; for *we shall see Him as He is.*
>
> *And every man that hath this hope in him purifieth himself even as He is pure.* (1 John 3:2-3)

> [To mine own elect]: for they will hear my voice, and *shall see me, and* shall not be asleep, and *shall abide the day of my coming: for they shall be purified, even as I am pure.* (D&C 35:21)

Be it a comforting assurance or a visual witness, it is the great and last promise of the temple that draws me to the summit of Mount Zion. It is the same promise that drew our patriarch fathers to the summit of holy mounts and made Moses declare: "Now for this cause I know that man is nothing" (Moses 1:10). It is as much a reality to me as the reality of this promise was to the children of Israel in the Sinai. We should yearn so deeply to be purified, by Him who so deeply wants to purify us, that this promise comes true for each of us even in this life:

> Sanctify yourselves; Yea, *purify your hearts, and cleanse your hands and your feet before me, that I may make you clean;*
>
> *That I may testify unto your Father, and your God, and my God, that you are clean from the blood of this wicked generation;* That I may fulfill this promise, *this great and last promise,* which I have made unto you. (D&C 88:74-75)

A Great and Last Sacrifice for the Great and Last Promise

The price for this "great and last promise" had to be great enough to pay for our purification and sanctification. The ultimate price already has been paid through the atoning blood of Jesus Christ (*see* 1 Corinthians 6:20). This is the price that will purify and sanctify us. *It is because of the great and last sacrifice of Christ that we have the great and last promise of the temple.*

Yet for His blood to miraculously wash our garments white and purify us of all sin, we too must pay a price (*see* D&C 19:16). This obligation on our part is discredited by many Christian religions as heresy, but as Lehi told Jacob: "*he offereth himself a sacrifice for sin, . . . unto all those who have a broken heart and contrite spirit"* (2 Nephi 2:7), and as Alma told Shiblon: *"none but the truly penitent are saved"* (Alma 42:24).

The Savior Himself proclaimed that *"my blood shall not cleanse them if they hear me not"* (D&C 29:15). This is why He admonished His messengers to "say nothing but repentance" (D&C 6:9). *It is only on condition of repentance that Christ can bring all men to His level, having cleansed them with His blood (see* D&C 18:12; 19:16; 29:44).

In the *Lectures on Faith*, Joseph Smith insisted on a sacrifice to God in order to obtain the kind of faith necessary to obtain the promise. It requires a sacrifice of "all things" (mortal objects, precepts, actions, and wills) in obedience to God. The Prophet explained what happens when we are unable to make this essential sacrifice:

> *But those who have not made this sacrifice to God do not know that the course which they pursue is well pleasing in his sight;* for whatever may be their belief or their opinion, it is a matter of doubt and uncertainty in their mind; and where doubt and uncertainty are there faith is not, nor can it be. *For doubt and faith do not exist in the same person at the same time;* so that persons whose minds are under doubts and fears cannot have unshaken confidence; and where unshaken confidence is not there faith is weak; *and where faith is weak the persons will not be able to contend against all the opposition, tribulations, and afflictions which they will have to encounter in order to be heirs of God, and joint heirs with Christ Jesus; and they will grow weary in their minds, and the adversary will have power over them and destroy them.*[7]

Many religions today discredit the importance of ordinances, and require only a sacrifice of confession in coming to Christ. Others look only to rituals as the source of purification. Neither spiritual manifestation without the Lord's ordinances, nor rituals without the presence of the Spirit is the "pattern" acceptable to the Lord (*see* D&C 52:14-29). Therefore, Joseph Smith said that *"Being born again comes by the Spirit of God through ordinances."*[8]

Some devout Jews in Israel are seeking purification in preparation for the restoration of the temple by reviving the sacrifice of the red heifer as set forth in the Law of Moses (*see* Numbers 19:19-20). It is fascinating that an American evangelist has arranged to provide a herd of red Angus cattle for this ritual.[9] It is not some concoction of water and ashes that will purify us today, any more than that same concoction purified the Jews under the law of Moses. *The red heifer was symbolic of the purification afforded by the Atonement of Christ. The rituals of purification are symbolic of obedience to the words of Christ that He might purify us.*

The importance that Latter-day Saints place on works (performing required ordinances and being obedient to commandments) is the ultimate expression of faith in Christ that works demonstrate (*see* James 2:17-26). Not that works will save us, but our obedience to Christ and His true messengers, with the real intent of a broken heart and contrite spirit will convince Him that we are truly penitent. By works obedient to His will, we take the name of Christ upon us, demonstrating that we believe on His name and love Him (*see* John 14:15). *Then* His grace will save us:

> And behold, this is the whole meaning of the law, every whit pointing to that *great and last sacrifice; and that great and last sacrifice will be the Son of God, yea, infinite and eternal.*
>
> And thus *he shall bring salvation to all those who shall believe on his name;* this being the intent of this last sacrifice, *to bring about the bowels of mercy, which overpowereth justice, and bringeth about means unto men that they may have faith unto repentance.*
>
> And thus mercy can satisfy the demands of justice, and encircles them in the arms of safety. . . .
>
> For behold, justice exerciseth all *his* demands, and also mercy claimeth all which is *her* own; and *thus none but the truly penitent are saved.* (Alma 34:14-16; Alma 42:24)

The comparison of gender in verse 24 is interesting. When I was growing up, my father was justice and my mother was mercy. When mercy pled with justice, promising that I would do better, mercy usually prevailed. However, did I become "truly penitent?" The truly penitent are those who "believe on His name," learning to sacrifice all in obedience to the Lord. The truly penitent are those who would sacrifice all in keeping covenants with the Lord, much like the father of king Lamoni, who asked, "What shall I do that I may have this eternal life? Yea, what shall I do that I may be born of God? Behold, said he, *I will give up all that I possess,* I will forsake my kingdom *that I may have this great joy.*" Ultimately, however, what it took was for Lamoni to "give away all my sins to know thee" (Alma 22:15, 18).

The price of the great and last promise for us is that we must be will-ing to offer our own great and last sacrifice: all our sins, and even our own lives if necessary, in obedience to the Lord.

The Sacrifice of a Broken Heart

As the rituals of the old covenant demanded specific animal sacri-fice, so the new covenant also demands a specific sacrifice. When Christ appeared to the Nephites at the temple in Bountiful, He declared that the Mosaic ritual of sacrifice could end, but that the principle of sac-rifice would continue under the new covenant:

> And ye shall offer up unto me no more the shedding of blood; yea, your sacrifices and burnt offerings shall be done away;
> And *ye shall offer for a sacrifice unto me a broken heart and a con-trite spirit.* (3 Nephi 9:19-20)

The Nephites understood the principle of sacrifice in the law of Moses. Even the Jews of the Old Testament should have understood this principle requiring "a broken spirit: a broken and a contrite heart" (*see* Psalms 51:16-17; 34:18).

The prophet Samuel warned King Saul that acceptable expression of a broken and contrite heart to the Lord is obedience to His word:

> Hath the Lord as great delight in burnt offerings and sacrifices, as in obeying the voice of the Lord? Behold *to obey is better than sacri-fice, and to hearken than the fat of rams.*
> For *rebellion* is as the sin of witchcraft, and *stubbornness* is as ini-quity and idolatry. Because thou hast rejected the word of the Lord, he hath also rejected thee from being King. (1 Samuel 15:22-23)

With strong messianic imagery, the prophet Micah taught the ele-ments of the sacrifices of a broken heart which are acceptable to the Lord:

> Wherewith shall I come before the Lord, and bow myself before the high God?
> Will the Lord be pleased with thousands of rams, or with ten thou-sands of rivers of oil? Shall I give my first born for my transgression, the fruit of my body for the sin of my soul?
> *He hath shewed thee, O man, what is good; and what doth the Lord require of thee, but to do justly, and to love mercy, and to walk humbly with thy God.* (Micah 6:6-8)

This same instruction on sacrifice which is acceptable to the Lord was given to Hyrum Smith, as a revelation through his brother Joseph:

> And now verily, verily, I say unto thee, put your trust in that Spirit which leadeth to do good—yea, to *do justly, to walk humbly, to judge righteously;* and this is my Spirit. . . .
>
> I will impart unto you of my Spirit, which shall enlighten your mind, which shall fill your soul with joy. (D&C 11:12-13)

"My Spirit," the "Spirit" of the Lord, refers to the gift of the Holy Spirit—the guidance of the Holy Ghost, the third member of the Godhead. This is the recompense for the sacrifice of a broken heart and contrite spirit. This is the Lord's promise in the sacramental covenant. Before we partake of the sacrament, however, and even before we are baptized, we are to offer the Lord a sacrifice of our broken hearts and contrite spirits (*see* D&C 59:8-13; 20:37).

Just as Hosea turned to and accepted Gomer for his wife (*see* Hosea 1:2), the Lord will turn to us and edify us if we turn to Him with a broken heart. Through the prophet Hosea the Lord declared, "For *I desired mercy, and not sacrifice; and the knowledge of God more than burnt offerings*" (Hosea 6:6).

The Hebrew word for mercy, *hesed*, refers to a "deep spiritual and emotional bond." The Hebrew words for knowledge, *yada* and *daat,* both mean "to learn by close experience."[10]

Therefore, to have mercy and knowledge are key concepts in the type of sacrifice required by the Lord—the terms indicate that we should have a bonding relationship with Him and with each other. It is the gift of the Holy Spirit that gives us the knowledge and shows us the merciful graces of Jesus Christ so that we will want to have a close relationship with Him.

King David understood that having the right or "clean heart," is having the right spirit, and this comes by following the Holy Spirit. He pled for the spirit when he prayed, "*Create in me a clean heart, O God; and renew a right spirit within me.* Cast me not away from thy presence; and take not thy holy spirit from me" (Psalm 51:10-11).

It is the Holy Spirit within the temple, be it a building or an individual, not its physical makeup, who justifies (makes right) and enlightens the structure with the right spirit. This truth of the sacrifice of a broken heart to obtain a heart enlightened and justified by the Holy Spirit is immutable in any temple dispensation. Even during the construction of the Tabernacle, this sacrifice was required when "every one whose heart stirred him up, and every one whom his spirit made willing [came] to the work of the Tabernacle" (*see* Exodus 35:21).

As we make a true change from our hard hearts to broken hearts, sacrificing the selfish and consuming animals within us, our hearts stir us to receive the right and willing spirit through the sanctifying gifts of the Spirit. Then we are "stirred" to the work of the temple and the discipleship of Christ (*see* Luke 14:26).

A Sacrifice of Sweet Savor

When Moses was given instructions about burnt offerings, an unlikely term was used by the Lord to describe the sacrifice: "And thou shalt burn the whole ram upon the altar: It is a burnt offering unto the Lord: *It is a sweet savour,* an offering made by fire unto the Lord" (Exodus 29:18).

The term "sweet savour" hardly fits a burning ram until we understand how the Lord considers this burnt offering a "sweet savour." Paul helped us come to that understanding when he said, "And walk in love, as Christ also hath loved us, and hath given Himself for us an offering and a sacrifice to God for a sweetsmelling savour" (Ephesians 5:2).

Here, a sacrifice to God of "sweet savour" or "sweet-smelling savour" is defined. It is not the sacrifice that is sweet. It is the diligently obedient and heart-felt intent to "walk in love" by the one offering sacrifice that can find sweet acceptance with the Lord.

The intent of sacrifice must be love of God and fellowman, sacrificing for their benefit. This is emulation of the sacrifice of Christ. Even if our sacrifice to the Lord does not result in a completed work, He will "accept of (our) offerings" if we "cease not (our) diligence" in obeying the Lord (D&C 124:49).

There are notable examples in the scriptures of this sweet-smelling sacrifice, even when the desired result seemed illusive. Oliver Granger was physically handicapped. He helped construct the Kirtland Temple, then returned to Kirtland as an emissary of the Prophet in order to help rectify financial problems. How we would like to hear these few sweet words of the Lord to describe our sacrifices:

> I remember my servant Oliver Granger; behold *his name shall be had in sacred remembrance . . .* for *his sacrifice shall be more sacred unto me than his increase,* saith the Lord." (D&C 117:12-13)

Just as sweet to our ears would be the words of assurance that Joseph Smith received from the Lord because of his sacrifices:

I seal upon you your exaltation, and prepare a throne for you in the kingdom of my Father, with Abraham your father.

Behold, I have seen your sacrifices, and will forgive all your sins; I have seen your sacrifices in obedience to that which I have told you. Go, therefore, and I make a way for your escape, as I accepted the offering of Abraham of his son Isaac." (D&C 132:49-50)

Abraham had such love for the Lord that he would sacrifice his own son to be obedient. Joseph Smith sacrificed his own life with the same Abrahamic love and obedience. In the temple, we covenant to sacrifice with this demonstration of love and obedience, that our sacrifices will be a sweet savor to the Lord.

Specific Sacrifices that Heal the Broken Heart

A sacrifice of sweet savor to the Lord is the broken heart. *The broken heart is broken or tamed because it sacrifices the ungodly and consuming animal of the natural man. The natural heart, thus broken of pride and ungodliness, becomes a meek heart, willing, learning, and forgiving. It can then be taught and trained by the Holy Spirit.* We, who are broken, can then receive a new heart, even a "mighty change of heart," for God "healeth the broken in heart" (Psalms 147:3). The Lord has told us specifically what we must sacrifice, along with the hard heart of the natural man, to heal our broken hearts and obtain a new heart: "And again, verily I say unto you that it is your privilege, and a promise that I give unto you that have been ordained unto this ministry, that *inasmuch as you strip yourselves from jealousies and fears, and humble yourselves before me,* for ye are not sufficiently humble, *the veil shall be rent and you shall see me and know that I am*—not with the carnal neither natural mind, but with the spiritual" (D&C 67:10). Notice again the great and last promise of the temple in this verse. The price for this promise is to sacrifice our jealousies and fears, as well as pride.

Because of Christ, there is no place for comparison, and its resulting jealousy, between us as human beings. We need only compare our own stature and will to God's. Therefore only understanding, edification, and love should be the relationship between each other.

Fear is a natural human reaction, but it takes the place of lost faith (*see* D&C 63:16). We have nothing humanly possible to fear if we have complete faith in Christ. All we really need to fear is disobedience: *"And if ye have no hope ye must need be in despair [fear]; and despair cometh because of iniquity [disobedience]"* (Moroni 10:22).

Hope in Christ, even a perfect brightness of hope, comes through preparation on our part. This preparation will dispel fear: *"If ye are prepared ye shall not fear"* (D&C 38:30).

Preparation on our part specifically means following the commandments of God. *"For if you will that I give unto you a place in the celestial world, you must prepare yourselves by doing the things which I have commanded you and required of you"* (D&C 78:7). The specifics of the preparation for our redemption are found in multiple verses of the scriptural temple (*see* Alma 5:7-8, 27-28; 34:32; Ether 12:33-34; D&C 78:6-7, 11-13, 17-18; 105:9-13).

As I stood on the roof of the house of Simon the Tanner in the old seaport of Joppa and looked at the rocky, protected enclosure of the port and the vanishing expanse of the blue Mediterranean beyond, I thought of the two scriptural men of Joppa. Jonah, whom I have already mentioned, feared the Assyrians and had little faith in the Lord. He boarded a ship at Joppa to escape, only to find himself in the belly of hell. The other, a man who also stood on the roof of Simon the tanner, had not yet comprehended the extent of his calling until he understood the great vision of the sheet descending from heaven (*see* Acts 11:5-7). At that moment the protected port of Joppa was no longer the limit for Peter. Now he saw beyond the horizon of the blue Mediterranean.

In the ports of our lives, we may find protection and refuge but unless we venture into open water, we limit our horizons because of fear. The real purpose of this life is to leave our ports of Joppa and go through tribulation—and let tribulation go through us—in order to discover what kind of men and women we really are.[11] We should sail out of our ports without fear, like a great ship, because our exposure to peril is covered by the Atonement, and we have "an anchor of the soul" (Hebrews 6:19) and a sail billowing "perfect brightness of hope" (2 Nephi 31:20) in our Savior, Jesus Christ.

"In the world ye shall have tribulation," Christ said, "but be of good cheer; I have overcome the world" (John 16:33). If we do not have this anchor and this hope, then we are "tossed to and fro by every wind of doctrine" (Ephesians 4:14) as we venture into open sea.

Like a sailing ship, we must move about even in open and dangerous water to be effective true messengers. Like a buoy, however, unless we are tethered to a solid foundation with the rope (hope) of the anchor of our souls, we would be at the mercy of the wind and soon lose our effectiveness and our souls. We must look to the horizon, beyond our weakness and fears, with a perfect brightness of hope, to the rising sun, believing that all is possible through the Atonement of the Son of God. We must hope, even as we fail, because the reality is, as the story of Jonah teaches, even in great sin and great fear we can have hope through simple obedience to Christ. As we grasp His rope, He will make us whole, and clean, and fearless.

Humility is the basic quality of the heart broken of pride. This attribute opens the door to all other spiritual qualities. It is the heart broken of pride that invites the Holy Spirit to teach and train in the qualities which permit us to sacrifice ("submit") all in obedience to the Lord: *"unless he yields to the enticings of the Holy Spirit, and putteth off the natural man and becometh a saint through the atonement of Christ the Lord,* and becometh as a child, submissive, meek, humble, patient, full of love, *willing to submit to all things which the Lord seeth fit to inflict upon him,* even as a child doth submit to his father" (Mosiah 3:19).

The Book of Mormon teaches that pride of the natural man is the most difficult to sacrifice. Therefore, sufficient humility is the most difficult to obtain.

Could ye say, if ye were called to die at this time, within yourselves, that ye have been sufficiently humble?

Behold, *are ye stripped of pride? I say unto you if ye are not ye are not prepared to meet God.* (Alma 5:27-28; *compare* Alma 34:32)

Our Great and Last Sacrifice for the Great and Last Promise

Once we have sacrificed jealousy, fear, and pride to obtain a broken heart, we must make one final sacrifice of sweet savor to the Lord in order to obtain the great and last promise: "Verily, thus saith the Lord; it shall come to pass that *every soul who forsaketh his sins and cometh unto me and calleth on my name, and obeyeth my voice, and keepeth my commandments, shall see my face and know that I am"* (D&C 93:1).

Again, the great and last promise is the result of this sacrifice, and it is for "every soul." The sacrifice talked about in this verse is the sacrifice made by the father of King Lamoni—*to forsake all our sins and worldliness, then come unto Christ.* The essence of this great and last sacrifice for the prize of eternal life, the great and last promise of the temple, is captured in the dialogue between Christ and the rich man:

> And when he was gone forth into the way, there came one running and kneeled to him, and asked him, Good Master, what shall I do that I may inherit eternal life? . . .
> Thou knowest the commandments, . . .
> And he answered and said unto him Master, all these have I observed from my youth.
> Then Jesus beholding him loved him, and said unto him, One thing thou lackest; *go thy way, sell whatsoever thou hast, and give to the poor, and thou shalt have treasure in heaven: and come, take up the cross, and follow me.* . . .
> It is easier for the camel to go through the eye of a needle, than for a rich man to enter into the kingdom of God. (Mark 10:17, 19, 20-21, 25)

The image of the camel going through the narrow gate (the eye of a needle) is the camel shedding all excess baggage in order to pass. We are all "rich men" if we have excess baggage. Death is a sudden shedding of our excess baggage, as though the loaded camel suddenly ran through the narrow gate. If we are not prepared, death—like birth—can strip us naked, unworthy for the promise. We need the covering that will pass through the eye of the needle. It is the garment of salvation and the robes of righteousness. Therefore, selling whatsoever we have that is excess *to acquire the gifts of the Spirit that He provides in the temple* is the final sacrifice in preparation to pass the narrow gate.

Shedding excess baggage, *we can also edify others with material needs and with devotion of time to their needs.* Be it material wealth, idleness, pride, sin, or even our own lives (*see* Luke 14:26), we must be willing to sell all that is excess and unnecessary to pass through the narrow gate and claim eternal life. *It is not sufficient to just rid ourselves of the excess. We must do it in a way that edifies others, including ourselves.* Shedding our excess baggage is an act of edification to ourselves if we repent. To rid ourselves of sin is only half the cleansing. *We must cover ourselves with righteousness.* To give material wealth to the poor is only half the giving. *We must also cover them with righteousness.*

To "take up the cross" is to abandon the false messengers of the precepts of men and take upon us the name of Christ. *It is to take upon us Christ's cross in the form of suffering, rejection, and sacrifice for the sake of bringing forth and establishing the cause of Zion* (*see* D&C 6:6; 11:6; 14:6). When we take up the cross, our own will is sacrificed for obedience to His will.

To follow the Savior is to do the will and works of Christ. It is to remain obedient to the True Messenger through mortal tribulation by *obeying and keeping His covenants with a perfect brightness of hope. To be "perfect" in this life is to keep His covenants with precision, having a joyful brightness in doing so. To endure to the end is to follow Him to the end.*

To take up the cross and follow is the great and last sacrifice that we must make through temple covenants in order to obtain the great and last promise of the temple. In sum, it is the sacrifice of all forms of idolatry (excess baggage) in our lives so that we are able to turn completely to the one true God. *In Book of Mormon terms, this sacrifice is called "yielding our hearts unto God"* (*see* Helaman 3:33-35).

Notice in this scriptural account of Helaman that those with a broken heart (the more humble part of the people) continued to sacrifice in obedience to the Lord because they became "firmer and firmer" in their faith in Christ. *This firmness of faith is a gift for sacrificing in obedience to the Lord.* It is the gift of the spirit of prophecy and revelation. Then these broken-hearted people became a pure-hearted people because they "yielded their hearts unto God." They yielded completely their will to God's will. This is the great and last sacrifice of the temple for those who are willing to sacrifice all, yielding their hearts to God. This is the ultimate sacrifice required for the great and last promise of the temple. It was the sacrifice required by the Lord in the sermon on the Temple Mount when He said, "therefore, if he shall come unto me, . . . then *come unto me with full purpose of heart, and I will receive you*" (3 Nephi 12:23-24).

It was the same sacrifice required by the Lord in "straitening" the children of Israel whose fathers rejected the great and last promise of the temple because they "err in their heart." Therefore, the Lord lamented, "O, that there were such an heart in them, that they would fear me, and keep all my commandments always" (Deuteronomy 5:29).

Full purpose of heart occurs by yielding our hearts to God. It comes by making a great and last sacrifice of the many facets of stubborn pride of the natural man. It is shedding all forms of idolatry, even the human relations that we idolize (*see* Luke 14:26), by completely taking Christ's name upon us, emulating Him with full purpose of heart (*see* D&C

18:27-28). Christ is the only one we should idolize because His name is written always in our hearts (*see* Mosiah 5:12). Then the Lord will "receive" us, which implies the blessing of His presence.

Since one of Christ's titles or names is the "Bridegroom" (*see* D&C 33:17), there is an interesting correlation to the gift or sacrifice given to the Jewish bridegroom by the bride. It is her heart.[12] *It is dedication to her husband with full purpose of heart. This is how the woman "gives herself" to the man in the Holy Order of Matrimony. Of course, the man must "receive" this sacrificial gift of his bride with full love and devotion to her as his most prized and holy possession.*

This great and last sacrifice begins with a broken heart, then continues until a sacrifice of the full heart is made. This is "such an heart" that is acceptable to the Lord. We offer this sacrifice of self and this gift of full purpose of heart when we "offer [our] whole souls" (*see* Omni 1:26) to God on the altars of the temple.

Before we can offer our whole souls as this gift of total obedience, yielding our own wills to His on the temple altar, we must first be reconciled with our "brother" (the priesthood authorities to whom we are accountable as well as all those with whom we have "ought").

> Therefore *if thou bring thy gift to the altar,* and there rememberest that thy brother hath ought against thee;
>
> Leave there thy gift before the altar, and go thy way; *first be reconciled to thy brother, and then come and offer thy gift.* (Matthew 5:23-24)

The greatest expression of a broken heart is the ability to completely forgive others. The object and desired result of complete forgiveness is reconciliation. This requires confession and forgiveness on both sides (*see* D&C 42:88). The power of pure love from a heart without guile (*see* D&C 41:11) is usually needed to produce this kind of reconciliation. *This is the gift: the reconciled heart, which is full sacrifice of the proud heart to a pure heart without guile, that we must bring to the mercy seat, the altar of the temple. This is the gift that we must bring even to the sacrament altar before partaking of the sacred emblems* (*see* D&C 46:4). Then we can be reconciled to God and obtain His mercy through the pure love of His Son (*see* 2 Nephi 10:24).

The Mighty Change of Heart on Mount Zion: The Pure Love of Christ

In making this great and last sacrifice to the Lord, *our broken hearts become pure hearts because they are filled with pure love.* This is " such an heart" that the Lord requires of us. It is only with this pure heart of pure love that all fear is dispelled (*see* 1 John 4:18; Moroni 8:16) so we can truly be reconciled with our brother and with God. Mormon called this pure love charity. *"But charity is the pure love of Christ, and it endureth forever; and whoso is found possessed of it at the last day, it shall be well with him"* (Moroni 7:47).

Mormon further exhorted us to obtain this gift, this pure love, with "all the energy of heart." He was telling us to make a great and last sacrifice to the Lord, yielding our hearts to God, to obtain this pure love in which all the "graces" of holiness are found. *We then become "true followers," the sons and daughters of God, seeing Him as He is because we are "purified as He is pure"* (Moroni 7:48). *This is the great and last promise of the temple.*

These words of Mormon are similar to the words of the Apostle John (*see* 1 John 3:2). Mormon however, specifically said that to be like Christ, we must fill our hearts with charity, the pure love of Christ. When we receive Christ, taking His name upon us, His pure love becomes part of our nature through the power of the Atonement. This is how we make the mighty change of heart (Alma 5:12) and become the sons and daughters of God (*see* 3 Nephi 9:17). The great and last promise of the temple, mentioned both by Mormon and John, can be our view of the summit of Mount Zion even as we climb, when our hearts become "such an heart."

The Lord clearly connected the temple with the quality of charity and the great and last promise:

> And inasmuch as my people build a house unto me in the name of the Lord, and do not suffer any unclean thing to come into it, that it be not defiled, my glory shall rest upon it.
>
> *Yea, and my presence shall be there, for I will come into it, and all the pure in heart that shall come into it shall see God.* (D&C 97:15-16)

This scripture recalls the words of the Savior in the Sermon on the Temple Mount, where he stated, "Blessed are all the pure in heart, for they shall see God" (3 Nephi 12:8).

The setting of these beatitudes was the temple, and the sermon was what John Welch calls *a "temple text."*[13] *Such a text contains sacred ordinances and teachings of the fulness of the gospel, which lead men and women to covenant with the Lord.* Unlike the information provided about the New Testament "Sermon on the Mount," the "Sermon on the Temple Mount" is *prefaced with two beatitudes* that provide the context for the subsequent beatitudes: *"Blessed are ye if ye shall give heed unto the words of these twelve whom I have chosen . . . Blessed are ye if ye shall believe in me and be baptized"* (3 Nephi 12:1).

In other words, the Lord is saying, "Blessed are ye if you follow true messengers in hearing my word." We cannot reject His true messengers and expect to come unto Christ. This is an extremely important temple doctrine. It is how we come to know God. Then, we are truly blessed if we give heed to the words of true messengers by taking Christ's name upon us in joining His Church.

Thereafter, the Nephites who heard this sermon were prepared to make temple covenants with the Lord, just like the Nephites at the temple in Zarahemla who had heard King Benjamin. It is not surprising, then, that in the beatitudes of this great temple sermon are the steps, the basic and advanced principles of the gospel, leading to the great and last promise of the temple[14] (*compare* Moroni 8:25-26):

1. *"Poor in spirit who come unto me:"* Only in comparison to Christ do we learn how poor in spirit we are. We are all spiritual orphans who should be seeking our spiritual parents. Only by coming to Christ with *faith in Him*, to spiritually beget us, can we find them.

2. *"They that mourn:"* This means godly sorrow that worketh repentance (*see* 2 Corinthians 7:10). *This is the kind of sorrow that produces fruit meet for repentance because it not only empties us of unrighteousness (the comfort of confession), but fills us with righteousness (the miracle of forgiveness).* This miracle produces the fruits of the Spirit that not only comfort but give the great joy of righteousness.

3. *"Meek:"* This term also means *having enough spiritual confidence and control to go beyond a respecting relationship with the Savior* (*see* Moroni 7:39). The meek seek the Lord because they have faith in Him. In Him alone is their justice and righteousness. Therefore, they can go through tribulation in full control with a perfect brightness of hope. They have a craving for an emulating relationship with Christ, a relationship built by obeying all His covenants and ordinances: first,

baptism, then the higher laws and ordinances. *When the meek obey the everlasting covenant, the Abrahamic covenant, they shall inherit the earth.*

4. *"**Hunger and thirst after righteousness:**" This is the definition of fasting with the right heart.* Then we will be filled with the *Holy Ghost.* The Holy Ghost is the one who teaches us about the qualities of a little child that are necessary to obtain a pure heart, pass the final judgment, and enter the celestial kingdom (*see* Mosiah 27:25-26). Remember who is the greatest in the kingdom of heaven (*see* Matthew 18:3-4). To become a little child is to covenant with the Lord and *build upon His rock, or His atonement and His temple covenants* (*see* 3 Nephi 11:38-39). *Rock is another word for covenant.* When we build upon His rock, we are not just any little children (*see* Ephesians 4:14-15), but the children of light (*see* John 12:36). This means *we become the children of Christ, His sons and daughters, because of the covenants we make and keep with Him* (*see* Mosiah 5:7). *We become the spiritually begotten children of Christ because He changes our hearts to pure hearts, filled with pure love, as we keep covenants of love with Him.* Then we are prepared for the great and last promise of the temple!

5. *"**Blessed are all the pure in heart, for they shall see God:**" It is in the temple that we covenant to sacrifice all, yielding our hearts unto God, that we may learn how to obtain charity, the pure love of Christ.* This mighty change of heart, *from a proud to a broken and then to a pure heart,* is the process of obtaining the pure love of Christ. It is the sacrificial path to the summit of Mount Zion.

Charity is the pinnacle of the temple paradigm. President Howard W. Hunter, who diligently directed the Church to the temple, said that charity, the pure love of Christ, "is the highest pinnacle the human soul can reach and the deepest expression of the human heart."[15] Charity is the greatest of all spiritual qualities that will permit us to receive the great and last promise of the temple.

Paul captured the essence of charity in one word, when he said, "Now as touching things offered unto idols, we know that we all have knowledge. Knowledge puffeth up, but *charity edifieth*" (1 Corinthians 8:1).

Charity is not the show of giving alms, being a self-righteous martyr, or boasting in knowledge (*see* 1 Corinthians 13:3). *It is the ability to edify others,* having mastered all the qualities of charity enumerated by Paul:

> Charity suffereth long, and is kind; charity envieth not; charity vaunteth not itself, is not puffed up;
> Doth not behave itself unseemly, seeketh not her own, is not easily provoked, thinketh no evil;
> Rejoiceth not in iniquity, but rejoiceth in the truth;
> Beareth all things, believeth all things, hopeth all things; endureth all things;
> Charity never faileth. (1 Corinthians 13:4-8)

Using the words of his father, Moroni repeated the qualities of charity listed by Paul (*see* Moroni 7:45). Michael Wilcox, a well-known author and teacher, offered his own version of Moroni's verse, *substituting the word "Christ" for the word "charity:"* "And Christ suffereth long, and is kind, and envieth not. Christ is not puffed up, seeketh not his own, is not easily provoked, thinketh no evil, and rejoiceth not in iniquity but rejoiceth in the truth. Christ beareth all things, believeth all things, hopeth all things, endureth all things."[16]

Christ never faileth! When we comprehend the fulness of charity, we comprehend the "stature of the fulness of Christ." He is full of grace because He is full of charity. We then understand the meaning of the Savior's parting commandment to his apostles: "A new commandment I give unto you, That ye love one another; as I have loved you" (John 13:34).

We understand His words by the example He showed:

> You call me Master and Lord: and ye say well; for so I am.
> If I then, your Lord and Master, have washed your feet; ye also ought to wash one another's feet.
> For *I have given you an example, that ye should do as I have done to you.* (John 13:13-15)

Climbing Mount Zion: Building an Edifice of Pure Love on a Sure Foundation

The word *edify* comes from edifice, suggesting a structure built upon a solid, sure foundation. *To edify therefore means to "build up" upon a solid foundation.* We are edified or built up upon the foundation of the gospel of Jesus Christ: "Build upon my rock, which is my gospel" (D&C 11:24; *see also* D&C 10:50-52, 62).

In Helaman's supplication to his sons, Nephi and Lehi, he declared that the rock of Christ is a "sure foundation, whereon if men build they cannot fall" (Helaman 5:12).

This rock is the fulness of Christ's gospel. It is the fulness of the stature of His love and power expressed through His atonement. With His love and power, built upon His foundation, we can build a structure of perfect love within us. To build up this structure of perfect love, we must precisely follow His perfect plan (*see* Psalms 127:1).

Isaiah prophesied that this sure foundation is the foundation of Zion. "Therefore thus saith the Lord God, Behold, *I lay in Zion for a foundation a stone, a tried stone, a precious corner stone, a sure foundation*" (Isaiah 28:16).

The foundation stone of Zion is the "rock" of Christ. He is the rock upon which the structures of Zion are built. He is also the chief cornerstone that makes one out of two opposing walls.

Paul alluded to Abraham and "the heirs with him of the same promise" looking for such a foundation when he said, "For he looked for a city which hath foundations, whose builder and maker is God" (Hebrews 11:10).

The city mentioned in this verse is Zion, specifically the city of Enoch:

> Wherefore, hearken ye together and let me show unto you even my wisdom—the wisdom of him whom ye say is the God of Enoch, and his brethren,
> Who were separated from the earth, and were received unto myself—*a city reserved until a day of righteousness shall come—a day which was sought for by all holy men, and they found it not because of wickedness and abominations.* (D&C 45:11-12)

The foundation of Zion was laid by the Lord, "who hath established the foundations of Adam-Ondi-Ahman" (D&C 78:15). Having dwelt with Adam, Enoch probably patterned his city after Adam-ondi-Ahman. Zion, the New Jerusalem, will be built on these same foundations established by the Lord. As we seek to establish Zion, we must learn the sure foundation of the Lord and lay the foundation of "the Zion of God" (D&C 58:7).

If we are to become a Zion-like people with pure hearts filled with pure love, we need to look for the structures built on a sure foundation that will edify us to become such a people. When our hearts respond to the Holy Spirit and we build our lives on the spirit of prophecy and revelation, which is the rock of the testimony of Christ, we become such a structure as true messengers. The Church of Jesus Christ of Latter-day Saints is such a structure, built on a foundation of these true messengers—the apostles and prophets, with Christ the chief cornerstone. Our homes, built on the foundation of the gospel with parents who live the Holy Order of Matrimony, are such structures. The House of the Lord is such a structure, built on the foundation of the fulness of the Melchizedek Priesthood, with Christ leading the way to the presence of God. Interestingly, all these "structures," built on the rock of Christ, are the temples in our lives (*see* 1 Corinthians 6:19; Isaiah 4:5-6).

Becoming "fitly framed and joined together" on this foundation and cornerstone means that *we build upon the rock of Christ's Atonement by making covenants with Him through priesthood ordinances.* When we keep these covenants, *we as saints become, collectively and individually, temples where God and His Spirit can dwell.*

> Now therefore ye are no more strangers and foreigners, but fellow-citizens with the saints, and of the household of God;
>
> And are built upon the foundation of the apostles and prophets, Jesus Christ himself being the chief cornerstone;
>
> In whom all the building fitly framed together groweth unto an holy temple in the Lord:
>
> In whom *ye also are builded together for an habitation of God through the Spirit.* (Ephesians 2:19-22)

Paul said that we become part of the structure "fitly joined together" as we learn to edify others. "From whom the whole body fitly joined together and compacted by that which every joint supplieth, according to the effectual working in the measure of every part, maketh increase of *the body unto the edifying of itself in love*" (Ephesians 4:16).

Being a physician familiar with muscles, bones, and joints, I interpret Paul beautifully describing the edifying function of a joint as a symbol of our relationships with each other. For as a bone supports a muscle, whose edifying action is conveyed across a joint to another bone, so must our relationships be with others. The joint is the interface of our relationships. It may be constrained or free as needed, but it must have smooth interactions, being well lubricated with the pure oil of charity. Then our efforts are well received to the edification of others. The whole relationship is then edified; the whole, being greater than the sum of its parts. The whole body then moves with the grace of a holy temple.

We "grow unto a holy temple" (Ephesians 2:21) as we are filled with a full measure of light reflecting the pure love of Christ. This light is the "marvelous light of His goodness" (*see* Alma 19:6). In the temple, the Holy Spirit of Truth enlightens us with the truth about the marvelous light of Christ's perfect love (*see* D&C 6:15). As we learn the words of Christ in our hearts and minds from the Holy Spirit of Truth, we are filled with light, which light fills our soul with the goodness and joy of Christ's perfect love (*see* D&C 11:11-13). Then we become the "children of light" because we "edify one another" (*see* 1 Thessalonians 5:5, 11).

There is an intimate relationship between truth, light, and love. Spiritual light is the truth that enlightens us about the power of perfect love. The fulness of the light of Christ is the power to love perfectly. Truth and light from the Holy Spirit provide the plan and power we need to construct an edifice of pure love on the rock of Christ as we climb Mount Zion.

> And that which doth not edify is not of God, and is darkness.
> *That which is of God is light; and he that receiveth light, and continueth in God, receiveth more light and that light groweth brighter and brighter until the perfect day.* (D&C 50:23-24)

The perfect day in our lives is the day we acquire perfect love.

Our Lead Climber: The Master of Grace and Truth

Christ's ability to edify through love is declared with a particular description in the scriptures. "And I, John, bear record that I beheld his glory, as the glory of the Only Begotten of the Father, full of grace and truth" (D&C 93:11). The teachers I admire the most are those who are full of grace and truth. They are full of knowledge, but they are most gracious to me as a student, considering my needs and ability to learn. I want to learn from them because I feel they respect me as an individual and love me as a student. *The Savior's grace, His ability to edify us with His love, is what draws us to Him (see 2 Nephi 26:24-25) as The Great Teacher.* Therefore, we follow Him as the lead climber in our ascent of Mount Zion because He is the Master of Grace and Truth. He commanded that we in His church do likewise when he said, "*Ye shall* instruct and edify each other that you may know how to act and direct my church" (D&C 43:8). Now I understand why Paul and Mormon taught that knowledge (truth) without charity (grace) is nothing (*see* 1 Corinthians 8:1; Moroni 7:44).

The greatest application of a pure heart that we make in this life is the sacrifice of self for the edification of others. According to President Hinckley, "the greatest selfless act of Christian service that we can perform in this mortal life" occurs in temple service.[17]

We desire consistently to make a sacrifice of self when our hearts are filled with this pure grace, the pure love of Christ. This transformation in our hearts occurs in the temple as we keep the covenants of our Savior, receiving grace for grace. "For if you keep my commandments you shall receive of his fulness, and be glorified in me as I am in the Father; therefore, I say unto you, *you shall receive grace for grace*" (D&C 93:20).

Perhaps this is why Christ spent so much time in His Father's House during His mortal ministry—because it was there He "continued from grace to grace" (D&C 93:13).

A Contrast Between Priestcraft and Charity

The Book of Mormon offers a striking contrast between priestcraft and charity. *Priestcraft sacrifices others for oneself. This is the great secret of Satan to get gain. Charity sacrifices the interests of oneself for the edification of others. This is the great secret to obtain God's power.*

Those who practiced priestcraft, such as Nehor (*see* Alma 1:12-16), were contrasted to priests, true messengers, preaching the word of God to edify the people of God: "And when the priests left their labor to impart the word of God unto the people, the people also left their labors to hear the word of God . . . *for the preacher was no better than the hearer, and thus they were all equal*" (Alma 1:26).

In the following verses we see the qualities of people who were striving to serve God. They serve as excellent criteria by which we can discern whether individuals are laboring to further God's work or whether they are practicing priestcraft. These attributes definitely *do not* describe those who are practicing priestcraft:

> And they *did impart of their substance,* every man according to that which he had, . . . and *they did not wear costly apparel,* yet *they were neat and comely.*

And now, because of *the steadfastness of the church* they became exceedingly rich . . .

And they *did not set their hearts upon riches;* therefore *they were liberal to all . . . having no respect to persons* as to those who stood in need. (Alma 1:27, 29, 30)

In contrast, Nephi, prophesying of the last days and the times of the Gentiles, described the pride of priestcraft as their great stumbling block:

And the Gentiles are *lifted in the pride of their eyes,* and *have stumbled,* because of the greatness of their stumbling block, that they have *built up many churches;* nevertheless, *they put down the power and miracles of God,* and preach up unto themselves their own wisdom and their own learning, that they may get gain and grind upon the face of the poor.

. . . for, behold, priestcrafts are that *men preach and set themselves up for a light unto the world, that they may get gain and praise* of the world; but *they seek not the welfare of Zion. . . .*

Wherefore, the Lord God hath given a commandment that *all men should have charity, which charity is love.* (2 Nephi 26:20, 29-30)

Nephi contrasted the pride and priestcraft of the Gentiles with the Savior's charity when he wrote:

For behold, my beloved brethren, I say unto you that *the Lord God worketh not in darkness.*

He doeth not anything save it be for the benefit of the world; for he loveth the world, even that he layeth down his own life that he may draw all men unto him. (2 Nephi 26:23-24)

In the temple, this contrast between priestcraft and charity is taught. As Satan entices us with money, we must choose to satisfy our selfish, carnal desires or be true messengers, holding the gifts of God sacred while acting with charity to edify the lives of others. Money may advance us in this life, but it is sacred gifts and ordinances of God which cannot be purchased with money (*see* Acts 8:20) that advance us to God's presence.

The Price to Reach the Summit of Mount Zion: A Sacrifice for the Oneness of Pure Love

We also learn in the temple that *we cannot reach the summit of Mount Zion alone. We must learn to edify others in our climb so that we all acquire the oneness of pure love at the summit.* Moroni was concerned about their weakness in writing of his people, and he worried that their writings might be mocked by the Gentiles. Nevertheless, he said the Lord would show the weakness of the Gentiles in that faith, hope, and charity is the fountain of all righteousness (*see* Ether 12:28). Then Moroni used great words, similar to Nephi, in describing the charity of Christ:

> And again, I remember that thou hast said that thou hast loved the world, even unto the laying down of thy life for the world, that thou mightest take it again to prepare a place for the children of men.
>
> And now I know that this love which thou hast had for the children of men is charity; wherefore, *except men shall have charity they cannot inherit that place which thou hast prepared in the mansions of thy Father.* (Ether 12:33-34)

The Apostle John also expressed the depth of Christ's love for us when he wrote, "Greater love hath no man than this, that a man lay down his life for his friends" (John 15:13). The sacrifice of self for the edification of others is the essence of charity.

Richard L. Evans, a former apostle and neighbor, described charity as a sacrifice: "*Sincere love is something that sacrifices—not something that indulges itself. Sincere love is responsible. It would never knowingly hurt, but would heal.*"[18]

I like to think that a physician who loves to fully heal his patients understands this kind of love. A marriage where husband and wife are one knows this kind of love. It is the love of edification, lifelong and beyond, with the partners sustaining and affirming one another so that such love forges one flesh.

Viktor Frankl, describing a poignant moment in his German concentration-camp experience, painted with his pen a scene of pure love and oneness with his wife. The separation of husbands, wives, and families in these camps was sudden, brutal, and usually final. While being marched to a work site early one morning, the man in front of Frankl said: "If our wives could see us now! I do hope they are better off in their camps and don't know what is happening to us."

"That brought thoughts of my own wife to mind," said Frankl. "And as we stumbled on for miles, slipping on icy spots, supporting each other time and again, dragging one another up and onward, nothing was said, but we both knew: each of us was thinking of his wife. Occasionally, I looked at the sky, where the stars were fading and the pink light of the morning was beginning to spread behind a dark bank of clouds. But my mind clung to my wife's image, imagining it with an uncanny acuteness. I heard her answering me, saw her smile, her frank and encouraging look. Real or not, her look was then more luminous than the sun which was beginning to rise. A thought transfixed me: for the first time in my life, I saw the truth as it is set into song by so many poets, proclaimed as the final wisdom by so many thinkers. The truth— that love is the ultimate and highest goal to which man can aspire. Then I grasped the meaning of the greatest secret that human poetry and human thought and belief have to impart: *the salvation of man is through love and in love. I understood how a man who has nothing left in this world may know bliss, be it only for a brief moment, in the contemplation of his beloved.*"[19]

One of my favorite hymns, "O Love That Glorifies the Son," describes the sincere love of charity that should fill our soul. It is the love of the Son in obedience to the Father, making them one. It is the love that comes from the Savior to us, to bind our families as one. It is pure love that fills our hearts and makes us like Him. It is the love that overcomes adversity and edifies our lives and those around us to make us one. It is the love that makes within us the mighty change of heart and sustains us to the end:

> O love that glorifies the Son,
>> O love that says, "Thy will be done!"
> Pure love whose spirit makes us one
>> Come, fill my soul today; Come, fill my soul today.

> O love that binds our family,
>> O love that brings my heart to thee,
> Pure love that lasts eternally
>> Come, fill my soul today; Come, fill my soul today.

> O love that overcomes defeat,
>> O love that turns the bitter sweet,
> Pure love that makes our lives complete
>> Come, fill my soul today; Come, fill my soul today.
> O Lord, give me the will to mend;
>> O Lord, change me from foe to friend;
> Dear Lord, sustain me to the end
>> Come, fill my soul today; Come, fill my soul today.[20]

When we seek the pure love of Christ and are founded on the rock of Christ, we can say, as Paul, that *we are "rooted and grounded with love" until we "know the love of Christ."* (*See* Ephesians 3:17-19.)

After dedicating the temple, King Solomon told his people to *"let your heart therefore be perfect with the Lord our God, to walk in his statutes, and to keep his commandments"* (1 Kings 8:61). The Kirtland Saints were rebuked by the Lord for failure to build a temple, because without a temple the Lord is unable to prepare us and bring about His "strange act" that will clearly distinguish good from evil in the world (*see* D&C 101:95). It is the knowledge and power of perfect love that will make this distinction.

> For ye have sinned against me a very grievous sin, in that ye have not considered the great commandment in all things, that I have given unto you concerning the building of mine house;
>
> For the preparation wherewith I design to prepare mine apostles to prune my vineyard for the last time, that I may bring to pass my strange act, that I may pour out my Spirit upon all flesh—
>
> But behold, verily I say unto you, that there are many who have been ordained among you, whom I have called but few of them are chosen.
>
> They who are not chosen have sinned a very grievous sin, in that they are walking in darkness at noon-day. (D&C 95:3-6)

The message of these verses is a powerful message about the temple. Temple worship is the great command in all things because the great commandment is to love perfectly (*see* Matthew 22:36-40). It is in temple worship that we learn to love perfectly.

When we make the ultimate sacrifice of yielding our hearts to God, then they will be filled with the pure love of Christ, thus "all the fullness of God" (Ephesians 3:19). Then we can say they are perfect. When our hearts are perfect, we have made the sacrifice to climb to the summit of Mount Zion and receive its great and last promise.

10

Yielding Our Hearts to God— Lord, How Is It Done?

While struggling to sacrifice our pride, fears, jealousy, and dis-obedience, desiring to yield our hearts to God, that we might have the pure love of Christ, we often say as Enos said: *"Lord, how is it done?"* (Enos 1:7).

This is the question I asked myself concerning the "mighty change." Is it possible in this life? Can I make the great and last sacrifice for this mighty change? Am I a man to match Mount Zion? Many of us are content to answer that "we are what we are." This is the mistaken precept of men that is used to justify any behavior.

The important question is: *What are we really?* Until this question is answered, we cannot say "we are what we are." We cannot honestly rationalize any human behavior as a normal and acceptable part of our intrinsic nature until we answer the question of the reality of our intrinsic nature. *What is our true nature? What is "the measure of man, according to his creation before the world was made?"* (D&C 49:17).

Volumes have been and are being written attempting to answer this fundamental question. True, we all are individually different, but have we discovered how individually important we are? I prefer to believe in the uniqueness I learned in Primary: I am a child of God. I was taught this truth by true messengers of God who learned it from other true messengers who ultimately learned it from God. This truth is confirmed to my heart, my spiritual self, in such unwavering conviction that I would be under condemnation to deny it.

Another true messenger, the Apostle Paul, along with the Holy Spirit, confirmed what I learned in Primary. *"The Spirit itself beareth witness to our spirit that we are the children of God"* (Romans 8:16).

Notice how we learn this truth. It is by spiritual recall of pure knowledge of things as they really are, when we let the Spirit of revelation and prophecy teach us.

The true answer to the question of our identity automatically leads to an even more important question: *What is the measure of the stature of the fulness of man's creation?* (*Compare* Ephesians 4:13 with D&C 49:16-17.) Verse 16 implies that a full measure of the creation of a man and woman is to become greater than themselves alone, by becoming "one flesh" together. This oneness is part of the great gathering in one of all things in Christ (*see* D&C 27:13). What can we really become? Paul also answered this question. "And if children, then heirs; *heirs of God, and joint-heirs with Christ*" (Romans 8:17; *see also* Psalms 82:6).

President George Q. Cannon taught that no sin or weakness need be permanent because God can give gifts (*see* D&C 46:11) to correct any imperfection.[1] *The great gift that God gave to all men is the Atonement of His Son. Therefore, with this gift of Christ, we can become perfect. When perfected, we become heirs with Christ and inherit eternal life.*

Both of these questions about our true nature must be examined and answered in light of the apparent reality of mortality. Life is hard, then we die. Yet Amulek said to live well is to prepare to die (*see* Alma 34:32-34). Christ has told us and promised us that He has overcome the world and mortality (*see* John 16:33). If we have faith in Him and follow Him, then we also can overcome the world (*see* 1 John 5:5). To live in Christ by following Him is to prepare to die (*see* Galatians 2:20). The peace of His assurance is pure knowledge and joy of things as they really are!

Climbing to the Summit by Growing Up in the Lord

As we grow up in mortality, most of us struggle to answer these questions in our own lives. At 16 we are given permission to drive a car. We think we are grown up until the first accident or citation reminds us of our responsibility to others. Between the ages of 18 and 21, we gain a new sense of being grown up when we decide for ourselves at the ballot box, or leave our parents for matrimony, matriculation, or missions. This sense of independence quickly meets reality as we feel the responsibility for ourselves and others.

Within the question "Can I really change?" is the question "Can I really grow up?" It is in the scriptural temple that I found the Lord asking me, an adult who had passed the maturity markers of 16 and 21, to "grow up!"

> *That we henceforth be no more children,* tossed to and fro, and carried about with every wind of doctrine, by the sleight of men, and cunning craftiness, whereby they lie in wait to deceive;
> But speaking the truth in love, *may grow up into Him in all things, which is the head, even Christ.* (Ephesians 4:14-15)

Paul was telling the Ephesian saints not to be vulnerable children, saying, "we are what we are." Instead, Paul urged his followers to become the children of Christ and obtain the stature of Christ by growing up in Him.

Again, I did not recognize this scripture as a great truth of the *scriptural temple* until I began to "grow up" and see the temple in the scriptures. Then, for me, the following scripture came alive: "*that they may grow up in thee,* and receive a fulness of the Holy Ghost, and be organized according to thy laws, and be prepared to obtain every needful thing" (D&C 109:15).

Joseph Smith prayed for this growing-up blessing in the dedication of the Kirtland temple. It is in the temple that we can receive a fulness of the Holy Ghost, and we can be taught how to become the children of Christ and how to "grow up" in Him. This verse is the answer to Enos's question and to my question. The growing-up process of the temple is how we can really change in this life. As Enos learned, this mighty change is based on faith in Christ.

The Apostle Paul taught us about growing up in the Lord when he said, "Furthermore we have had fathers of our flesh which corrected us, and we gave them reverence: shall we not much rather be in subjection unto the Father of spirits, and live?" (Hebrews 12:9). The growing-up corrections from our mortal fathers are preliminary to the real growing-up corrections from the Father of spirits.

Mormon taught his son Moroni that growing up in the Lord starts with the first four principles of the gospel and ultimately leads to "perfect love:"

> And the first fruits of repentance is baptism; and baptism cometh by faith unto the fulfilling the commandments; and the fulfilling the commandments bringeth remission of sins;
> And the remissions of sins bringeth meekness and lowliness of heart; and *because of meekness and lowliness of heart cometh the*

visitation of the Holy Ghost, which Comforter filleth with hope and perfect love, which love endureth by diligence unto prayer, until all the saints shall dwell with God. (Moroni 8:25-26)

This perfect love is the sweet fruit of the tree of life, of which we can partake if we follow the commandment to be baptized unto repentance (*see* Alma 5:62).

If we grow up by the Father of spirits and are corrected by Him, we will have "eternal life" and dwell with Him. Elder Henry B. Eyring described growing up in the Lord as an "upward pull" requiring a mighty change:

> Our Heavenly Father has created a way for us to follow the feeling that there is something better, through the atonement. *Self-improvement is a longing for home, a desire to be with our Heavenly Father. The exchange is all He has for all we have.*[2]

Growing up in the Lord is to climb to the summit of Mount Zion.

Growing up in Grace and Truth

The Lord tenderly invites us to grow up in Him when he says, "Behold, *ye are little children* and ye cannot bear all things now; *ye must grow in grace and in the knowledge of the truth*" (D&C 50:40).

This growing-up process of the Lord in "grace and truth" is found in His holy temple, where we learn from the master of "grace and truth." An important part of this growing-up process is the endowment of the temple. The purpose of the endowment is to endow us with the graces of charity and the truths of eternal life. In the temple, we are led to grasp all the qualities (graces) of charity, as listed by Paul and Mormon. *As we make these graces part of our lives, we are given the keys that unlock the truths of eternal life.*

The Apostle Peter described the growing-up process of the endowment when he taught that the "divine nature" is reached in this life when we obtain the quality of charity:

> Whereby are given unto us exceeding great and precious promises: *that by these ye might be partakers of the divine nature . . .*
> And beside this, giving all diligence, add to your faith virtue; and to virtue knowledge;
> And to knowledge temperance: and to temperance patience: and to patience godliness;

And to godliness brotherly kindness; and to brotherly kindness charity." (2 Peter 1:4-7)

A revelation on the priesthood received through the Prophet Joseph Smith teaches the attributes of the doctrine of the priesthood (*see* D&C 121:36-42) and also the same "growing-up" qualities taught by Peter (*see* D&C 107:30).

Then the Prophet Joseph Smith told us, using tree-of-life imagery, about the ultimate blessing in Peter's "promises," received when we have these divine qualities. The "ultimate" is the great and last promise of the temple: the promise of eternal life. "Because the promise is, if these things abound in them they shall not be unfruitful in the knowledge of the Lord" (D&C 107:31).

The sequence of qualities listed by Peter and Joseph Smith closely reflect the spiritual qualities obtained when we keep the major covenants of the temple endowment. The sequence of covenants we make in the law of obedience, the law of sacrifice, the law of the Gospel, the law of chastity, and the law of consecration is the growing-up process of the endowment. It is through this "growing up" that we become men and women to match His mountain and "climb up" Mount Zion.

As we climb, we are endowed with virtue, which is obedience and conformity to moral, ethical and celestial principles (the law of the Lord). We are endowed with patience and temperance because of the moderation and self-restraint we learn from obedience and sacrifice. We are endowed with godliness or holiness because we live the law of the gospel, learning the "graces" as taught in the Sermon on the Mount. We are endowed with brotherly kindness as we live the principles of the law of the gospel, specifically the law of chastity as we apply it to our marriage relationships. Because of this brotherly kindness, we would do nothing to destroy relationships with others; we strive only to edify. Literally, the law of chastity will be fulfilled in the Lord's definition of a "legal and lawful marriage." It is for those who have become one in love in the Holy Order of Matrimony.

Finally, we are endowed with the quality of charity. This pure love of Christ comes to us because we have mastered the preceding laws, *then the power of the love of Christ makes a mighty change in our hearts, even to the consuming of our flesh* (*see* 2 Nephi 4:21) as we become "new creatures." We are then prepared to live the law of consecration, which is a law of the celestial kingdom.

We are not asked by the Lord to fully live the law of consecration at the present time. We are asked to accept it by living the law of sacrifice and the law of the gospel (see D&C 104:18). We must first learn to sacrifice our avarice, then edify others with pure love before we can fully live the law of consecration. In preparation for the celestial law of consecration, today we live a law of sacrifice by living the law of tithing. This law will "sanctify the land Zion" (*see* D&C 119:6) as we grow up and fully live the law of consecration.

In his book, *Temples in the Last Days,* Elder Royden Derrick described the "growing-up" transformation in the temple:

> In the temple, through the power of the Holy Spirit, *knowledge is transformed into virtues. A person who attends the temple regularly grows more patient, more long-suffering, and more charitable . . .* In the temple *knowledge is transformed into feelings of the heart resulting in actions that build character.*[3]

The character built in the temple is that of a divine nature: the perfect man or woman in "the measure of the stature of the fulness of Christ" (Ephesians 4:13).

Growing Up on Mount Zion of the Old Testament

The growing-up message of the book of Leviticus can be hidden by the tedious rituals and carnal commandments of the Levitical laws given to Moses for those who rejected the "rest" of the Lord. Yet *the dominant theme of the Book of Leviticus is holiness through atonement.* In Leviticus chapters 2, 4-11, 14, 16, 19-23, and 27, the term "holy" or "atonement" is used. The Lord was still trying to separate this group of people who "err in their hearts" and make them holy (*see* Leviticus 10:10, 11:45, 20:24).

Near the middle of Leviticus (perhaps suggesting the Atonement in the meridian of time), the laws of the rituals of the Day of Atonement are described (*see* Leviticus 16:30-34). In the context of the law of Moses, *the laws of the Lord found in Leviticus reflect the growing-up process of the endowment.* These laws focused on rituals and worship in the holy place, the tabernacle of the congregation: *worship of the Lord through sacrifice (see* Leviticus 1-7, 17); *holy living, loving one's neighbor (see* Leviticus 19); *avoiding blasphemy (see* Leviticus 24);

living the law of chastity (*see* Leviticus 18, 20); and *living the law of consecration* (*see* Leviticus 25-27).

On the plains of Moab, before crossing the Jordan, Moses revealed the contents of Deuteronomy to the children of Israel. Deuteronomy means the law repeated or the second law, implying that the law of the Lord is to be repeated and not forgotten. In fact, *the specific law of repetition in Deuteronomy was a gathering of the people every seven years in consecration to the Lord and to each other to hear again the words of this great book* (*see* Deuteronomy 31:10-13). Specifically, the words of the law of Deuteronomy, which is the first and great commandment (*see* Mark 12:29-30), were to be kept in the hearts of the people (*see* Deuteronomy 6:5-6). These words contained in detail the rules of successful relationships in this life so the people, as a people set apart by the Lord, would obey the first and great commandment with full purpose of heart.

Deuteronomy contains the rules of application of the law of consecration in this life. They are based on this truth: As God has freely consecrated all for our well-being, so we should freely share His gifts for the well-being of our fellowmen. This we must do out of love for God and all men.

As Latter-day Saints, we often hear the phrase "in the world but not of the world." Yet in light of 1 John 2:16 ("For all that is in the world, . . . is not of the Father, but is of the world"), can we be in the world and not be part of the world? No! *The Lord is continually trying to separate Zion from Babylon. He does this by having us grow up in Him, learning how to consecrate all that we have to His will.* While we must pass through Babylon as we seek Zion, we would do well to liken the laws of the Lord in Deuteronomy to our own lives. Then we should apply them as best we can so that one day we will be prepared to observe and keep the law of consecration.

Concerning this Old Testament foundation of our "growing up" in the Lord, John Welch draws our attention to its value: "Not being steeped in the ethical and spiritual dimensions of the law of Moses, modern LDS readers tend to overlook the profound religious legacy of these underlying purposes of the law that have enduring relevance to the temple."[4]

Just like those who worshiped at the tabernacle under the law of Moses, we become separate and holy by growing up in the grace and truth of the Lord in His holy house. "Do ye not know that they which minister about holy things live of the things of the temple?" (1 Corinthians 9:13).

Grown-up on Mount Zion: Endowed with Charity

The laws and covenants of the endowment prepare us to one day fully live the laws of the celestial kingdom because charity will have become the crowning quality of our divine, holy nature. Therefore, the *purpose of the endowment is to endow us with the celestial quality of charity.* The Apostle Paul captured this truth in one verse of scripture: *"Now the end of the commandment is charity out of a pure heart"* (1 Timothy 1:5). The end result of growing up in the Lord is a divine nature. The quintessential quality of this divine nature is "charity out of a pure heart."

Alma instructed his son Shiblon to grow up in the Lord when he said, "Use boldness, but not overbearance; and see that ye bridle all your passions, that ye may be filled with love" (Alma 38:12).

The words of the tongue are a particular passion, even a "world of iniquity" (James 3:2) when untamed (*see* James 1:26; 3:8). We can bridle "the whole body" (James 3:2) to show that we are filled with love when we bridle our tongue, because not only what we say but how we say it expresses sincere love that edifies (*see* D&C 52:16). Edifying words can lift "the spirit of heaviness" by covering our fellowmen with "the garment of praise" (Isaiah 61:3) and sustaining them with the "fruits of praise" (D&C 52:17).

The laws and covenants of the endowment teach us how to bridle our passions so that we may be filled with the love of charity. In an article titled "Bridle All Your Passions," Bruce and Marie Hafen beautifully explained why the Lord wants us to grow up and learn the art of self control. "The truth is not that worldly gratifications are too satisfying, but they are not satisfying enough. . . . The Lord desires that we find fulfillment to the height of human capacity. . . . The Lord seeks to satisfy everlastingly our deepest human longings. . . . If we accept the disciplined yoke of the Gospel, one day we will have a divine nature and a fulness of joy."[5] The disciplined yoke is the commandments and covenants of the gospel, particularly the growing-up covenants of the temple which result in a divine nature and the full joy of charity.

Growing Up in the Lord Is Preparing to Meet God

When Amulek said, "Now is the time for men to prepare to meet God," (*see* Alma 34:34), he didn't have last-minute preparation in mind. Amulek was not warning of an impending return of the Savior even though this return was implied in his warning. The world continues to be warned that the Savior will return to earth. Similar to the anticipation of many Jews in the meridian of time, many today look forward to this event as a solution to the world's and their problems. However, *most people don't understand that prophetic warnings like those of Amulek usually warn about how we use the time of our mortal probation in preparation to meet God (see D&C 78:7).*

Brigham Young focused Amulek's warning, emphasizing the growing-up process of the temple as the preparation to meet God. "Do not be too anxious for the Lord to hasten His work. *Let our anxiety be centered upon one thing: the sanctification of our own hearts, the purifying of our own affections.*"[6]

The temple is where we learn to "grow up" in the Lord. It is where we learn to "climb up" Mount Zion. The temple is where we learn the qualities of a divine nature and acquire pure hearts filled with a pure love. With this mighty change of heart, we are worthy for the great and last promise of the temple and all that eternal life means. Therefore, the temple should be the center of our lives, teaching us the way of salvation.

Growing Up in the Preparatory Redemption of Zion

Brigham Young had a great understanding of the redemption of Zion, which began with his Zion's Camp experience. Therefore he must have understood the meaning of D&C 105:5: *"Zion cannot be built up unless it is by the principles of the law of the celestial kingdom;* otherwise I cannot receive her unto myself."

Brigham Young knew, as Moses knew, that a Zion society requires the celestial law of consecration. In order to live this law on a celestial level, we must have pure hearts filled with the pure love of charity. The failure to establish a holy nation of Zion in both the Sinai and in Missouri came about because the saints "erred in their hearts." Whether rich man or poor man, greed is an impurity of the heart (*see* D&C 56:16-18). When the Lord's people have impure hearts, they will fail to keep the law of consecration. They will not be "gathered in one" at His coming (*see* D&C 42:36).

The law of consecration was promised to the Latter-day Saints as early as 1831 before the exodus to the Ohio (*see* D&C 38:16, 25-27, 34-35), and then fulfilled in working application for a brief period, one month later in Kirtland (*see* D&C 42:2, 30-39; 53-55). One of the reasons that some of the Kirtland Saints were sent to Missouri to establish the foundation of Zion was that their "hearts might be prepared" for "the things which are to come" (D&C 58:6). This is why Brigham Young called for "the sanctification of our hearts, the purification of our affections." This sanctification and purification of hearts produces a unity and equality that is required of a Zion people on the celestial level (*see* D&C 78:6-7; 105:3-4).

Worshiping in the temple prepares us for this unity and equality. Susan Savage captured this feeling of unity in her poem *Temple Snow:*

> To one who loves winter this pilgrimage is so white.
> Gone the cut and color of difference, the clatter of humanity
>   that wars with birdsong and gentle thought.
> Hearts toward heaven, voices hushed to sacredness
>   focus in unity.
> We are one—all alike before Him, as snow shapes line to line,
> White truth sifting softly, drink for our seasons.[7]

It is in the temple that we drink the "white truth" that makes us one with each other and the Lord.

I love the expression of this unity that existed with Alma and his followers:

> And he commanded them that *there should be no contention one with another,* but that they should look forward with one eye, having one faith and one baptism, *having their hearts knit together in unity and in love one towards another. . . .*
>
> They should impart of their substance of their own free will . . . imparting to one another both temporally and spiritually. (Mosiah 18:21, 28-29)

The Apostle Paul used the same terms in addressing the Saints of Colosse. "That their hearts might be comforted, *being knit together in love and unto all riches of the full assurance of understanding,* to the acknowledgement of the mystery of God, and of the Father, and of Christ" (Colossians 2:2).

The power of the pure love of Christ to change behavior was manifest in the remarkable state of unity between the Nephites and Lamanites. For nearly 200 years after the appearance of Christ to these people, they were unified in peace and love:

> And it came to pass that there was no contention in the land, *because of the love of God which did dwell in the hearts of the people.* . . .
>
> There were no robbers, nor murderers, neither were there Lamanites, nor any manner of -ites; but they were in one, the children of Christ, and heirs to the kingdom of God. (4 Nephi 1:15, 17)

It is a powerful message to recall that this pure love of the Savior was shown and taught to these people when He appeared to them at the temple in the land Bountiful. How profound and long lasting His marvelous love was! How profoundly changing His love is today as we learn of it in the temple and practice it in our own lives, keeping "church covenants" to "establish" us now and in the New Jerusalem (*see* D&C 42:67) as His "covenant people" (*see* D&C 42:36).

In order to bring His Latter-day Saints to this state of pure hearts with pure love, knit together in unity, the Lord promised the Missouri Saints, who failed in their attempt for a Zion society, the redemption of Zion. "Therefore, in consequence of the transgressions of my people, it is expedient in me that mine elders should wait for a little season for the redemption of Zion" (D&C 105:9).

It is interesting that this revelation came through a prophet who led Zion's camp. The formation of Zion's camp in Kirtland was the beginning of the redemption of Zion (*see* D&C 103:12, 14-15). While this 1000-mile march of hardships from Ohio to Missouri did not achieve its intended purpose, it did provide a foundation of valuable experience for Brigham Young and other future Church leaders. It was a camp where unity was learned and the welfare of others was sought.

The Lord compared the redemption of Zion in the latter days to His attempt at creating a holy nation, a Zion, in the Sinai:

> Therefore, I will raise up unto my people a man, who shall lead them like as Moses led the children of Israel.

> For ye are the children of Israel, and of the seed of Abraham, and ye must needs be led out of bondage by power, and with a stretched-out arm.
>
> And as your fathers were led at the first, even so shall the redemption of Zion be. . . .
>
> . . . Mine angels shall go up before you, and also my presence, and in time ye shall possess the goodly land. (D&C 103:16-18, 20)

The Lord specifically says in these verses that Zion will be redeemed as the children of Israel were led at first (before the provocation), with power and an outstretched arm, with the Lord Himself going before them. The Lord explained to those of Zion's camp why He would wait for a little season, and what He meant by power and an outstretched arm with His presence before them (*see* D&C 105:9-13). *Clearly the power, the outstretched arm of the Lord in His presence, is the endowment of the temple with its great and last promise.* Unlike the children of Israel in the Sinai, the Lord Himself goes before us today with the fulness of the Melchizedek Priesthood in His holy house and with the great and last promise of the temple.

Nestled in a rather long verse about temple ordinances, the redemption of Zion is the focal point of D&C 124:39:

> Therefore, verily I say unto you, that your anointings, and your washings, and your baptisms for the dead, and your solemn assemblies, and your memorials for your sacrifices by the sons of Levi, and for your oracles in your most holy places wherein you receive conversations, and your statutes and judgments, *for the beginning of the revelations and foundation of Zion,* and for the glory, honor, and endowment of all her municipals, are ordained by the ordinance of my holy house, which my people are always commanded to build unto my holy name.

The beginning of the revelations and foundation of Zion, therefore the beginning of the redemption of Zion as promised by the Lord, comes to pass through the ordinances and endowment of the temple. This is the Lord's expedient course through tribulation to Zion. D&C 124:39 was given in reference to the Nauvoo Temple, but Elder Bruce R. McConkie noted that "all subsequent *temples are for the express purpose of preparing and purifying the Lord's people, freeing them from the blood and sins of the world, so they will be ready in due course to build the New Jerusalem and the temple on that center place.*"[8]

In the dedicatory prayer of the Manti Temple, given May 21, 1888, Lorenzo Snow prayed for freedom from persecution so that temple worship could be a "purpose" of the Lord for the redemption of Zion: "We ask thee, Righteous Father, to so control this present persecution *that thy purposes may be accomplished in the redemption of thy Zion.*"[9]

As the Missouri Saints and the Nauvoo Saints were led by Moses-like prophets, Joseph and Brigham, so are we led today by a living prophet. If we will obey his voice and become a temple-loving people, then shall we possess the goodly land and enter into the rest of the Lord through the temple endowment.

How does the endowment of the temple prepare us for the redemption of Zion? The scriptural definition of Zion gives the answer: "Therefore, verily, thus saith the Lord, let Zion rejoice for *this is Zion— the pure in heart*" (D&C 97:21).

The ultimate purpose of the endowment is to endow us with the quality of charity, the pure love of Christ, which changes a broken heart to a pure heart. With this celestial quality, we are prepared to be a Zion people. The pure heart permits us to live in a unity and equality required by celestial law.

The formula for the redemption of Zion is straightforward:

Zion is the pure in heart.
The endowment produces a pure heart.
The endowment is the preparatory redemption of Zion.

Zion's Redemption: The Rainbow Connection

The *scriptural temple* informs us that unity of heart and mind was the essence of Enoch's Zion. "And *the Lord called his people Zion, because they were of one heart and one mind, and dwelt in righteousness:* and there was no poor among them" (Moses 7:18).

The scriptures also indicate that Enoch and the people of a former Zion knew of the redemption of Zion in the fulness of times:

And righteousness will I send down out of heaven; and truth will I send forth out of the earth, to bear testimony of mine only begotten; . . . *And righteousness and truth will I cause to sweep the earth as with a flood, to gather out mine elect from the four quarters of the earth, unto a place which I shall prepare, an holy city,* that my people may gird up their loins, and be looking forth for the time of my coming; for *there shall be my tabernacle, and it shall be called Zion, a New Jerusalem.* (Moses 7:62)

The beginning of this scripture was fulfilled in the First Vision of Joseph Smith and the coming forth of the Book of Mormon. The restoration of the fulness of the gospel is a testimony of the Savior, Jesus Christ, and a preparation for the ultimate witness of the Savior, the Second Coming. This witness will be given first to the jewels of the Lord, His elect, who have been prepared as were the people of Enoch to live in a Zion society, the New Jerusalem. There the Savior will appear in His tabernacle, fulfilling the great and last promise of the temple for all present.

In reference to the blessings of Enoch's Zion, Joseph Smith said of our preparation to become like Enoch's elect people, "yet if we are . . . called with the same calling . . . and embrace the same covenant . . . *we can . . . obtain the same promises . . . because we, ourselves, have faith . . . even as they did.*"[10] Therefore, in preparation to be gathered to the millennial Zion, we must first be gathered on Mount Zion to Christ, the Master of pure love, who can make us a Zion people.

While I was driving over Big Mountain from East Canyon recently, a severe rainstorm lifted. I saw the setting sun in the west refract through the mist in the atmosphere. Then, a full, brilliant rainbow spanned the air from Big Mountain to Wyoming. This glorious wonder of nature reminded me of a special witness that I had had in the temple.

While sitting in the celestial room of the Bountiful Temple, the sun broke from behind a cloud and penetrated an upper window. Like a laser beam, it pierced the crystal jewels of the chandelier. The whole celestial room was filled with miniature rainbows. As I contemplated this wondrous show of light, I realized that the rainbow is more than the sign of the end of the earth's baptism. It is also the sign of the redemption of Zion. In connection with this sign of the rainbow, Noah was reminded of the "everlasting covenant" given to Enoch, who wept when he saw Noah's day. Perhaps Enoch was also given the sign of the rainbow: And "the bow shall be in the cloud, and I will look upon it, that I may remember the everlasting covenant, which I made unto thy father Enoch: *that, when men should keep all my commandments, Zion should again come on the earth, the city of Enoch*" (JST Genesis 9:21). The reality of the return to the earth of Zion, the city of Enoch, is confirmed in revelation given in our dispensation: "a city reserved until a day of righteousness" (*see* D&C 45:11-12).

While I sat in the celestial room flooded with rainbows, recalling the promise given to Enoch, I understood the real meaning of the rainbow. For, *as the full rainbow rises from the earth and then returns to the earth in the distance, so Enoch and his Zion people were taken from the earth and will return to the earth in the future.*

I no longer look at a rainbow and think only of Noah and the great flood. I think of Enoch and the great event of the redemption of Zion that he and the people of the city of Enoch are anticipating. I think of how I want to be there to meet them, for it will be a joyous meeting as though there were a pot of gold at the end of the rainbow:

> And the Lord said unto Enoch: *Then shalt thou and all thy city meet them there, and we will receive them into our bosom,* and they shall see us; and we will fall upon their necks, and they shall fall upon our necks, and we will kiss each other. (Moses 7:63)

At that marvelous moment in the celestial room, when I made the rainbow connection, I began to gain yet another realization of the importance of the temple. It was becoming the center of my life, teaching me the way of salvation and preparing me for the redemption of Zion. I wanted to grow up and become a man who could match Mount Zion.

11

The Bond of Perfectness: The Only Way to the Summit of Mount Zion

Binding to Christ, that None Be Lost

On Mother's Day, while talking long distance with my daughter Lys-An who was serving a mission in Poland, I asked her what scripture had become a favorite to her. She said she found comfort in D&C 50:40-43:

> Behold, *ye are little children, and ye cannot bear all things now; ye must grow in grace and in the knowledge of the truth.*
> Fear not, little children, for you are mine, and I have overcome the world, and you are of them that my Father hath given me;
> And none of them that my Father hath given me shall be lost.

After quoting this scripture, Lys-An expressed her love for the Polish people. She so much wanted to share her joy, being a true messenger of the true message. At that time, only a precious few had seen the great view with the courage to change. Others had glimpsed the light, but not enough to embrace it. These she considered the "little children" who somehow, sometime, would grow in grace and knowledge of the truth to become the children of Christ. These, she hoped, because of her love for them, would be given by the Father that none would be lost.

I was greatly moved by her love and desire to bind her Polish friends to Christ, that none would be lost. I feel that same concern for those who are like I once was—temple drop-outs and temple inactives. I desire that we as members of His church understand the importance of diligently following our Savior, binding ourselves to Him in His holy house, that none be lost.

> Verily, verily, I say unto you, *ye are little children, and ye have not as yet understood how great blessings the Father hath in his own hands and prepared for you;*

And ye cannot bear all things now; nevertheless, be of good cheer, for I will lead you along. *The kingdom is yours and the blessings thereof are yours, and the riches of eternity are yours.* (D&C 78:17-18)

It is our guide and Savior, Jesus Christ, who will lead us along a sure path to the summit of Mount Zion. If, with faith, we grasp and bind the rope of His Atonement to us and obediently follow Him, none will be lost.

Sealing of Hearts: The Great Welding Link of Mount Zion

I often look at a cherished portrait of my family and think that these are the people I love and want to be with. The pose in this photograph is a pyramid shape, as though we were all linked together. I see in this family that is linked together the image of the temple, the mountain of the Lord. Perhaps this is why King Benjamin had the people of Zarahemla and Mosiah arranged in families in front of the temple, so its image would reflect on them (*see* Mosiah 2:5-6).

The symbolism of this portrait projects backward and forward for infinity, like the mirrors of a sealing room. We are gathered as a family on the foundation of our ancestors. We will be remembered by many as their ancestral family. This welding link is not just genetic. Hopefully, we can all be bound or linked together with hearts turned to eternal relationships.

As a parent and husband, I desire that none of my family will be lost. I see us all bound together with the rope of our Savior's Atonement, following Him to the summit of Mount Zion. This is the image in my mind: of the great welding link, the whole and complete and perfect union envisioned by Joseph Smith (*see* D&C 128:18). This is the vision in portrait of the prophecy of Malachi (*see* Malachi 4:5-6; D&C 2; D&C 110:14-15; JSH 1:39) concerning the "turning of hearts."

Once I turn my attention from my immediate family to my ancestors, I realize I want to be sealed to them in eternal relationships. Because my identity is fixed to my ancestors and I desire that none of them be lost, I seek to turn my heart—to perfect it with pure love. Then, with this pure love, I seek to turn my heart to my ancestors and seal them in the eternal relationships of the temple.

Joseph Smith explained that the word *turn* in Malachi's prophecy (*see* Malachi 4:5-6) is correctly translated to mean bind or seal.[1] As we turn our hearts to our fathers and they turn their hearts to us, we can be bound or sealed together. Therefore, the turning of hearts leads to the sealing of hearts: "And *seek diligently to turn the hearts* of the children to their fathers, and the hearts of the fathers to the children" (D&C 98:16). Ultimately we can be bound or sealed to our Eternal Father. This great binding or sealing occurs in the temple as our hearts become purified by being bound to our Savior.

The Great Sealing of Mount Zion: Birth into the Kingdom of God

The temple has a great attraction for families because in it they can bind or seal the relationships they develop in this life for time and eternity. The promise, through worthiness, that none will be lost through this temple sealing, is a great blessing and comfort. It is a promise, like the promise of the resurrection, that takes the sting out of death. This is especially true when our children die young, voiding the privilege to raise them in mortality.

As much as we talk about and desire the sealing of families that occurs in the temple, little do we consider the most profound sealing that occurs in His holy house. It is the sealing of us, spirit children, to our Heavenly Parents. In the temple we make great progress in finding our Spiritual Parents, filling the void of spiritual orphans. As King Benjamin explained in his temple sermon, this sealing occurs through the mediation of Christ, by being spiritually born of Him:

> And now, because of the covenant which ye have made ye shall be called the children of Christ, his sons, and his daughters; for behold, this day he hath spiritually begotten you; for ye say that your hearts are changed through faith on his name; therefore, ye are born of him and have become his sons and his daughters. (Mosiah 5:7)

We are born of Christ through his Atonement when we are bound to His everlasting covenants. When we follow the words of Christ through our teacher, the Holy Spirit (*see* 2 Nephi 32:3-5) and climb to the summit of the temple mount, Christ will "deliver" us to His Father's kingdom.

The process of being born into the celestial kingdom of God through the temple has a beautiful correlation to being born into the earthly kingdom of God. Into both kingdoms we are born by "water, and blood and the spirit" (*see* Moses 6:59). The unborn child is cleansed in the living water of the womb and survives by the blood of its mother. Yet the child is animated and becomes a new and living creature by its own spirit. Likewise, we all must be cleansed by the living water of the womb of baptism, to witness that we keep the commandment, survive to sanctification by the blood of Jesus Christ, and become a new justified creature by the power of the Holy Spirit (*see* Moses 6:60) renewing our spirits. This is the plan of salvation because the Spirit, water, and blood are the "three that bear witness in earth" (*see* 1 John 5:6-8) and heaven of Jesus Christ. He is the central focus of the plan of salvation.

We are born through a temple into the kingdom of God on earth when we are born through a woman bound to the everlasting covenant of marriage. *Part of the ancient Hebrew concept of a betrothed woman was that she represented a holy temple. This is why she was veiled. A veiled woman in the temple represents the presence of God. Since the Glory of God is the glory of man and a woman is the glory of man, then to man, a woman should represent the glory of God (see* 1 Corinthians 11:7, 10, 12, 15). Like an holy angel, the woman was created for the man (*see* 1 Corinthians 11:9), as a holy temple to whom he can go for the refuge of her love and the counsel of her heart. She will not be defiled if he treats her with holiness. Now we understand why the Lord said: *"I, the Lord God, delight in the chastity [holiness] of women"* (Jacob 2:28). The greatest sin and atrocity in the world today, by both men and women, is desecration of the temple.

To his betrothed bride, the Hebrew groom would say, "Thou art set apart for me according to the law of Moses and Israel." The woman was like a temple in being set apart for holiness. It was the great holiness of making a new life and bringing it to the earthly kingdom of God.[2] Likewise, through the temple a new creature with a mighty change of heart is made and delivered to the presence of God. Appropriately, a woman first witnessed mortal life and a woman first witnessed immortal life on this earth.

It takes two in both the earthly kingdom (a man and a woman) and heavenly kingdom (the Son of Man and mankind) to make a new life. In both kingdoms this new life is made in a temple. A most wonderful description of a temple is Adam's description of Eve when he called her "the Mother of all living." Truly in a temple all living, mortal and eternal beings, are created.

Catherine Thomas has beautifully expressed our birth through the "narrow channel" of the temple into the celestial kingdom of God by the travail and power of the Atonement. This is the sealing power of perfection that occurs in the temple so we will be delivered in perfection to our Father in Heaven:

> The temple is the narrow channel through which we must pass to reenter the Lord's presence. A mighty power pulls us through that channel, and it is the sealing power of the at-one-ment of the Lord Jesus Christ. The Savior's atonement is another word of sealing power. By the power of the atonement, the Lord draws and seals his children to himself in the holy temples.[3]

The final words of King Benjamin's temple sermon expressed this great and profound sealing to our Heavenly Father, which occurs through our sealing to His Only Begotten Son, being born of Him by faith on His name:

> Therefore, I would that ye should be steadfast and immovable, always abounding in good works, that Christ, the Lord God Omnipotent, *may seal you his, that you may be brought to heaven,* that ye may have everlasting salvation and eternal life. (Mosiah 5:15; *compare* Alma 34:35)

The declaration of the resurrected Christ to the Nephites must have revived the words of King Benjamin in their minds: "And as many as have *received me,* to them have I given to become the sons of God; and even so will I to as many as shall *believe on my name.*" (3 Nephi 9:17).

Binding to Christ and Following Him to the Summit of Mount Zion

In binding through obedience to Christ's covenants of grace and truth we grow up straight, to a fullness of perfection and reach the summit of Mount Zion. This is why the Savior gave the following commandments to the Ohio saints in 1831 and 1832 in preparation for the binding that would occur in temples:

> And thus ye shall become instructed in the law of my church, and be sanctified by that which ye have received, and *ye shall bind yourselves to act in all holiness before me—*

That inasmuch as ye do this, glory shall be added to the kingdom which ye have received. (D&C 43:9-10)

Wherefore, a commandment I give unto you, *to prepare and organize yourselves by a bond or everlasting covenant that cannot be broken.* . . .
Behold, this is the preparation wherewith I prepare you, and the foundation, and the ensample which I give unto you, whereby you may accomplish the commandments which are given you. (D&C 78:11, 13)

As an orthopedic surgeon, I see practical application of binding a crooked limb to a sturdy, straight device. The term *orthopedic* means straight child. I have straightened out many broken and twisted bones by binding them to a straight rod or other fixation device. Sometimes this must be done in stages, by gentle persuasion, so the soft tissues around the bone will tolerate the straightening. The principle of binding to something straight and perfect is engraved in the "Tree of Andry"—a symbol of orthopedics.

The image of a crooked tree bound to a straight rod, or a crooked child bound to a fixation device, that they might grow straight and tall is the perfect image for the growing-up process of the temple. This image gives new meaning to Nephi's expression about the Israelites in the Sinai and the rod of the Lord that straitens: "And he did straiten them in the wilderness with his rod; for they hardened their hearts, even as ye have; and the Lord straitened them because of their iniquity" (1 Nephi 17:41).

The term *rod* gives the image of an instrument that physically gets our attention as a sign of authority or a tool of correction. *The "rod" of the Lord is His "word," like the iron rod.* It is the rod of His mouth (*see* D&C 19:15) that demands our attention and corrects us with His commandments and covenants. His rod is a straight rod because it tells us all that we must do to grow straight (*see* 2 Nephi 32:3).

The term *straiten* means confined or limited. Our wandering, disobedient nature becomes confined or limited as we are bound to the straight rod or word of the Lord. We can at first lean on His "rod" for support, but we must ultimately take His yoke upon us by keeping His commandments to be straightened. *The straitening that makes us straight, is with gentle persuasion and chastisement.*

We should remember that the Lord chastens or straitens those He loves (*see* Hebrews 12:6) and those who are His people (*see* Mosiah

23:21). He prepares for them a way of deliverance from temptation through chastening (*see* D&C 95:1). Finally, if we cannot bear the Lord's chastening, we cannot be sanctified (*see* D&C 101:5) and be worthy of His kingdom (*see* D&C 136:31).

Hopefully, the result of chastening or straitening is repentance and meekness. Then we can be straightened or grow straight as we are taught by the Spirit and obey the words of Christ (*see* 2 Nephi 32:5). This obedience gives us a fulness of freedom because we grow straight to a fulness of power and joy. Of course we have our agency in deciding to bind ourselves to our Savior and to be straitened and straightened by His rod.

In making and keeping righteous covenants (*see* Mosiah 5:6) as we do in the temple, we are bound to Christ. We should "cleave unto the covenants" (D&C 25:13), so in binding to Christ He can straiten and straighten us. In cleaving to the covenants, we are bound to Christ in the sense that we take His name upon us in trying to emulate Him.

Christ has many names or titles suggesting the various ways in which we must bind to Him and emulate Him. *He warns that when we take His name upon us, we must use His name with reverent sincerity and proper authority (see D&C 63:61-62; Exodus 20:7).*

It is not only how the name of the Lord passes through our lips, but also how it passes through our hearts, as expressed in our actions, that may condemn us. Unless we keep the covenants of the Lord in His Holy House, by authority of His Holy Order, with "full purpose of heart and real intent" (2 Nephi 31:13), we use His name in vain.

The message of the hymn "Come Thou Fount of Every Blessing" beautifully expresses the desire and need to be bound (fettered) and sealed to the Lord:

> Come thou fount of every blessing.
>> Tune my heart to sing thy grace.
> Streams of mercy never ceasing.
>> Call for songs of loudest praise.
> Teach me some melodious sonnet.
>> Sung by flaming tongues above.
> Praise the mount, I'm fixed upon it.
>> Mount of thy redeeming love.
>
> Here I raise my ebenezer.
>> Hither by thy help I'm come.

And I hope by thy good pleasure
    Safely to arrive at home.
Prone to wander, Lord, I feel it.
    Prone to leave the God I love.
Here's my heart—O take and seal it.
    Seal it for thy courts above.

Jesus sought me when a stranger
    Wandering from the fold of God.
He to rescue me from danger
    Interposed his precious blood.
Prone to wander, Lord I feel it.
    Prone to leave the God I love.
Here's my heart—O take and seal it.
    Seal it for thy courts above.

O to grace how great a debtor
    Daily I'm constrained to be.
Let thy goodness, like a fetter
    Bind my wandering heart to thee.
Prone to wander, Lord, I feel it.
    . Prone to leave the God I love.
Here's my heart—O take and seal it,
    Seal it for thy courts above.[4]

Being fixed upon the mount of the Atonement, we realize what debt to His grace we owe. We then want to be bound to Him and have His seal of approval upon us. This will only occur if we fetter or straiten our wandering by keeping His covenants. In taking the name of Christ upon us through these covenants we promise to grow straight by emulating Him. As we keep this promise we will receive His power (*see* D&C 39:4) to perfect us and imbue us with a "new spirit" and a "new heart" filled with His perfect love (*see* Ezekiel 36:25-27). By this power, He will seal or preserve our pure hearts for the courts of His Father above if we are obedient to Him "unto the end of our lives."

Therefore, I would that ye should *take upon you the name of Christ, all you that have entered into the covenant with God that ye should be obedient unto the end of your lives.*

And it shall come to pass that whosoever doeth this shall be found at the right hand of God, *for he shall know the name by which he is called;* for he shall be called by the name of Christ. (Mosiah 5:8-9)

Knowing the name by which we are called, we are led by the power of Christ to the right hand of God, perfected for celestial glory in the fold of the Father.

The Power of Christ to Heal Us and Make Us Holy on Mount Zion

The Savior has the "holy hands" (D&C 60:7) of a holy "potter" (*see* Jeremiah 18:6; Isaiah 64:8) with "all power unto the fulfilling of all his words" (1 Nephi 9:6). Out of "vessels of wrath," He can make of us "vessels of mercy" (*see* Romans 9:21-23). Then, when he "makes known the riches of His glory on the vessels of mercy," like He did to Paul, we can become "chosen vessels" (*see* Acts 9:15; Ephesians 1:4; Moroni 7:31). Therefore, Christ can mold us as clay and endow us with power from on high (*see* D&C 38:32) if we will bind ourselves to act in all holiness before Him (*see* D&C43:9).

The Savior can truly make us whole by making us holy. This is what He taught the infirm man at the pool of Bethseda:

And a certain man was there, which had an infirmity thirty and eight years.

When Jesus saw him lie, and knew that he had been now a long time in that case, he saith unto him,Wilt thou be made whole? . . .

And immediately the man was made whole, and took up his bed, and walked: . . .

Afterward Jesus findeth him in the temple, and said unto him, *Behold, thou art made whole: sin no more, lest a worse thing come unto thee.*

The man departed, and told the Jews that it was Jesus, which had made him whole. (John 5:5-6, 9, 14-15)

It is in the holy temple that we hear the Savior say to us "be whole by being holy and sin no more." It is in the temple that we can say "it was Jesus that made us whole." It is in the temple that we come to understand and feel the power of Christ to make us whole by purifying and perfecting our hearts, that we do all in "holiness of heart" (D&C 46:7). In His Holy Order, we are made " whole" as we are "sanctified by the Spirit unto the renewing of [our] bodies" (D&C 84:33).

During his great temple sermon, King Benjamin described the power of Christ to maintain and even renew the mortal body as a "matchless and marvelous power" (*see* Mosiah 1:13; 2:11). It is by the matchless and marvelous power of the Atonement, through His Holy Order, that Christ can make us holy. He tenderly and enticingly invites us to Him, to understand His purifying power: "Learn of me, and listen to my words; walk in the meekness of my Spirit, and you shall have peace in me" (D&C 19:23).

As we listen to Christ's words, he desires that we reason with Him "that [we] may understand" (*see* D&C 50:11-12).

> For after this manner doth Lord God work among the children of men. For the Lord God giveth light unto the understanding; for he speaketh unto men according to their language, unto their understanding. (2 Nephi 31:3)

In reasoning with the Lord, we come to understand His power to make us holy. "*Come now, and let us reason together, saith the Lord:* though your sins be as scarlet, they shall be as white as snow; though they be red like crimson, they shall be as wool" (Isaiah 1:18).

We must reason the words of Christ not only in our mind, but also in our hearts. "By the Spirit" (D&C 50:10) is how the Lord finally reasons with us to our understanding. *The wisdom of God can only be understood if it comes by the Spirit and is received by the spirit (see* D&C 50:17-22). When we accept the everlasting covenant and come unto Christ in the temple, we receive through the spirit of prophecy and revelation the "strong reasoning" and "wisdom" of the Lord (*see* D&C 45:9-11). Then we come to understand the power of the redemption of Christ, and see ourselves with an eye of faith raised to immortality and incorruption:

> *Do ye exercise faith in the redemption of him who created you?* Do you look forward with an eye of faith, and view this mortal body raised in immortality, and this corruption raised in incorruption, to stand before God? (Alma 5:15)

If we keep an eye of faith single to the glory of God, then one day the veil will be lifted from our minds and we will see with eyes of understanding (*see* D&C 110:1).

Those who cannot understand Christ's matchless power in their hearts, with an eye of faith, should at least acknowledge it in their minds. The creation of this earth, from matter unorganized, to be a sphere glorious and beautiful is an evident reality. There is no place like it in the known solar system or near galaxy. All forces of the universe seem to be concentrated on this speck of organized matter, to maintain life. And for what purpose? To testify that God, by the matchless power of His Son, can take us from matter unorganized to a state glorious and beautiful if we will bind ourselves to the Son and sin no more.

The world still believes in the geocentric theory. From the surface of the earth, it appears the sun revolves around us every day. But alas, Copernicus, one who sought the truth, was right. Everything revolves around the Son! (*See* D&C 88:7.)

Joseph Smith expressed the need to "revolve around the Son" in our daily lives when he said that "*we need the temple more than anything else.*"[5] Why? Because we need Christ more than anything else. For the "living deaths" of everyday life, we need the healing and sealing power of the Atonement through Jesus Christ (*see* Isaiah 53:3-6; 61:1-3), that only the temple can fully provide. This truth was expressed by Truman Madsen when he wrote: "*All 'living deaths' require atonement and healing. The Atonement of Christ through ordinances of the temple* 'reverses the blows of death.' *If his healing the wounds is the beginning then His sealing of families [and us to Him] is the end.*"[6]

It is a marvelous healing of "living deaths" as the wounds of resentment, rejection, and conflict disappear in the temple when we can draw near to the Savior and emulate Him. The Savior assures those who draw near to Him that He will draw near to them (*see* D&C 88:63) because even in this life Christ has the power that we "be lifted up" (Mosiah 23:22) above the depressions of mortality. Therefore, Mormon said to his son, "May Christ lift thee up" (Moroni 9:25). I wish, as a physician, I could lift my patients and heal their physical and mental wounds as well. Unfortunately, as Francis Bacon said, many do not want to be healed because they prefer to keep "deaths" living. "This is certain, that a man that studieth revenge keeps his own wounds green, which otherwise would heal and do well."[7]

The wounds of "living deaths" must be healed if we are to be sealed to each other and to our Heavenly parents (*see* 3 Nephi 12:23-23; Matthew 5:23-24). We must be reconciled to each other if we are to be reconciled to God. These wounds are healed by the power of the Atonement through temple covenants.

The healing of "living deaths" in telestial temples is a reflection of the ultimate healing that will occur when the earth becomes a celestial temple and God Himself shall be there!

> And God shall wipe away all tears from their eyes; and there shall be no more death, neither sorrow, nor crying, neither shall there be any more pain: for the former things are passed away. (Revelation 21:3- 4)

Notice the great and last promise of the temple in these verses. The temples of mortality, extensions of the celestial temple, are the healing hospitals for our souls.

Once we understand the healing and sealing power of the Atonement through temple covenants, we then want to cry for joy as did those covenant people at the temple with King Benjamin, who "all cried aloud with one voice, saying: O have mercy, and apply the atoning blood of Christ that we may receive forgiveness of our sins, and our hearts may be purified" (Mosiah 4:2).

A Full Moon Over Mount Zion

When we cry for joy like the people of King Benjamin, we have finally understood the heralding message that Moroni is trumpeting from the temple. It is the music of a full moonlight sonata captured in Don Busath's most beautifully significant picture of the Salt Lake Temple with a full moon silhouetting the angel Moroni. The symbolic meaning of the full moon is the fullness of Christ's love which is the fullness of the power of the Atonement. The message of Moroni's full moonlight sonata is the music of his trumpet in his own words:

> *Yea, come unto Christ, and be perfected in him, and deny yourselves of all ungodliness; and if ye shall deny yourselves of all ungodliness, and love God with all your might, mind and strength,* then is his grace sufficient for you, that by his grace ye may be perfect in Christ. (Moroni 10:32)

Then the real secret of the mighty change in this life comes to our understanding, as Moroni further explained with the second verse of his full moonlight sonata how the grace of Christ can perfect us:

> And if men come unto me I will show unto them their weakness. I give unto men weakness that they may be humble; and *my grace is sufficient for all men that humble themselves before me;* for if they

humble themselves before me, and have faith in me, *then will I make weak things become strong unto them.* (Ether 12:27)

In the finale of Moroni's trumpet solo, the power of the full moon, the Savior's perfect love in His perfect Atonement, shines in all its glory. By this power we can again become the holy sons and daughters of God:

> And again, if ye by the grace of God are perfect in Christ, and deny not his power, *then are ye sanctified in Christ by the grace of God, through the shedding of the blood of Christ, which is in the covenant of the Father unto the remission of your sins,* that ye become holy, without spot. (Moroni 10:33)

Christ loves us and is our advocate because He "knoweth the weakness of man and how to succor them" (D&C 62:1). If we search diligently in the full moonlight of Christ and receive every good thing from Christ, He will give us the power to make the mighty change in our weak hearts to become His sons and daughters (*see* Moroni 7:19; D&C 29:4).

The Binding Power of Love

While love binds us to our mortal parents, so *it is love that will bind us to our Heavenly parents—their love for us and our love for them.* However, to be sealed or bound to our Heavenly Father, we must have within us the kind of love that He has. It is the pure love of His Only Begotten Son. Paul expressed this truth in one precise verse. "*And above all these things put on charity, which is the bond of perfectness*" (Colossians 3:14).

This is the kind of bonding love that exists between the Father and the Son. It is the same love that the Father has for all His children in the world. To those who believe on His Son, becoming one in Him (*see* D&C 35:2), He gives the fulness of His love expressed in the perfect oneness and unity that the Father and Son have. This unity, even as the Father and Son are one, is beautifully expressed in the Son's prayer to His Father (*see* John 17:5, 20-26).

Notice the great and last promise of the temple, when the Son says that "*they may behold my glory*" (John 17:24) in these deeply moving words of His prayer to the Father. The Son desired to reveal His glory (His rest), which also is the glory of the Father. This promise can come to us when we seek the Son (*see* D&C 76:19). It will most certainly come when "the love wherewith thou hast loved me may be in them"

(John 17:26), and we develop the kind of ultimate, all-encompassing love that the Father and Son have.

We can develop within us the celestial love and unity required as we are bound to Christ, keeping His covenants. This is because He knows the love of the Father. Therefore, with the power of the love of Christ, we can be sealed to our Heavenly Parents with the "bond of perfectness."

Jacob profoundly described the power of the Atonement as "infinite" (*see* 2 Nephi 9:7-10, 12). The power of the Atonement is the power of love, an infinite love that is the "bond of perfectness." Joseph Smith described the Lord God Almighty in his dedicatory prayer as having "an infinity of fulness" (D&C 109:77). *The fulness of God is the infinite measure of His love* (*see* Ephesians 3:19). It is "the measure of the stature of the fulness of Christ" (*see* Ephesians 4:13). The Lord God Almighty and His Son are infinitely full of the power of perfect love. Therefore, John the Beloved wrote, "*Beloved, let us love one another: for love is of God; and every one that loveth is born of God, and knoweth God. He that loveth not knoweth not God; for God is love*" (1 John 4:7-8).

God's powerful bond of love binds us to Him and to each other, bringing all things to a perfected state never again to be corrupted. It is the ultimate power to overcome the force of telestial entropy that, as Jacob stated, causes all mortal matter to "rot and crumble" (2 Nephi 9:7).

We learn to a degree, in mortality, that with great love comes great oneness. *Growing up in mortality, hopefully, we pass from a stage of entropy to a state of edification. Without the temple and the Atonement, we cannot fully arrive at this state.* We, however, should learn in mortality that the love that edifies is a power that elevates unorganized matter and relationships to a creative, organized, lasting state.

As curious toddlers, we succumb to the forces of entropy. Everything seems to crumble in our hands. Later, when we are given responsibility for material possessions, respect for maintenance and even love of ownership develops. When this responsibility includes others, we can learn of the powerful, lasting bond that edification creates.

We can only learn of the power of love with the law of agency. After reading Moses 4:1, where Satan proposed his plan to "redeem all mankind, that one soul shall not be lost," I wondered about the details of his plan. How was he going to force spirit beings, who seem to respond best to the power of love, to all be saved? Like many of his followers talked about in the Book of Mormon, he must have had a powerful rhetoric, because he "turned away a third part of the hosts of heaven because of their agency" (D&C 29:36).

The only way Satan's plan could be implemented would be through the elimination of the law of agency (*see* Moses 4:3). Besides their mortal bodies, these "hosts of heaven" who followed Satan also lost their agency, because he would "lead them captive at his will" (Moses 4:4).

In all dispensations of man on earth, Satan's plan under varying philosophies has been presented. Unlike the Lord's law of consecration, all of these philosophies have a basic element: the elimination to some degree of free agency. Therefore, *like the intimate relation between truth, light, and love, the power of love is intimately related to the law of free agency.* No accountable spirit can be forced by the power of love!

There are many inspiring stories, written and personal, that verify the power of love. A favorite story of mine that demonstrates the binding power of love is *Cry, the Beloved Country,* by Alan Paton.

In South Africa, during the 1940s, a prominent white man and a black minister both lost their sons. The white man's son was shot to death by the minister's son. The minister's son was executed because of this crime, which occurred out of fear. Eventually, the white man's heart turned from prejudice and hate and the minister's heart turned from fear and grief to the point that they began to respect, then love, then edify each other. Finally the white man built a new church for the black minister.

A sacrifice was necessary for both of these fathers to come together in love. It was a sacrifice not only of their sons but of their proud hearts—changed first to broken hearts, then to hearts filled with pure love. This change of heart necessary to produce the binding oneness of pure love is based on the infinite sacrifice and pure love of Jesus Christ (*see* Galatians 3:28). The glory of God's love is expressed in love for enemies. It is the victory of divine love over the powers of evil by patient suffering and sacrifice, until evil quells itself (*see* Matthew 5:38-48; Romans 12:17-21).

Pure love is a will to act on behalf of others. Therefore it is a power. It is not only the power of knowledge, but the graces of edification such as self-discipline, sacrifice, patience, hope and faith.[8] It is the power that repels the forces that cause all matter and relationships to rot and crumble. Jacob said that the power of the infinite Atonement, this infinite love, not only overcomes our physical but also our spiritual degradation. Therefore by the Atonement, "this corruption [can] put on incorruption" (2 Nephi 9:7), overcoming "the death of the body, and also the death of the spirit" (2 Nephi 9:10).

The connection between the power of love and the powers of heaven is the doctrine of the priesthood (*see* D&C 121:36-46; 107:30-31). Christ is the perfect example of the powers of heaven manifest through the power of love. It is with love unfeigned, our bowels full of charity towards all men, that the rights of the priesthood we hold become inseparably connected with the powers of heaven.

The fact that God desires to bestow upon his children the powers of heaven through the rights and doctrine of the priesthood, that we might wax strong in His presence, is ample proof that He wants us to become like Him. Because the promise is if "these things" (the virtues of the doctrine of the priesthood) are part of us, then *by the power of the Atonement, we shall have eternal life, which is to know and become like God* (*see* D&C 107:31). The promise for having the power of the Atonement and the doctrine of the priesthood distill upon our souls is "all that my Father hath" (D&C 84:38).

At the Summit Veil:
The Mercy Seat of Mount Zion

Within the Holy of Holies of the early Old Testament temples was the mercy seat, the throne of God. *The Hebrew word for the gold covering of this seat is* kapporeth, *which, as we have seen, means a covering of acceptance through atonement and forgiveness.* Therefore, this seat was appropriately called a "mercy seat." Paul directed us to this throne, calling it *"the throne of grace," that we might obtain the grace and mercy of Christ* (*see* Hebrews 4:16).

The Lord accepted the Kirtland Temple with a promise of His manifestation "in mercy in this house" (D&C 110:7). *Nephi taught that the "tender mercies" of Christ are sufficient to make the faithful "mighty" with the "power of deliverance" from the Fall and the bitter results of the forbidden fruit* (*see* 1 Nephi 1:20).

The real deliverance is from our weaknesses, that we may be made strong (*see* D&C 50:16), even with the "power to overcome all things which are not ordained of God" (D&C 50:35).

As we are delivered from things not ordained of God, we become "strangers and pilgrims" (Hebrews 11:13; D&C 45:13), traveling through this life, seeking a life of righteousness as did the patriarchs of old. With images of "kapporeth," Catherine Thomas has expressed our search as "strangers and pilgrims": "This was the very search for which they [and we] were put on earth: to rend the veil of unbelief, to yield to the pull of the Savior's sealing power, to stand in the Lord's presence, encircled about in the arms of his love"[9] (*see also* Acts 17:27-28).

With faith and hope in Christ, Joseph Smith taught that Christ's mercy enables us to endure the deserts and fleshpots of mortality during our pilgrimage to the promises: "They are enabled by faith to lay hold on the promises . . . And wade through all the tribulations and afflictions . . . believing that the mercy of God will . . . lay hold of them and secure them in the arms of His love."[10]

Christ's mercy expressed as the "arms of His love" is what enabled Father Lehi to exclaim at his mortal parting the assurance of his deliverance, having seen and felt the great and last promise of the temple (*see* 2 Nephi 1:15).

The fruit of the tree of life is the love and mercy of Christ. Jacob taught that as our hearts become purified, we feast upon this fruit. It is this fruit that kept Job (*see* Job 19:21-27) and Jacob (*see* Jacob 3:1-2) steadfast in their afflictions with "firmness of mind." Christ's love and mercy also will console us in our afflictions and plead our cause.

The hymn "I Stand All Amazed" also mentions the mercy seat and teaches that worshiping in the temple will lay hold and secure us in the love of God at His glorified throne: "I will praise and adore at the mercy seat, until at the glorified throne I kneel at His feet."[11]

As we return to the temple, worshiping at the mercy seat, we lay hold of the healing and sealing power of the Atonement. We feast upon the love and mercy of God. We learn that Christ is the one who leads us to the glorified throne, the presence of the Father, because He is sealed to the Father (*see* John 6:27). Therefore we must ultimately report to the Savior and be sealed or bound to Him; He will then lead us through the veil to the presence of the Father:

> *The keeper of the gate is the Holy One of Israel;* and he employeth no servant there; and there is none other way save it be by the gate; for he cannot be deceived . . .
>
> And whoso knocketh, to him will he open; . . . And save they shall cast these things away and consider themselves fools before God, and come down in the depths of humility, he will not open unto them. (2 Nephi 9:41-42)

The temple veil is the final strait and narrow gate. The Savior is the gate keeper.

In a Church Education Week address, Michael Wilcox revealed a vision of his own judgment. He entered a waiting room and saw about 20 people seated. When he looked closely, they were all Michael Wilcox. There was Michael Wilcox the husband, and Michael Wilcox the father, and teacher, and priesthood holder, and so forth. All of these seemed to go through judgment without incident. In the last seat was a trembling, wretched man. It was Michael Wilcox the man, stripped of all titles. As he fearfully made his way to the door of judgment, the Savior put an arm of love around him, saying, "Michael, do not fear. I am your advocate with the Father because you have believed on my name."[12]

This same love and mercy of the Savior experienced by Brother Wilcox is expressed in the *scriptural temple:*

> *Listen to Him who is the advocate with the Father, who is pleading your cause before him—*
>
> Saying: Father, behold the sufferings and death of him who did no sin, in whom thou wast well pleased; behold the blood of thy Son which was shed, the blood of him whom thou gavest that thyself might be glorified;
>
> *Wherefore; Father, spare these my brethren that believe on my name, that they may come unto me and have everlasting life.* (D&C 45:3-5)

It is at the veil that we really see the mercy and power of the Atonement. Even if we must finally cry, as Nephi did, "O wretched man that I am" (2 Nephi 4:17), we who believe on His name have the greatest advocate of all who is pleading our cause because of His Atonement (*see* D&C 38:4). If in us, He finds the fruits of the spirit because we believe on His name by taking His name upon us, He will joyfully plead, for against such there is no law (*see* Galatians 5:22-23).

If the Lord finds in us the pure heart and devotion to Him that is required, then another type of sealing will occur. It is the seal of assurance, the stamp of approval from the Holy Spirit of Promise, a calling and election made sure, "shed forth upon all those who are just and true" (*see* Ephesians 1:13; D&C 76:53).

The Bond of Perfectness:
A Sure Way to Stand in the Presence of the Lord

The bond of perfectness is the infinite power of a "perfect atonement" that can perfect us. "These are they who are just men made perfect through Jesus the mediator of the new covenant, who wrought out this perfect atonement through the shedding of his own blood" (D&C 76:69).

The bond of perfectness, the bonding and equalizing power of a perfect love, is a requirement even in this life, to live the laws of the celestial kingdom, that we "may be equal in the bonds of heavenly things" (*see* D&C 78:5). For this bond of perfectness, we must make a great and last sacrifice, yielding our hearts to God by keeping temple covenants. We must keep the everlasting covenant, which is the everlasting bond (*see* D&C 78:11). *Then the Savior will encircle us with the arms of His love and clothe us with the robes of righteousness by filling our hearts with His perfect love. This is the ultimate expression of "kippur" as we are clothed with the bond of charity, becoming His spiritually begotten children.* "And above all things, clothe yourselves with the bond of charity, as with a mantle, which is the bond of perfectness and peace" (D&C 88:125).

The bond of perfectness is the bond of perfect love that binds us to our Savior and to each other. It is the bond required to live the celestial law, becoming truly equal in preparation for the redemption of Zion and the great and last promise of the temple.

These thoughts are captured in wonderful verses of instruction for the ambiance of the "school of the prophets" held in the house of God. They mention an "everlasting covenant, in which covenant" we receive each other "to fellowship in determination that is fixed, immovable, and unchangeable, to be your friend and brother through the grace of God in bonds of love" (*see* D&C 88:130-133).

May we return often to the house of God where we receive the bond of perfectness through the everlasting covenant from our friend and brother, Jesus Christ. This bond comes to us by the power of a perfect love, expressed in a perfect Atonement which can spiritually beget us as the children of Christ. As we become the children of Christ (*see* Mosiah 5:7), we can become the sons and daughters of God (*see* Mosiah 27:25; 3 Nephi 9:17; Moroni 7:48; D&C 25:1; Moses 6:68). By the powers of heaven through temple ordinances and the endowment of the doctrine of the priesthood, our confidence will wax strong in the presence of God.

In the Garden, Adam and Eve stood in the presence of God. After the Fall, they knelt at the altars of sacrifice. As the plan of redemption was revealed to them and they obeyed it, their confidence waxed strong so they could again stand in God's presence. This confidence came by the power of the priesthood, the Order of the Son of God (*see* JST Genesis 14:30-31).

This is the same sequence we enact in the temple being frequently reminded that we can stand in the presence of God. This sequence is symbolic of our heavenly birth, our fall, and our redemption. As our confidence grows with the power and bonds of God's perfect love, we will stand in His presence. Returning often to the temple, we will desire to return to our Father in Heaven, standing in His presence.

12

The Wells of Salvation— Sustaining the Ascent of Mount Zion

Feeling my way along the chiseled walls of Hezekiah's tunnel and wading through the knee-deep, cool water of the Gihon spring to the pool of Siloam, I recalled the miracles of the rocks at Horeb and Meribah (*see* Exodus 17, Numbers 20). Moses smote these rocks with his rod and water gushed forth to satisfy the thirst of the Israelites. *Giha* in Hebrew means "gush forth."

The spring of Gihon in the Kidron valley and the springs of the Jordan valley, such as En Gedi, seem to gush out of desolate ground or rocks as reminders of the water miracles of Moses. This image of water gushing from rock reminds those who drink the water, that in this land precious water flows because the Lord said:

> It shall come to pass, if ye shall hearken diligently unto my commandments . . .
> That I will give you the rain of your land in his due season. (Deuteronomy 11:11-14)

The annual rainfall of Jerusalem is equivalent to the rainfall of London, but in Jerusalem, rain falls in winter months.[1] The remainder of the year is relatively arid. Therefore stored water from the ground-supplying springs is important. Even the water that feeds the Jordan River comes from a rock—the aquifers of Mount Hermon. The precarious edge between wet and drought on which Judea balances is evidenced by the many cisterns around Jerusalem. There are 37 cisterns under the Temple Mount courtyards capable of holding 10 million gallons of water.[2]

The Nourishing Word of God

The water that gushed from the rocks struck by the rod of Moses was a type of Christ symbolizing the Atonement and the spiritual truths that would flow from the "rock of Israel" to everlastingly quench the spiritual thirst of those that follow Him. This truth was frequently taught by the Savior during His mortal ministry. After Christ fed the five thousand and was sought by those receiving this miracle, He taught them the truth about nourishment from God: "And Jesus said unto them I am the bread of life; he that cometh to me shall never hunger; and he that believeth on me shall never thirst" (John 6:35).

The prophets of old have compared lack of the knowledge of God to famine and drought. "Therefore, my people are gone into captivity, because they have no knowledge; and their honorable men are famished, and their multitude dried up with thirst" (2 Nephi 15:13; *see also* Isaiah 5:13).

The Prophet Amos foretold that the worst drought and famine of all, even for the young and the strong, is the drought and famine of the word of God:

> Behold, the days come, saith the Lord God, that I will send a famine in the land, not a famine of bread, nor a thirst for water, but of hearing the words of the Lord.
>
> In that day shall the fair virgins and young men faint for thirst. (Amos 8:11, 13)

Knowledge of Christ and His works is what nourishes us everlastingly. It is a spring of water that will never dry up because His works and words "never cease" (Moses 1:4).

A Well of Living Water Within Us

A beautiful bas relief on a front court wall of the Alberta Temple shows the scene of Christ with the Samaritan woman at Jacob's well. Christ's profound scriptural message is referenced below this scene: "But whosoever drinketh of the water that I shall give him shall never thirst; but the water that I shall give him shall be in him a well of water springing up into everlasting life" (John 4:14).

The Savior explained the source of this well of water within us:

> Jesus stood and cried, saying, If any man thirst, let him come unto me, and drink.

He that believeth on me, as the scripture hath said, out of his belly shall flow rivers of living water.

But this spake he of the Spirit, which they that believe on him should receive. (John 7:37-39)

The Spirit, the fulness of the Holy Ghost, the spirit of prophecy and revelation, is the source of this well of living water within us. This personal well of living water was further defined by the Lord, through a revelation of the Prophet Joseph Smith: "But unto him that keepeth my commandments I will give the mysteries of my kingdom, and the same shall be in him a well of living water springing up unto everlasting life" (D&C 63:23).

The location of the source of the well of living water is the Mountain of the House of the Lord for "a fountain shall come forth of the house of the Lord" (Joel 3:18). It is from His house that His living waters will flow like the waters flowing from the caverns of Mt. Hermon, symbolizing the celestial temple. It is in the temple that we receive a fulness of testimony and knowledge of Jesus Christ, because in the temple we receive a fulness of the Holy Ghost (*see* D&C 109:15).

As we are taught by the Holy Ghost and covenant in the fulness of the Melchizedek Priesthood through temple ordinances, we learn of the mysteries (the revealed truths) of God's celestial kingdom. This knowledge, this great view, becomes in us a well of living water that gushes forth quenching our thirst for eternal life. It then gushes forth, out of our belly, as our "bowels shall be a fountain of truth" (*see* D&C 85:7)

We will become fountains of truth with the words of eternal truth for our fellow men as we draw from the deep well of the Lord in Mount Zion. For "counsel in the heart of man [is like] deep water; [and] a man of understanding will draw it out" (Proverbs 20:5), then we will become mouths of righteousness to quench the thirst of our fellow men from the well of life within us, since "the mouth of a righteous man is a well of life" (Proverbs 11:10).

On a wall of the hospital at which I work are framed the following words of Tennyson:

More things are wrought by prayer than the world dreams of.
Wherefore, let thy voice rise like a fountain night and day.[3]

Not only should we testify eternal words to our fellowmen, but our bowels should also be a fountain of prayer for them, especially for our enemies (*see* Matthew 5:44). By praying for our enemies, Deitrich Bonhoffer said, we vicariously edify them with love: "For if we pray for them, we are taking their distress and poverty, their guilt and perdition upon ourselves, and pleading to God for them. We are doing vicariously for them what they cannot do for themselves.[4]

Mount Zion Has the Fountain of Truth

Isaiah's vivid description of the righteousness of the Millennial era seems to center at the temple: "They shall not hurt nor destroy in all my holy mountain; for the earth shall be full of the knowledge of the Lord, as the waters cover the sea" (Isaiah 11:9; 2 Nephi 30:15).

It is from the temple, the holy mountain, that the knowledge of the Lord will flow. It will cover the earth in the millennium as water covered the earth during the Great Flood. It is from the temple that we draw living water from the well of salvation because there we learn of the truths of eternal life that gush forth from the One who saves. When we understand this truth we understand what Isaiah meant when he declared, "Therefore with joy shall ye draw water out of the wells of salvation" (Isaiah 12:3).

A traditional Irish melody, entitled "Take Time to Be Holy," describes the well of salvation. To be holy is to be with and to emulate the Savior. It is to be led to His fountains of love:

> Take time to be holy, speak oft with thy Lord;
> Abide in Him always, And feed on His word,
> Make friends of God's children, Help those who are weak,
> Forgetting in nothing His blessing to seek.
> Take time to be holy. The world rushes on;
> Spend much time in secret with Jesus alone;
> By looking to Jesus, Like Him thou shalt be;
> Thy friends in thy conduct His likeness shall see.
> Take time to by holy. Let Him be thy guide,
> And run not before Him, whatever betide;
> In joy or in sorrow, still follow thy Lord,
> And looking to Jesus, still trust in his word.
> Take time to be holy. Be calm in thy soul,
> Each thought and each motive beneath His control;
> Thus led by His Spirit to fountains of love,
> Thou soon shall be fitted for service above.
> Thou soon shall be fitted for service above.[5]

The temple is a fountain of truth from the well of salvation. The water of that well is the mysteries of God in the truth of things as they really are, the covenants of eternal life, and the power of the Atonement. It is, in sum, the testimony of Jesus Christ.

The well of salvation is a fountain of love with "living" water because by the love of God, the Atonement, we can become forever "living." Therefore, the well of salvation is the real fountain of youth because by drinking its spiritual water we become eternal lives.

In contrast to the fountain of truth in a true messenger, false prophets are called a "bitter fountain" (Moroni 7:11) and "wells without water" (*see* 2 Peter 1:1, 17-18).

A favorite movie of mine, *Jean de Florette*, tells the tragedy of greed for lack of water. Its incredible sequel, *Manon of the Spring*, exposes Sobeyrand who, over greed for a water source, unknowingly caused the death of his own son in the first movie.

The remarkable story in *Jean de Florette* and *Manon of the Spring* vividly portrays man's ability to destroy his greatest possessions out of pride and greed.

Charity, the ability to edify others out of love and sacrifice, could have been the source of a happy ending to this story. If the invitation by Jacob to come to the wells of salvation and drink freely were the attitude of Sobeyrand and his neighbors, then all would have found a well of salvation and none would have perished.

> Come, my brethren, every one that thirsteth, come ye to the waters; and he that hath no money, come buy and eat; yea, come buy wine and milk without money and without price.
>
> Wherefore, do not spend money for that which is of no worth, nor your labor for that which cannot satisfy. Hearken diligently unto me, and remember the words which I have spoken; and come unto the Holy One of Israel, and feast upon that which perisheth not, neither can be corrupted, and let your soul delight in fatness. (2 Nephi 9:50-51; see D&C 10:66)

The "fountain of the water of life" from the well of salvation is free for all who are "athirst" (*see* Revelation 21:6). The water from this well will eventually provide a "feast of fat things" through the laws of consecration so that poverty and inequality will be abolished (*see* D&C 58:8; Isaiah 25:6). This feast is the feast of the fruit of the tree of life, the bread and waters of life, which can be enjoyed freely (*see* Alma 5:34).

The well of salvation is a well that does not deplete nor depend on another source. It fills the meek and lowly heart that has faith and hope in Christ with His love, the quality of charity (*see* Moroni 7:43-44). It is the fountain of all righteousness because with faith and hope in our Savior, we desire to attain all His righteousness. "And I will show unto them that faith, hope and charity bringeth unto me—the fountain of all righteousness" (Ether 12:28).

Faith, hope, and charity summarily describe our climb to the summit of Mount Zion through temple worship. There we will find the fountain of all righteousness that will forever quench our thirst for righteousness and holiness with eternal lives.

The Healing Water Flowing from the Well of Salvation

The water of the well of salvation is not contained by its walls. The power and message of the temple is not confined by its walls. Thus King Benjamin had to build a tower outside the temple to accommodate those gathered to hear him (*see* Mosiah 2:7).

Ezekiel had a marvelous vision of water flowing from a future temple built on Mount Moriah. It is reminiscent of the river flowing from the Garden of Eden to the four corners of the earth, and the knowledge of the Lord flowing from the millennial temple covering the earth like a sea. This vision teaches us of the cleansing and healing power of the water of the well of salvation. This water must flow through our everyday lives to heal us and make us grow, even as it made the Judean desert flourish and healed the waters of the Dead Sea:

> Afterward he brought me again unto the door of the house; and, behold, waters issued out from under the threshold of the house eastward;
>
> . . . at the banks of the river were very many trees on the one side and on the other.
>
> These waters issue out toward the east country, and go down into the desert, and go into the sea; which being brought forth into the sea, the waters shall be healed.
>
> . . . And there shall be a very great multitude of fish, and every thing shall live wither the river cometh. (Ezekiel 47:1, 7-9)

Having traveled the route from the temple mount eastward through the barren Judean hills to the Dead Sea, I realized that the imagery in Ezekiel's vision is miraculous. I can see his vision literally fulfilled as Joseph Smith prophesied,[6] but the message for me in this vision is that wherever the waters of salvation flow from the well of salvation (the temple), there is healing and growth.[7] The power of the temple heals the hurts and weaknesses of our lives and makes us grow spiritually.

The image of the "many trees" on both sides of the river is a vivid image in an arid geographic setting. The tallest, greenest trees grow near the river bank because the river brings "goodly land" to the banks. Likewise, if we plant a seed (the word of God) in "goodly land" (the mind and heart) and nourish it with water from the wells of salvation by being "planted in the house of the Lord" (Psalm 92:13), we "shall be like a tree planted by the rivers of water" (*see* Psalm 1:1-3). We shall become "a very fruitful tree which is planted in goodly land by a pure stream that [yields] much precious fruit" (*see* D&C 97:9). As Alma taught, we can grow a tall tree of life within us, producing a most delicious fruit even in this spiritually arid world.

The image of the association in mortality of a nourishing river producing growth of trees is a reflection of this association in the celestial realm:

> And he shewed me a pure river of water of life, clear as crystal, proceeding out of the throne of God and of the Lamb.
>
> In the midst of the street of it, and on either side of the river, was there the tree of life, which bare twelve manner of fruits, and yielded her fruit every month: and the leaves of the tree were for the healing of the nations. (Revelation 22:1-2)

The healing water of life (knowledge of God's power and love) and the healing leaves of the tree of life (the power of the atonement) are found in earthly temples. They cast a reflection of the ultimate healing of our suffering and weaknesses, which will occur in the celestial temple. (*see* Revelation 7:14-17).

Because of this ultimate healing promise of the temple, we should not be so concerned with tribulation surrounding us, hoping, like the Jews, for the overthrow of our oppressors. Rather, we should be more concerned about the faults within us that can be healed by water from the well of salvation. Through temple ordinances and covenants we drink pure, living water from the well of salvation. This water is the power of an infinite Atonement and the knowledge of the fullness of Christ. With this pure water we become "the trees of righteousness, the planted of the Lord" (Isaiah 61:3).

To Be Healed: Flowing to the Well of Salvation

In imagery reverse to that of healing waters flowing from the temple, Lehi exhorted his son Laman to flow to the temple. "And when my father saw that the waters of the river emptied into the fountain of the Red Sea, he spake unto Laman, saying: O that thou mightest be like unto this river, continually running into the fountain of all righteousness." (1 Nephi 2:9).

It is interesting that Lehi saw this same image of a river running to the "fountain of living waters" (1 Nephi 11:25) in his tree of life vision: "And as I cast my eyes round about, that perhaps I might discover my family also, I beheld a river of water and it ran along, and it was near the tree of which I was partaking the fruit" (1 Nephi 8:13).

This river of water was accompanied by a "rod of iron" and a "strait and narrow path," which also led to the tree of life (*see* 1 Nephi 8:19-20)

In Nephi's vision and interpretation of his father's dream, the fountain of living waters was contrasted to a fountain of filthy water (*see* 1 Nephi 11:25; 1 Nephi 12:16). Clearly there is a contrast between a river of filthy water that flows into a fountain of filthy water representing the depths of hell and a river of living water flowing into a fountain of living water representing the love of God. It is not clear in Lehi's dream how many rivers are represented. Perhaps there is one river that divides. If it divides, this occurs when we choose between the forbidden fruit and the fruit of the tree of life.

The river of living water represents the Atonement. Without the Atonement, holding the iron rod and walking the strait and narrow path would not get us to the tree of life. The healing and cleansing water of the Atonement is the only water that can extinguish the flaming sword that guards the tree of life. This flaming sword as a "flaming fire" represents the justice of God (*see* 1 Nephi 15:30).

Only the Atonement extinguishes or appeases the demands of justice. "And now the plan of mercy could not be brought about except an atonement should be made; therefore God himself atoneth for the sins of the world, to bring about the plan of mercy, to appease the demands of justice, that God might be a perfect, just God, and a merciful God also" (Alma 42:15).

Only the Atonement of Christ can open the way that we might fully partake of the fruit of the tree of life.

The full effect of the Atonement can be realized in our lives if we take hold of the rod of iron, in following true messengers and walk the strait and narrow path in obeying the Lord's covenants. These acts of holding fast and strictly following make the difference between filthy and living water in our lives. They make the difference between good and evil in our lives as a consequence of partaking of the fruit of the tree of knowledge of good and evil. If we hold to the words of true messengers and are obedient to the covenants we make with the Lord, then His Atonement will wash us clean of all sin with living (healing) water (*see* Ezekiel 36:25).

The river of living water leads to and comes from the fountain of living water and all righteousness in God's temple. When we are healed and grow because of living water from the temple, tasting the sweetness of the love of God, we want to become rivers of living water continually "running" to the temple. It is in the temple, the living water within us, the spirit of prophecy and revelation, is renewed.

Stand in Protected Places of Holiness

Curiously, in the midst of the Missouri persecution, the Lord commanded the Saints to build a temple. The Lord explained the necessity of this commandment:

> Verily I say unto you, that it is my will that a house should be built unto me in the land of Zion, like unto the pattern which I have given you.
>
> Yea, let it be built speedily, by the tithing of my people. Behold, this is the tithing and sacrifice which I, the Lord, require at their hands, that there may be a house built unto me for the salvation of Zion—
>
> And, now, behold, if Zion do these things she shall prosper, and spread herself and become very glorious, very great, and very terrible. (D&C 97:10-12, 18)

One can strongly speculate that the fate of the Saints in Missouri would have been different had they heeded this commandment.

The fate of the Northern Kingdom, which was carried away by Assyria in the fourth year of King Hezekiah, would have been different had they heeded the invitation of King Hezekiah to go to the temple and "enter into His sanctuary" (*see* 2 Chronicles 30:8).

When the Assyrian army besieged the Southern Kingdom, the people of Jerusalem renewed their worship of the Lord. Hezekiah went into the House of the Lord and prayed for his people. The Lord responded with the miraculous decimation of the Assyrian army (*see* 2 Kings 19:32-36).

Clearly the Lord was telling both the Missouri Saints and the Israelites of the Northern and Southern kingdoms that faith in building a temple and worshiping in the temple would be a great protection to them. He is sending us the same message today:[8] "Behold it is my will, that all they who call on my name, and worship me according to mine everlasting Gospel, should gather together and stand in holy places" (D&C 101:22).

Isaiah told us what these holy places are and why we should stand in them and for them and "be not moved" (*see* D&C 45:32, 87:8):

> And the Lord will create upon every dwelling place of Mount Zion, and upon her assemblies, a cloud and smoke by day, and the shining of a flaming fire by night; for upon all the glory shall be a defense.
>
> And there shall be a tabernacle for a shadow in the daytime from the heat, and for a place of refuge, and for a covert from storm and from rain. (Isaiah 4:5-6)

The holy places are our homes (dwelling places), our churches (assemblies), and our temples (tabernacle). A holy place is also within us as we become holy like a temple. To the Jew the place where he stands is holy if he is righteous. From all of these holy places can flow living waters of growth and healing if we keep them holy and righteous like a temple. Therefore, they can be a defense, a refuge, and a covert against the doctrines of men and the temptations of Satan.

In a special temple address, Elder Vaughn Featherstone beautifully expressed the power and protection of the temple:

> Just as this is the dispensation of the fulness of times, so *it is also the dispensation of the fulness of evil . . .*
>
> *As the evil night darkens upon this generation, we must come to the temple for light and safety.* In our temples we find quiet, sacred havens where the storm, cannot penetrate to us. *There are hosts of unseen sentinels watching over and guarding our temples. Angels attend every door . . .*

Before the Savior comes the world will darken. There will come a period of time when even the elect will lose hope if they do not come to the temples . . .

There will be greater hosts of unseen beings in the temple. Prophets of old as well as those in this dispensation will visit the temples. Those who attend will feel their strength and feel their companionship . . .

The Savior will come and will honor his people. Those who are spared and prepared will be a temple loving people. They will know Him. They will cry out "blessed be the name of him that cometh in the name of the Lord, thou art my God and I will bless thee, thou art my God and I will exalt thee". . .

Come, come, oh come up to the temples of the Lord and abide in His presence.[9]

Protection from the Power of Satan While Ascending Mount Zion

A dramatic scene from the endowment is a warning from Satan. It is a warning of bad news, but hidden in the bad news is good news. The good news is that we are protected from the power of Satan if we will worship in the temple and keep temple covenants. Therefore to put on the robes of righteousness is to put on the whole protecting armor of righteousness (*see* 2 Nephi 1:23; Ephesians 6:13-17; D&C 27:15-18). Elder John A. Widtsoe expressed the protective power of the temple with the following words: "Men grow mighty under the results of temple service; women grow strong under it; the community increases in power; until the devil has less influence than he ever had before."[10]

Adam and some of his righteous posterity received a special blessing from the Lord. It was the blessing of having Satan cast out of their lives. Certainly this blessing removes a great barrier in tasting the good in the fruit of the tree of knowledge of good and evil and, ultimately, growing a tree of life within us. Perhaps this is why Enoch and his people could so completely live the celestial law. They must have been a temple-loving people because "they were blessed upon the mountains, and upon the high places" (Moses 7:17).

The many years of peace experienced by the Nephites after the appearance of the Savior was the result of having Satan cast out. This is implied in the Savior's sermon on the temple mount when He said "he that hath the spirit of contention . . . is of the devil. Behold . . . this is my doctrine that such things should be done away" (*see* 3 Nephi 11:29-30).

If the spirit of contention is done away in our lives then Satan, the source of that spirit, is also removed.

To receive this blessing of having Satan removed from our lives starts with obedience to the Lord and His prophets. Then the Lord will "disperse the powers of darkness from before [us]" (*see* D&C 21:5-6). The Savior's great message in His temple sermon at Galilee and Bountiful was the message of the great commandment: to love perfectly even with love of enemies. The power of love is the power that removes Satan from our lives. Our expression of love to God is obedience to Him and His messengers (*see* John 14:15). Then we will live in righteousness and Satan will have no influence upon us (*see* 1 Nephi 22:26).

If we are to prepare for the redemption of Zion, we must acquire pure hearts and live celestial laws as did Enoch's Zion. They grew up in the Lord "upon the high places," having Satan cast out of their lives. So it is with us today:

> But before the great day of the Lord shall come . . .
> Zion shall flourish upon the hills and rejoice upon the mountains, and shall be assembled together unto the place which I have appointed. (D&C 49:24-25)

Literally, Satan can be cast out of our lives, that we have no more disposition to do evil, if we stand in holy places, rejoicing upon the temple mountains.

Wells of Salvation from Heaven and Earth

Those doing and receiving the great missionary work in the world of spirits have great interest in temple activity on earth because redemption of the dead comes through temple ordinances (*see* D&C 138:58). These may be the unseen sentinels and beings mentioned by Elder Featherstone. There are many reports, some personal and sacred, which verify the reality of these beings.

A good friend of mine shared a special experience with me when an ancestor spent a weekend with him in close communion because my friend had started to do temple work for hundreds of his Moravian ancestors. Promises of help in my friend's personal life came from this visitor of the spirit world as my friend promised to continue the temple work. These angelic visitors have great interest in our temple activity because of their salvation and our salvation. "For we without them cannot be made perfect, neither can they without us be made perfect. Neither can they nor we be made perfect without those who have died in the Gospel also; for it is necessary . . . that a whole and complete and perfect union, and welding together of dispensations . . . the dispensation of the fulness of times" (D&C 128:18).

Concerning the work of those who have died in the gospel. Brigham Young said, "the names of those who have received the Gospel in the spirit will be revealed by the angels of God and the spirits of just men made perfect; also the place of their birth, the age in which they lived, and everything regarding them that is necessary to be recorded on earth, and they will then be saved so as to find admittance into the presence of God.[11]

Commenting on that statement, President Joseph Fielding Smith noted that, "President Brigham Young has said that during the Millennium those on the other side will work hand in hand with those in mortality and will furnish the names of the dead which we are unable to obtain through our research . . . I fully believe that many among the dead, those who are worthy, are even now engaged in compiling records and arranging information, if it has not already been done, for this very purpose.[12]

On both sides of the veil, this temple work of a "complete and perfect union" of all dispensations and generations is now occurring in this pre-millennial dispensation of the fulness of times. Even in the meridian dispensation, after the Resurrection of the Savior, this great work began when Paul stated "that they without us should not be made perfect" (*see* Hebrews 11:40). It will continue throughout the Millennium to its completion.

The Shepherds of Mount Zion Drink from the Well of Salvation

In my Church callings, I have had the opportunity to prepare newly called missionaries for their own temple endowment. In this capacity, I told these new elders that an important preparation for the mission field is going to the temple. There they will receive a special blessing of power and protection from the Lord. It is like filling their spiritual bowels with the protecting and healing water from the well of salvation before they go into the world to be the Lord's shepherds:

That thy servants may go forth from this house armed with thy power, and that thy name may be upon them, and thy glory be 'round about them, and thine angels have charge over them;

And from this place they may bear exceedingly great and glorious tidings, in truth, unto the ends of the earth, that they may know that this is thy work, and that thou hast put forth thy hand, to fulfill that which thou hast spoken by the mouths of the prophets, concerning the last days. (D&C 109:22-23)

In the temple, these new shepherds of the Lord learn that they will be taught from on high as true messengers of the true message:

Again, I say, hearken ye elders of my church, whom I have appointed: Ye are not sent forth to be taught, but to teach the children of men the things which I have put into your hands by the power of my Spirit;

And ye are to be taught from on high. Sanctify yourselves and ye shall be endowed with power, that ye may give even as I have spoken. (D&C 43:15-16)

Then the Lord completes the blessing with a promise of companionship and protection:

And whoso receiveth you, there I will be also, for I will go before your face. I will be on your right hand and on your left, and my spirit shall be in your hearts, and mine angels round about you, to bear you up. (D&C 84:88)

When missionaries replace fear of men with faith in the Lord, this blessing is fulfilled (see D&C 3:7-8). The Lord commanded those who carry His gospel to the world to become His friends even as He becomes their most important companion (see D&C 84:77). They are His friends when they faithfully carry His testimony with the spirit of prophecy and revelation.

I had the great privilege to travel to Poland when my daughter Lys-An finished her mission. When I passed the border control and cleared customs in Warsaw, I walked between two packed columns of waiting Poles. At the end of this walk was an angel named Lys-An. After we embraced, I stepped back and looked at her from head to foot. On her feet were the most pathetic shoes I had ever seen. It was as though she had yielded to the ubiquitous European cobblestones and latched two of them about her feet. All the dirt and dust of 16 months in Poland had collected upon them. Then I wept as I recalled scriptures about beautiful feet.

> How beautiful upon the mountains are the feet of him that bringeth good tidings, that publisheth peace; that bringeth good tidings of good, that publisheth salvation; that saith unto Zion, Thy God reigneth! (Isaiah 52:7; *see also* D&C 128:19; Mosiah 15:14)

> And O how beautiful upon the mountains were their feet!
> And again, how beautiful upon the mountains are the feet of those that are still publishing peace!
> And behold, I say unto you, this is not all, For O how beautiful upon the mountains are the feet of him that bringeth good tidings, that is the founder of peace, yea, even the Lord, who has redeemed his people; yea, him who has granted salvation unto his people. (Mosiah 15:15-16, 18)

I then understood that feet of true messengers are beautiful not because of the shoes they wear but because their feet carry the testimony of Jesus Christ. It is the spirit of prophecy and revelation within true messengers that makes them beautiful. This is why my missionary daughter was beautiful beyond her natural beauty. It was witnessed by her well-worn shoes covering feet that carried the testimony of Jesus Christ, bringing "glad tidings of good things" (*see* Romans 10:14-15) to the Polish people.

The testimony of Jesus Christ is the living water of salvation that will gush forth from us as we become true messengers of the Lord. This is the glorious calling of my young missionary friends who are about to receive their temple endowment and dip into the well of salvation. For out of their bellies "shall flow rivers of living water." That is to say, "the Spirit" (*see* John 7:37-39), the spirit of prophecy and revelation. These beautiful missionaries are about to have beautiful feet that will carry the testimony of Jesus Christ: "And again, how beautiful upon the mountains are the feet of those who shall hereafter publish peace, yea from this time henceforth and forever!" (Mosiah 15:17).

When full-time missionaries are released, the full-time nature of this blessing is released. However some of the best missionary work a returned missionary can do, maintaining the spirit of this blessing, is to return to the temple often and do the work needed in the world of spirits. In doing this work, they refill their spiritual bowls with the living waters of the spirit of prophecy and revelation. President Kimball extended the missionary calling when he said, "I feel the same sense of urgency about temple work for the dead as I do about missionary work for the living, since they are basically one and the same."[13]

Whether we are returned missionaries or not. regardless of where we live, or what we do, the blessings, protection, and power of the temple can be ours if we become the Lord's covenant people in His temple. Then we become His shepherds who lead His sheep to the well of salvation. To seek the Lord and drink from His wells of salvation is a full-time calling, not only for missionaries but for all of God's children.

The Distilling Dews of Mount Zion

We drink of the water of the wells of salvation as the water of the firmament comes to the land of Israel. For a short season it comes in great bursts of rain, then gushes forth from dry ground. For the rest of the year, it distills upon the land as dew. In the temple, sometimes spiritual truths will gush forth to our understanding. More often these truths will slowly distill upon us like dew, keeping pace with our growing up.

Standing on the summit of Mount Carmel, overlooking the great view of the fertile Jezreel valley below and the misty Mediterranean to the west, I read a scripture that refers to this sacred natural temple with imagery of the distilling of the dews of eternal life: "Now, what do we hear in the gospel which we have received? . . . A voice of gladness for the living and the dead; How beautiful upon the mountains are the feet of those who bring glad tidings of good things, and say unto Zion: Behold, thy God reigneth! As the dews of Carmel, so shall the knowledge of God descend upon them" (D&C 128:19).

What distills upon us in the temple, as we come to understand the holy virtues of the endowment, is the "doctrine of the priesthood," which is the endowment of the quality of charity. "Let they bowels also be full of charity towards all men, and to the household of faith, and let virtue garnish thy thoughts unceasingly; then shall thy confidence wax strong in the presence of God; and the doctrine of the priesthood shall distil upon thy soul as the dews from heaven" (D&C 121:45; see also verse 46). Notice in these verses that the virtue of charity, the great doctrine of the fulness of the priesthood, leads to constant companionship of the Holy Ghost and confidence in the presence of God. This is the great and last promise of the temple.

The Power of the Lamb: A River of Love

In the temple, whether missionary or regular Church member, we continue to be taught from on high and endowed with power. This "power of the Lamb of God, descending upon the saints" in the dispensation of the fulness of times was foreseen by the prophet Nephi. "And it came to pass that I, Nephi, beheld the power of the Lamb of God, that it descended upon the saints of the church of the Lamb, and upon the covenant people of the Lord, who were scattered upon all the face of the earth; and they were armed with righteousness and with the power of God in great glory" (1 Nephi 14:14).

As we drink from the well of salvation in the temple and are healed by its living water flowing into our lives, our parched minds and hearts become refreshed with the words and blessings of the fulness of the gospel. This is why Peter, foretelling our dispensation, said, "Repent ye therefore, and be converted, that your sins may be blotted out, when the times of refreshing shall come from the presence of the Lord" (Acts 3:19).

In his book *House of Glory,* Michael Wilcox described the refreshing river of the temple. "Latter-day temples are the source of a powerful, deeply refreshing river. It is a river of peace, revelation, truth, light and priesthood power. But above all else, it is a river of love.[14] The power of the Lamb of God that distills upon and flows into us from the wells and dews of Mount Zion is the power of the Savior's love. This is the power that will sustain us as we ascend to the summit.

13

The Salt and Light of the Covenant

Not far from the city of Krakow in southern Poland is a large salt deposit under the town of Wieliczka. For centuries, this salt was mined from deep subterranean caverns. The mining was begun in the 14th century under the direction of King Kazimierz the Great. He permitted the miners to take a small, personal portion of salt when they came to the surface. This made the miners wealthy because salt, being an important preservative, was an expensive commodity.

Today the salt mine is a tourist attraction, with scenes from Polish history and the history of the mine preserved in salt carved by the miners. The grand carving is an entire cathedral. Even the chandeliers are salt crystals. The walls are carved with scenes from the life of Christ. Past and current use of part of the mine is a sanatorium for respiratory illnesses because of the medicinal effects of the salt.

After visiting this mine, I reflected on the preserving and healing qualities of salt. I recalled the scriptural uses of salt, and include them in the scriptural temple because the temple purges and preserves, by healing, then sealing like salt.

Salt was often used in Levitical rituals as a symbol of purging, preserving, healing, and flavoring, through covenants with the Lord. "All the heave offerings of the holy things, which the children of Israel offer unto the Lord, have I given thee, and thy sons and thy daughters with thee, by a statute for ever; *it is a covenant of salt for ever before the Lord unto thee and to thy seed with thee*" (Numbers 18:19).

Berith, the Hebrew word for covenant, is derived from the word meaning "to eat with salt."

The Abrahamic Covenant: An Everlasting Covenant of Salt and Light

The Abrahamic covenant, which has been preserved as a covenant between God and those who are obedient to His Gospel as an everlasting covenant (*see* Genesis 17:7), is a covenant of salt. This covenant has four main parts. The first three are blessings from the Lord. The last part is our obligation in order to receive and share the stated blessings.

To remember the parts of this covenant, I use mnemonic "P" words:

> Property (*see* Genesis 13:14-15)
> Posterity (*see* Genesis 22:17)
> Priesthood (*see* Genesis 17:7; Abraham 2:9, 11)
> Proselyte (*see* Genesis 22:18; Abraham 2:9, 11)

I take liberty with the word *proselyte*, using it to reveal a deeper meaning. The word *proselyte* can be considered a composite of three words: Pro-Sel-Light. Sel is the French word for salt, so in my mind proselyte means *"for salt and light."* The *scriptural temple* clearly states the obligation of those accepting the "everlasting covenant" to be for salt and light: "When men are called unto mine everlasting Gospel, and covenant with an everlasting covenant, *they are accounted as the salt of the earth and the savor of men*" (D&C 101:39). In the sermon on the mount, the Savior said, "*Ye are the salt of the earth . . . Ye are the light of the world*" (Matthew 5:13-14).

Salt only loses its savor when it becomes contaminated by other elements. Therefore, we keep our savor as long as God is our God and we yield our hearts to Him. We who keep the everlasting covenants of the temple are the pure salt that flavors the earth, because we preserve through our obedience the everlasting gospel in its purity and fullness. Referring to the importance of covenants that are to be preserved and obeyed, and the type of relationship they require, the Savior said, "*Have salt in yourselves* and have peace one with another" (*see* Mark 9:50; *see also* Colossians 4:61).

When we take the everlasting gospel and its everlasting covenants to the world, teaching the love of God, those who feel and accept it savor the sweetness of the fruit of the tree of life. Symbolic of the sweet fruit surrounding a seed of new life, those who eat the entire fruit will plant a seed from this fruit within them to grow a new tree of life.

This fruit was never meant to be hidden under a bushel. Therefore, we must keep our part of the Abrahamic covenant and let the love of God shed forth and be savored because we have a covenant of salt and light within us.

Those who hear and feel our testimonies of Christ *"as a lamp that burneth"* (*see* Isaiah 62:1), *taste the light* (*see* Alma 32:35) and *feel the power* (*see* 2 Nephi 33:1) of the Holy Spirit as His witness sheds forth (*see* Romans 5:5; D&C 100:8) in their hearts. In His Sermon on the Temple Mount, the Savior directed us to hold up His light to the world: *"Therefore, hold up your light that it may shine unto the world. Behold I am the light which ye shall hold up*—that which ye have seen me do" (3 Nephi 18:24).

Christ's Shepherds: The Savor and Saviors of Men

The Lord counseled Joseph Smith, Lyman Wight, and Parley Pratt with the following advice concerning the salvation and redemption of the saints in Missouri:

> Verily I say unto you, my friends, behold, I will give unto you a revelation and commandment, that you may know how to act in the discharge of your duties concerning the salvation and redemption of your brethren, who have been scattered on the land of Zion. . . .
>
> And by hearkening to observe all the words which I, the Lord their God, shall speak unto them, they shall never cease to prevail until the kingdoms of the world are subdued under my feet, and the earth is given unto the saints, to possess it forever and ever. . . .
>
> *For they [the obedient Saints] were set to be a light unto the world, and to be the saviors of men.* (D&C 103:1, 7, 9)

While this revelation was directed to a specific need in Missouri, it has general application as we learn our duty concerning the salvation and redemption of our brethren. *When we let the love of Christ and His gospel shine from us by sacrificing our own interests to edify others, then we are not only the savor of men but the saviors of men.* This truth has direct application when we perform the temple saving and exalting ordinances for the dead.

During His meridian ministry, the Savior taught the truth about our role in being saviors of men:

> He that entereth by the door is the shepherd of the sheep. . . .
> Verily, verily, I say unto you, I am the door of the sheep. . . .

I am the door; by me if any man enter in, he shall be saved, and shall go in and out, and find pasture. . . .

I am the good shepherd: the good shepherd giveth his life for the sheep. (John 10:2, 7, 9, 11)

In calling us to be the saviors of men, Christ is calling us to be shepherds. The calling to be a shepherd is what Christ desires most of His disciples (*see* Matthew 9:35-38; John 21:17). The shepherd stays with the flock. He knows all the sheep by name and loves them. He feeds them by leading them gently to green pastures. He seeks the one lost sheep and brings it back to the fold. Instead of fleeing from wolves, he gives his life for the sheep.

The shepherd leads the sheep with a mighty staff. It is an iron rod, a mighty sword, even the word of God (*see* Ephesians 6:17). The word of God protects the sheep from wolves and penetrates the hearts of the sheep, moving them to righteousness by the power of the Holy Spirit. To be a good shepherd (a true messenger, the savor and savior of men, the salt and light of the everlasting covenant), the shepherd must have compassion for the sheep and lead them with a gentle iron rod. This staff is a scepter of authority and power, even the "sceptre" of Jesus Christ (*see* Numbers 24:17), but it must be used with the doctrine of the priesthood and the power of the Holy Spirit, the spirit of prophecy and revelation (*see* 2 Peter 1:21).

The Burden Is Light when Climbing Mount Zion

Oliver Cowdery received the call to Pro-Sel-Light in the following revelation:

Now, as you have asked behold, I say unto you, keep my commandments, and *seek to bring forth and establish the cause of Zion;* . . . and if you desire, you shall be the means of doing much good in this generation.

And if thou wilt inquire, thou shalt know mysteries which are great and marvelous; . . . that thou mayest bring many to the knowledge of the truth, yea, convince them of the error of their ways. (D&C 6:6, 8, 11)

This revelation evokes the Prophet Joseph Smith's call to be true messengers as our imperative duty (*see* D&C 123:11-13).

When we covenant in the temple to accept the law of consecration, we covenant to become the salt, the preservers, of the Abrahamic covenant. We covenant to sacrifice all to establish the cause of Zion, that the glorious view of the kingdom of God will shine as a great saving light, for a "great benefit" (Mosiah 8:18) to the world. The greatest benefit and greatest miracle of all is that by the power of Christ we and all our fellowbeings can become the sons and daughters of God with eternal life (*see* D&C 45:9).

Since being a true messenger is not always easy or comfortable (ask any missionary), perhaps there was a deeper message for those who labor to climb Mount Zion when the Lord said:

> Come unto me, all ye that labour and are heavy laden, and I will give you rest.
>
> *Take my yoke upon you,* and learn of me; for I am meek and lowly in heart: and ye shall find rest unto your souls.
>
> For my yoke is easy, and my burden is light. (Matthew 11:28-30)

Our burden in the Abrahamic covenant is to be the salt (savor) and light (saviors) of the world, by emulating the Savior.

Heavy laden, laboring to rid ourselves of excess baggage in climbing Mount Zion, we find our rest in the Savior. For His rest or fullness, the burden we carry is to be the salt that preserves the full savor of the covenant and the light that shines as the Savior of the covenant. This burden we learned in Primary when we enthusiastically sang, "*I'll be a sunbeam for Him.*"

The burden to be a true messenger of the true message is a great responsibility. However, it is a responsibility that is joyfully carried because of the exquisite savor of joy and the taste of light (*see* Alma 32:35) that dissolves bitterness and darkness as we labor to save our fellow men (*see* Alma 36:24-26). Ammon expressed this exquisite savor of joy, even to the point his joy was "full," as he and his brethren had been "instruments in his hands of doing this great and marvelous work" (*see* Alma 26:14-16). Ammon's burden for this full joy was to bring the Lamanites from "everlasting darkness" to "everlasting light," freeing them from the darkness of the pains and chains of hell (*see* Alma 26:13-14).

The "instrument in His hand" is a trump, similar to the trump in the hand of the angel Moroni. The trump is His true messengers sounding "long and loud" (D&C 43:18) the true message "both day and night" (D&C 24:12). This trump heralds "with the sound of rejoicing, as with the voice of a trump" (D&C 29:4), lifting up "voices as with the sound of a trump" (D&C 42:6), even "the trump of God" saying, "Ye saints arise and live" (D&C 43:18).

Elder John A. Widtsoe said that not only in the mission field but in temple work we can savor exquisite joy in the great and marvelous works of redemption:

> *Men may rise through temple work to high levels of character and spiritual joy.* Once only may a person receive the temple endowment for himself, but innumerable times may he receive it for those gone from the earth. *Whenever he does so, he performs an unselfish act for which no earthly recompense is available. He tastes in part the sweet joy of saviorhood. He rises toward the stature of the Lord Jesus Christ* who died for all.[1]

Part of the joy of redemption Adam and Eve tasted was the same sweet joy of charity we taste as saviors to our fellowmen, when we offer them the joy of their redemption by our works. Therefore, that our joy may be full, let us become the "seed of Abraham," keepers and pre-servers of the everlasting covenant, and do the works of Abraham:

> This promise is yours also, because ye are of Abraham, and the promise was made unto Abraham; and *by this law is the continuation of the works of my Father, wherein he glorifieth himself.*
> *Go ye, therefore, and do the works of Abraham; enter ye into my law and ye shall be saved.* (D&C 132:31-32)

Preserving the Covenant: The Turning of Hearts

It is deeply significant that Malachi 4:5-6, the last recorded revela-tion in the Old Testament dispensation, became the first recorded reve-lation in the dispensation of the fulness of times (*see* D&C 2:1-3). Moroni's words to Joseph Smith, declaring the coming of Elijah, por-tended the restoration of this everlasting covenant in our dispensation: "And he shall plant in the hearts of the children the promises made to the fathers, and the hearts of the children shall turn to their fathers" (D&C 2:2).

This verse is a reflection of Adam seeking messengers from his Father. His heart was turned to the Father for truth and salvation. So should our hearts be turned to the Father and His true messengers who have received the promises. "The fathers" who received the promises are the patriarchal fathers, such as Adam and Abraham (*see* D&C 27:9-11). When we hear and respond to the voice of the Father in our hearts, these promises will be written or planted in our hearts through spiritual, everlasting covenants with the Father (*see* Jeremiah 31:31, 33; Hebrews 8:10).

The turning of the heart to God the Father starts at a very young age. Shortly after birth, we receive a name and a blessing as the hearts of our earthly fathers turn toward us as newborn in mortality. In Primary, our hearts begin to turn toward our Heavenly Father as we learn that we are His children. At baptism, we take upon us a new name. It is the name of Christ, the Father of our spiritual rebirth. As we emulate His name, Christ will spiritually beget us with a mighty change of heart. Our changed hearts will then turn to our Father in Heaven, because with this new heart we can again become the sons and daughters of God (Mosiah 5:7; 27:25).

Later, the blessing at the hand of a patriarch is an extension of the blessing and promises of the patriarch fathers, who received the promises by covenant from God. In this patriarchal blessing, we learn of our royal lineage and our obligation to become the seed of Abraham and to do the works of Abraham by proselyting the gospel. In this special way, the promises of the fathers are planted in our hearts.

When a young man receives the priesthood, he receives the oath and covenant of the Father. He is given the obligation to carry the keys of salvation to his fellowmen and his fathers by becoming a true messenger of the Father. The Father turns his heart towards those priesthood holders who become kings of righteousness, promising all that the Father hath.

When a young man and a young woman receive their temple endowments, they make covenants to be the salt and light of the world in bringing salvation for the living and the dead, and building up the kingdom of God. With these covenants written in their hearts, they turn to their fathers and fellowmen as kings and queens of righteousness. When a man and a woman enter the Holy Order of matrimony, they promise to turn their hearts first to each other, then to their children, planting in the hearts of these children the promises that they have received. Thus "great things" are required at the hand of these mothers and fathers (*see* D&C 29:48). Because of these promises and their parents' love, these children will turn their hearts to their earthly parents, and then to their Heavenly Parents.

When we perform temple ordinances and keep temple covenants, our hearts will not only turn to our Father in Heaven but eventually will be sealed to Him. To advance this great sealing of hearts, this welding link, the hearts of the fathers will be turned to us, their gospel seed (*see* Malachi 4:6) because we have accepted the obligation of the everlasting covenant. They turn their hearts to us with the spirit of Elias and Elijah to help the promises planted in our hearts turn to a mighty change of heart. This change of heart will turn our hearts to our fathers ("their fathers") who await the promises in spirit prison and to our fellowmen who are still in the prison house of mortality (*see* D&C 123:12).

The Prophet Joseph F. Smith, in his great vision of the redemption of the dead, saw the faithful spirits of the prophets and elect of God organized to continue pronouncing the Abrahamic covenant in the world of spirits. Elijah had an important role proselyting in the world of spirits at this time:

> The Prophet Elijah was to plant in the hearts of the children [in spirit prison] the promises made to their fathers [the patriarchs],
> *Foreshadowing the great work to be done in the temples of the Lord in the dispensation of the fulness of times, for the redemption of the dead, and the sealing of the children to their parents,* lest the whole earth be smitten with a curse and utterly wasted at his coming. (D&C 138:47-48)

Therefore, the hearts of many of our fathers had turned to us long before our hearts began to turn to them.

After explaining the allegory of the olive tree taught by Lehi to his "brethren," Nephi reminded them of the obligation of the "seed" of Abraham:

> Wherefore, our father hath not spoken of our seed alone, but also of all the houses of Israel, *pointing to the covenant which should be fulfilled in the latter days; which covenant the Lord made to our father Abraham,* saying: In thy seed shall all the kindreds of the earth be blessed. (1 Nephi 15:18)

Nephi had already explained to his brethren that in the latter days the fulness of the gospel of the Messiah would come to the Gentiles, and from the Gentiles to the remnant of the seed of Lehi.

This "pro-sel-lighting," to turn and seal hearts in temples, is our obligation in the Abrahamic covenant both in this world and in the world of spirits:

And thou shalt be a blessing unto thy seed after thee, that in their hands they shall bear this ministry and Priesthood unto all nations;

And I will bless them through thy name; for as many as receive this Gospel shall be called after thy name, and shall be accounted to thy seed. . . . for I give unto thee a promise that this right shall continue in thee, and in thy seed after thee . . . shall all the families of the earth be blessed, even with the blessings of the Gospel, which are the blessings of salvation, even of life eternal. (Abraham 2:9-11)

The charge to "pro-sel-light" was committed by the Lord "into [the] hands" (*see* D&C 110:16) of the elders of the Church in this dispensation, fulfilling the declaration to Abraham that "in their hands" (Abraham 2:9) the ministry and priesthood would go forth. The Lord is still telling the "elders of [His] church" today that the keys of salvation for our waiting fathers and fellow men are in our hands if the promises are planted in our hearts by the power of the Holy Spirit:

Again I say, hearken ye elders of my church, whom I have appointed: Ye are not sent forth to be taught, but to teach the children of men the things which I have put *into your hands* by the power of my Spirit. (D&C 43:15)

Our obligation in the everlasting Abrahamic covenant, as the gospel seed of Abraham, is to bear the ministry and priesthood unto all nations. We are to bless all the families and kindreds, from the beginning to the end of the earth, with the blessings of salvation, even eternal life. Those who embrace the fulness of the gospel will bless all the kindreds and families of the earth, dead or alive, with the blessings of eternal life through missionary work, both on earth and in the world of spirits. The purpose of this missionary work is to bring souls to base camp and prepare them to climb Mount Zion to do temple work. Through temple ordinances and covenants, all the families (sealed families) and kindreds (sealed relatives) of the earth shall be blessed with the fulness of the gospel.

We who embrace the everlasting covenant in the last days have the obligation of performing this temple work to bless all the kindreds and families who cannot do this work for themselves. This is our obligation and privilege because the dispensation of the fulness of times is "the dispensation of the fulness of the priesthood,"[2] therefore temples.

Thus the covenant with Abraham will be fulfilled in the latter days. By teaching the importance of the temple and the obligation of the everlasting covenant to our children, the works of Abraham and the gospel of Abraham will continue, fulfilling the promise pronounced by Elias in the Kirtland Temple: "After this, Elias appeared, and *committed the dispensation of the gospel of Abraham, saying that in us and our seed all generations after us should be blessed*" (D&C 110:12).

Grown-Up in the Lord: Receiving a Fulness of the Abrahamic Covenant

The Abrahamic covenant is a covenant of salt because it preserves in purity the knowledge and keys, thus the power of the priesthood of God. This knowledge and these keys are in the ordinances and covenants that we make in the temple, including the crowning covenant, the everlasting covenant of marriage. These keys are the "key to the knowledge of God" (D&C 84:19), which unlock the power to become as God, with eternal lives.

To become as God we must develop a divine nature. We develop this divine nature by growing up in the temple. There we acquire, through the power of Christ, all of the "graces" and "truths" of His divine nature. *Symbolically, in the endowment, we put on a divine nature as we are clothed with the robes of righteousness.* We are fully clothed when we have the divine nature of charity, which is fully practiced in the celestial law of consecration, the virtue and holiness of oneness (*see* D&C 38:24-27).

It is interesting that with the verses of scripture most often quoted as a calling to those who wish to become true messengers, carrying salt and light to the world, the graces of a divine nature are again mentioned:

> Remember faith, virtue, knowledge, temperance, patience, brotherly kindness, godliness, charity, humility, diligence. (D&C 4:6)

The endowment teaches us that as we become more righteous (symbolically more completely clothed in the robes of righteousness), we receive more priesthood power until we receive a fulness of the priesthood. When we receive and keep the fulness of the Melchizedek Priesthood in the temple, *we become kings and queens of righteousness* (Melchiah *means Jehovah is king,* Zadok *means righteous*),[3] truly emulating the Savior. The Savior taught the Nephites at the temple of the land Bountiful their obligation to "pro-sel-light" by emulating Him. "Verily, verily, I say unto you this is my gospel; and ye know the things that ye must do in my church: for the works which ye have seen me do that shall ye also do" (3 Nephi 27:21).

When we receive the fulness of the priesthood, then we receive the fulness of the Abrahamic covenant—the "oath and covenant of the Father" (*see* D&C 84:40), for "all that [the] Father hath shall be given unto him" (D&C 84:38). With this priesthood we have access to great power:

> God having sworn . . . with an oath . . . that *every one being ordained after this order and calling should have power, by faith, to break mountains, to divide the seas, to dry up waters, to turn them out of their course;*
>
> To put at defiance the armies of nations, to divide the earth, to break every band, *to stand in the presence of God; to do all things according to his will, according to his command,* subdue principalities and powers, and this by the will of the Son of God. (JST Genesis 14:30-31)

However, we are expected to practice what we learn in the temple and exercise the power of the priesthood in everyday life, with "kindness and pure knowledge" (D&C 121:41-42), and to succor the weak (*see* D&C 81:6). We are to use priesthood power only in accordance with the will and counsel of God, or "we shall have no power" (*see* D&C 136:19; 3:4).

Receiving signs and wonders with the power of the priesthood comes only by faith, as a benefit for our fellowmen and the glory of God. What a contrast this truth is with the practice of priestcraft in the world today: "Wherefore, I the Lord, am not pleased with those among you who have sought after signs and wonders for faith, and not for the good of men unto my glory" (D&C 63:12).

By following the counsel of the Lord for His glory we will grow up in the temple as the salt and light to the world. There we will receive the fullness of the Abrahamic Covenant. And thus, by "growing up" in the Lord in His temple, we become the salt and light of the earth, blessed with the powers of heaven.

14

Views from the Summit of Mount Zion

> If a writer's aim be logical conviction, he must spare no logical pains, not merely to be understood, but to escape being misunderstood; where his object is to move by suggestion, to cause to imagine, then let him assail the soul of his reader as the wind assails an aeolian harp. If there be music in my reader, I would gladly wake it.[1]

I hope the music of the scriptural temple has awakened the music within our souls, and that the temple becomes the most powerful spiritual motivation in our lives. I hope the heralding and mellifluous message from the trumpet of Moroni, which declares "come unto Christ," will draw us to the temple as the power of Christ draws us to Him (*see* D&C 88:63). There we will enjoy the entire composition.

Mount Zion:
The Ever-expanding Scriptural Temple

As we have journeyed through the scriptural temple, we have seen consistent temple messages through time and on both hemispheres. The messages are in the stick of Judah and the stick of Joseph. They are in the scriptures of the dispensation of the fulness of times, now one in our hands (*see* Ezekiel 37:16-17). *To read, ponder and pray is only the beginning of searching the scriptures (see John 5:39). Temple worship leads to the completion of this search for eternal life* as we come to see the great view of this ever-expanding *scriptural temple* through the spirit of prophecy and revelation.

A clear temple message woven through the scriptures explains how we make the mighty change in preparation to meet God. Since the law of Moses, a law of sanctification through atonement, was centered in the temple, even more should the fulness of the gospel in the dispensation of the fulness of times be centered in the temple. This is where we prepare to meet God.

The scriptural temple's warning message for us today is the same as in past dispensations. As the ancient Tower of Babel was in contrast to the tower or staircase seen by Jacob, today, Mount Babylon is in contrast to Mount Zion. One is formed by the hand of man for the purpose of selfish idolatry. The other is formed by the hand of God for the exaltation of man. We must choose which mount we will climb. We cannot stand on both (*see* 2 Corinthians 6:14-18).

The scriptures tell us of the fate of both Mount Babylon and Mount Zion in the last days:

Mount Babylon:

Behold, I am against thee [Babylon], O destroying [corrupting] mountain, saith the Lord, which destroyest all the earth: and I will stretch out mine hand upon thee, and roll thee down from the rocks, and will make thee a burnt mountain.

And they shall not take of thee a stone for a corner, nor a stone for foundations; but thou shalt be desolate for ever, saith the Lord. (Jeremiah 51:25-26; *compare* Isaiah 28:16)

Mount Zion:

Thou sawest till that a stone was cut out without hands, which smote the image upon his feet that were of iron and clay [Mount Babylon] and brake them to pieces.

. . . and the stone that smote the image became a great mountain, and filled the whole earth. (Daniel 2:34-35; *see also* D&C 109:72)

If we cannot stand on both Mount Babylon and Mount Zion, nor serve both God and mammon, then the song in our hearts should be the song of the elders of Israel:

O Babylon, O Babylon, we bid thee farewell; We're going to the mountains of Ephraim to dwell.[2]

The Great View of a Better World

As the stone cut without hands rolls forth to become the great Mount Zion that fills the whole earth, I hope we feel the urgency and responsibility for the preparation of the redemption of Zion and the gathering together in one all things in Christ. This preparation and gathering must pass up the spiritual Mount Zion, the mountain of the House of the Lord. It is this spiritual mount that each of us must climb, to see and be part of the great "gathering in one" of the Lord, that we will be prepared for the redemption of Zion. We can only climb Mount Zion with the Savior's rope: a "perfect brightness" and "full assurance" of hope in the Atonement of our guide Jesus Christ.

The prophet Ether exhorted the people of Coriantumr to have faith and hope in Christ for the great view of a "better world." Then, like the Apostle Paul (*see* Hebrews 6:18-19), Ether gave the image of the climb of Mount Zion to obtain the summit and see the great view:

> Wherefore, *whoso believeth in God might with surety hope for a better world, yea, even a place at the right hand of God, which hope cometh of faith,* maketh an anchor to the souls of men, which would make them sure and steadfast, always abounding in good works, being led to glorify God. (Ether 12:4)

Once we have seen even glimpses of the great view of this "better world," we will want to "lay aside the things of this world, and seek for the things of a better" (D&C 25:10). We will have no more disposition to do evil, but to do good continually:

> *Because of the Spirit of the Lord Omnipotent, which has wrought a mighty change in us, or in our hearts, that we have no more disposition to do evil, but to do good continually.*
>
> And we, ourselves, also, through the infinite goodness of God, and the manifestations of his Spirit, have great views. (Mosiah 5:2-3)

To Reach the Summit: Come Unto Christ

When we glimpse the great view, we will hear Moroni and the Holy Spirit calling us to come unto Christ. We will better understand the greatness of our Savior and His Atonement. The covering He provides for the nakedness of our fall is the garment of salvation. As we climb back to the presence of our Father in Heaven, the Savior clothes us with the robes of righteousness. As the Savior said: "Solomon, in all his glory, was not arrayed like one of these [lilies of the field] . . . Even so will I clothe you" (3 Nephi 13:28, 30). We should seek this holy covering of our Savior, eschewing the covering of the flesh, "the garments spotted with the flesh" (*see* D&C 36:6; Jude 1:23).

We are clothed in Christ's holy covering when we learn to take His name upon us and become His spiritually begotten children. Taking His name upon us and becoming His children is the key that will unlock the mysteries of God for our honor and glory. This spiritual birth to a mighty change only occurs through true temple worship where the fulness of the Melchizedek Priesthood is found (*see* D&C 84:19). For "*therein are the keys of the holy priesthood ordained, that you may receive honor and glory*" (*see* D&C 124:31, 34). Without Christ's covering, we could not climb Mount Zion to obtain the keys and make the mighty change necessary to return to our Father in Heaven.

In climbing Mount Zion, we will be endowed or filled with charity, the pure love of Christ (*see* Psalm 24:3-4). With this crowning quality, through the power of the Atonement, we will become "new creatures" with the mighty change of heart. This is the great paradigm shift of the gospel, and it occurs only within the temple paradigm. In the temple, by the matchless power of an infinite Atonement, our hearts and bodies are renewed and sanctified as we perform the ordinances and keep the covenants of His Holy Order. Paul, in verses laden with temple meaning, clearly understood the importance of being drawn to Christ with "true hearts" (real intent, broken hearts), that our hearts and bodies be purified by Him in the "house of God":

And having an high priest over the house of God;
Let us draw near with a true heart in full assurance of faith, having *our hearts sprinkled* [purified] from an evil conscience, and *our bodies washed* with pure water [the pure blood of Christ]. (Hebrews 10:21-22)

To be drawn to Christ with a true heart and to receive His gift of perfection, we must repent by obedience and sacrifice to His covenants:

For, behold, the Lord your Redeemer suffered death in the flesh; wherefore *he suffered the pain of all men, that all men might repent and come unto him.*

And he hath risen again from the dead, *that he might bring all men unto him, on conditions of repentance.*

And how great is his joy in the soul that repenteth! (D&C 18:11-13)

I hope we are men and women to match His mountain and His message through repentance. If so, we will receive the gift of the spirit of prophecy and revelation, even the more sure word of prophecy. With this gift, we will not only see the great view but become part of it. So, as Joseph Smith implied, let us climb to the summit: *"It is one thing to be on the mount and hear the excellent voice. &c., &c., and another to hear the voice declare to you, You have a part and lot in that kingdom."*[3]

The Bond of the Great Covenant

Through the *scriptural temple,* we begin to understand the importance of making *and* keeping covenants with the Lord. The Lord requires that we make covenants with each other and with Him, that we may be bound together as one, by the power of love:

> And I will bring you out from the people, and will gather you out of the countries wherein ye are scattered, with a mighty hand, and with a stretched out arm, and with fury poured out.
>
> And I will bring you into the wilderness of the people, and *there will I plead with you face to face.*
>
> Like as I pleaded with your fathers in the wilderness of the land of Egypt, so will I plead with you, saith the Lord God.
>
> And I will cause you to pass under the rod [be straitened by His word or commandments], and *I will bring you into the bond of the covenant.* (Ezekiel 20:34-37)

Again, our Guide and Savior led the way. He passed under the rod (the will) of His Father, that He would be brought into the bond of love, the covenant with His Father.

The greatest covenant of all was completed on the northern end of Mount Moriah, a natural and most sacred altar, and on the nearby Mount of Olives, where Jesus began the process of taking upon Himself the sins of all mankind. This covenant was between the Father and the Son:

> But, behold, my Beloved Son, which was my Beloved and Chosen from the beginning, said unto me—Father, thy will be done, and the glory be thine forever. (Moses 4:2; *see also* 3 Nephi 27:13-14).

> And this is the will of Him that sent me, that every one which seeth the Son, and believeth on Him, may have everlasting life; and I will raise him up at the last day. (John 6:40)

On this sacred Mount Moriah altar, Jesus Christ completed the covenant with His Father. Because of the bond of perfect love for us and His Father, He sacrificed His life that we might live.

> Which suffering caused myself, even God, the greatest of all, to tremble because of pain, and to bleed at every pore, and to suffer both body and spirit—and would that I might not drink the bitter cup, and shrink—
> Nevertheless, glory be to the Father, and I partook and finished my preparations unto the children of men. (D&C 19:18-19)

> I have glorified thee on the earth: I have finished the work which thou gavest me to do.
> And now, O Father, glorify thou me with thine own self with the glory which I had with thee before the world was. (John 17:4-5)

> When Jesus therefore had received the vinegar, he said, It is finished: and he bowed his head, and gave up the ghost. (John 19:30)

As the great example of one who keeps his covenants, Christ "suffered the will of the Father in all things from the beginning" (3 Nephi 11:11).

Nephi recognized the covenant relationship which exists between the Father and the Son, and the importance of the same relationship between us and the Son when he said, "For the Lord covenanteth with none save it be with them that repent and believe in his Son, who is the Holy One of Israel" (2 Nephi 30:2).

By keeping the fulness of our covenants with the Son, we keep the covenants that He kept with His Father. We do the will of the Father by entering, in the name of the Son, the narrow gate and following the strait path to eternal life.

The fulness of the bond of the covenants, in pressing forward with a steadfastness in Christ, feasting upon His words, and becoming spiritually begotten by Him, occurs in the temple. The effect of steadfastness in temple worship is to learn how to love God and all men. This is the "bond of the covenant," and this quality helps us endure to the end and seals us for eternal life:

> Know ye not that he was holy? But notwithstanding he being holy, he showeth unto the children of men that, according to the flesh he humbleth himself before the Father, and witnesseth unto the Father that he would be obedient unto him in keeping his commandments. . . .

And again, *it showeth unto the children of men the straitness of the path, and the narrowness of the gate, by which they should enter, he having set the example before them.*

And he said unto the children of men: *Follow thou me. Wherefore, my beloved brethren, can we follow Jesus save we shall be willing to keep the commandments of the Father? . . .*

And I heard a voice from the Father, saying: Yea, the words of my Beloved are true and faithful. *He that endureth to the end, the same shall be saved.*

And now, my beloved brethren, I know by this that unless a man shall endure to the end, in following the example of the Son of the living God, he cannot be saved. . . .

And now, my beloved brethren, after ye have gotten into this strait and narrow path, I would ask if all is done? Behold I say unto you, Nay; . . .

Wherefore, *ye must press forward with a steadfastness in Christ, having a perfect brightness of hope, and a love of God and all men. Wherefore, if ye shall press forward, feasting upon the word of Christ, and endure to the end, behold, thus saith the Father: Ye shall have eternal life.* (2 Nephi 31:7, 9-10, 15-16, 19-20)

Steadfastly Seeking the Summit: Being Drawn to Mount Zion

There is no written guideline for temple activity. An unwritten tradition is temple attendance once a month. However, as my understanding of the importance of the temple has grown, my desire to be in it has greatly increased. I now understand Luke's declaration of Christ in the temple when he said,

He taught *daily* in the temple . . .
For all the people were very attentive to hear him. (Luke 19:47-48)

If we knew that Christ were teaching daily in the temple, would we not eagerly and attentively go to hear Him? Yet, is He not still teaching daily in the temple? Is He not, through the power of the Holy Spirit in the temple, expounding all the scriptures, both great and small, unto one (*see* 3 Nephi 23:6, 14; 26:1) scriptural temple by expounding the things concerning Himself? (*See* Luke 24:27.) I wish I could go daily, but I would feel spiritually hungry if I did not attend the temple as much as I attend church on the Sabbath.

If, for reasons of inaccessibility, we cannot visit the House of the Lord, then we should at least make ourselves, our homes, and our assemblies as temples. Then the Lord, through His Holy Spirit, will visit us. Ascending to holiness in His house and our house is proof to the Lord of our desire to draw near to Him. We need to be drawn to the temple like King David: *"One thing I have desired of the Lord, that will I seek after; that I may dwell in the house of the Lord all the days of my life, to behold the beauty of the Lord, and to inquire in his temple"* (Psalm 27:4).

Surely goodness and mercy will follow us all the days of our lives because we seek to dwell in the house of the Lord forever. (*See* Psalm 23:6.)

The more we inquire in the temple and behold the beauty of the Lord, the more we are drawn out of Babylon into Zion. The more we acquire the quality of charity, the more we desire to renounce the laws of competition and profits for the oneness of the law of consecration, *"continuing daily with one accord in the temple"* (*see* Acts 2:44-46).

It is a glimpse of the reality of the great view, and of the great and last promise of the temple, that draws me to this sacred place. It is to the words of Christ, taught by the Holy Spirit, that I want to be very attentive while in the temple. There, I want to offer up my "most holy desires" (*see* D&C 95:16) that I might hear the "words of eternal life" and "peaceable things of immortal glory" (*see* Moses 6:59, 61), receiving "revelation upon revelation, knowledge upon knowledge" of the mysteries of God, and "that which bringeth life eternal" (*see* D&C 42:61).

I want to be able to say as Abraham: "Thy servant hath sought Thee earnestly; now I have found Thee." I want to be a true messenger and be called as Abraham "the Friend of God" (James 2:23). To this end, I want to climb Mount Zion and reach the summit, for I am beginning to see that "eye hath not seen, nor ear heard, neither have entered into the heart of man, the things which God hath prepared for them that love him" (1 Corinthians 2:9).

Certainly, the great view, even a glimpse of the summit of Mount Zion, is worth the climb, for as Joseph Smith said, *"Could you gaze into heaven five minutes, you would know more than you would by reading all that ever was written on the subject."*[4]

Let Us Go Up to the Summit of Mount Zion

May we find through the temple the path of salvation and exaltation to "the things which God hath prepared for them that love Him" (1 Corinthians 2:9). For this great view, we need to heed the words of true messengers and prophets of this dispensation, as foretold by the prophet of a former dispensation: "Many people shall go and say, Come ye, and *let us go up to the mountain of the Lord, to the house of the God of Jacob; and he will teach us of his ways, and we will walk in his paths*" (Isaiah 2:3).

While leaving the Salt Lake temple one day, I started up the exit stairs and looked at a portrait of a prophet of this dispensation. My eyes caught the penetrating words on a directional sign below the portrait of Lorenzo Snow, the first president of the Salt Lake temple. The sign read: "Up Only." *This is the temple message that Lorenzo Snow, a man who personally received the great and last promise of the temple, would leave for us today.*

Once we enter the gate, the path up Mount Zion is "up only." This does not mean that as we follow the Savior up Mount Zion, all in our lives will go up and go well. Even the Savior had to descend below all things to be the light of truth (*see* D&C 88:6). In our climb up Mount Zion, there will be tribulations and trials, but as we follow our Savior with a perfect brightness of hope, even the "downs" will transcend to up only. Therefore, let us look up and go up only to the summit of Mount Zion.

Enticed more and more by the fruit of the tree of life (the view of the love of God at the summit of Mount Zion), and less and less by the forbidden fruit (the views of the world), we will hear the call of the Prophet Joseph Smith, encouraging us to the summit of Mount Zion:

> Brethren, shall we not go on in so great a cause? Go forward and not backward. Courage, Brethren; and on, and on to the victory! Let your hearts rejoice, and be exceedingly glad . . . for the prisoners shall go free.
>
> *Let the mountains [temples] shout for joy, . . . Let all the sons of God shout for joy! And let the eternal creations declare His name forever and ever!* . . . How glorious is the voice we hear from heaven, proclaiming in our ears glory, and salvation, and honor and immortality, and eternal life; kingdoms, principalities, and powers!" (D&C 128:22-23)

The Great View at the Summit: The Fulness of the Lord's Work

As we steadfastly press forward to climb Mount Zion, the glorious view (*see* 2 Nephi 1:24) at the summit will become more and more real to us. It is upon the summit of Mount Zion that we will see the fulness of the Lord's work, *"when the Lord hath performed his whole work upon Mount Zion"* (2 Nephi 20:12).

To those who climb Mount Zion, in the dispensation of the fulness of times, is given the responsibility to be the savor and saviors of our fellowmen. We are to carry out the "whole work" of the Lord in gathering together all dispensations in one through temple work:

> For unto you, [the First Presidency, the Twelve and all those appointed with them] is the power of this priesthood given, for the last days and for the last time, in the which is the dispensation of the fulness of times.
>
> Which power you hold, in connection with all those who have received a dispensation at any time from the beginning of the creation. (D&C 112:30-31)
>
> For it [temple work] is necessary in the ushering in of the dispensation of the fulness of times, which dispensation is now beginning to usher in, that a whole and complete and perfect union, and welding together of dispensations, and keys, and powers, and glories should take place, and be revealed from the days of Adam even to the present time. (D&C 128:18)

Once "the whole work upon Mount Zion" is completed and all things become one in Christ, the earth will be celestialized, and temple work as we know it will no longer be needed. Then, the great and last promise of the temple—or dwelling in the eternal presence of God and His Son—will be granted to the righteous. The celestialized earth (*see* D&C 130:7-11), and the Father and the Son, will be our temple: "And I saw no temple therein: for *the Lord God Almighty and the Lamb are the temple of it*" (Revelation 21:22).

When we see this great view, we will "sing the song of the Lamb, day and night forever and ever" (*see* D&C 133:56), for He is the perfect reflection of the great view. Reaching the summit of Mount Zion and entering the "heavenly place," we will receive the fulness of the Lord:

> They are they who are priests and kings, *who have received of his fulness, and of his glory;* . . .
>
> *These are they who are come unto Mount Zion, and unto the city of the living God, the heavenly place, the holiest of all.* (D&C 76:56, 66)

The celestial city of God, a heavenly and holy place, is the great view before our eyes at the summit of Mount Zion. It is worth every obedient act, and every personal sacrifice, to climb the mountain of the house of the Lord. It is worth holding fast to the rod of iron, for it leads to the tree of life and fountain of living waters. These represent a fulness of the love of God found at the summit of Mount Zion (*see* 1 Nephi 25:11).

As we hold fast and climb, partaking of the fruit and drinking the water, we become holy. We become new creatures with a mighty change of heart. When we taste the exquisite sweetness of the fruit of the tree of life, our desire for righteousness will not be satisfied until we experience a fulness of joy that can only continue in the city of the living God with the full power of His love.

Thank God for the scriptural temple and the everlasting covenant. Thank God for the dispensation of the fulness of times, the dispensation of the fulness of temples.

> And for this cause, *that men might be made partakers of the glories which were to be revealed,* the Lord sent forth the fulness of his gospel, his everlasting covenant, reasoning in plainness and simplicity . . .
>
> *And unto him that repenteth and sanctifieth himself before the Lord shall be given eternal life.* (D&C 133:57, 62)

The Summit: Being Sealed to the Father with Eternal Life

Eternal life, the greatest gift of God, is the summit of Mount Zion. There we will come to know our Eternal Father and then, as Joseph Smith taught, "*we will come to know ourselves. We will see things as we really are.*"[5] Eternal life is the great and last promise of the temple:

> Wherefore, I now send upon you another Comforter, even upon you my friends, that it may abide in your hearts, even the Holy Spirit of promise; which other Comforter is the same that I promised unto my disciples, as is recorded in the testimony of John.
>
> *This Comforter is the promise which I give unto you of eternal life, even the glory of the celestial kingdom.* (D&C 88:3-4)

For this greatest of gifts, I hope we are beginning to glimpse, as President McKay said, the importance of the temple. At age 91, while addressing general authorities in the temple about the endowment, President McKay said, *"Brethren, I think I am finally beginning to understand."*[6]

Progressing from a glimpse to understanding can be a lifelong pursuit as we climb Mount Zion. Joseph Smith said the climb of Mount Zion will continue beyond this life:

> When you climb up a ladder, you must begin at the bottom, and ascend up step by step, until you arrive at the top; and so it is with the principles of the Gospel—*you must begin with the first, and go on until you learn all the principles of exaltation. But it will be a great while after you have passed through the veil before you will have learned them. It is not all to be comprehended in this world; it will be a great work to learn our salvation and exaltation even beyond the grave.*[7]

An important key to finding the Father of our spirits again, and becoming like Him, is to have the Holy Ghost as our constant companion. He is the one who gives us the knowledge of Jesus Christ, the grand key who unlocks the veil to the Father and His Kingdom of Heaven. This constant companionship occurs when our thoughts are garnished unceasingly with virtue and our bowels are filled with charity towards all men (*see* D&C 121:45-46).

As we grow up in the temple, we are endowed with virtues, the greatest of which is charity. A part of the great and last promise of the temple is to receive a gift for this virtue. It is the fullness (*see* D&C 109:15) or constant companionship of the Holy Ghost. *With this gift, we will be prepared, our lamps full, because with the constant companionship of the Holy Spirit, we will practice virtue and holiness before the Lord continually* (*see* D&C 46:33). Only then will our dominion be an everlasting dominion. Truth and righteousness will flow unto us forever and ever as the Holy Spirit leads us to the companionship of Christ, the Second Comforter. *These Comforters, Christ and the Holy Spirit, will plead our cause and seal us to the Father with eternal life.*

Fortunately, even a glimpse can be a powerful spiritual motivation to keep climbing. While we make this climb, the Holy Spirit will open our mind and heart in the temple, teaching us the way of salvation. He will lead us to Christ, who will take us to the the summit of Mount Zion, our Heavenly Father.

Joseph Smith taught that this will be accomplished through the great and last promise of the temple, when our knowledge of Christ parts the veil to the glories of the Kingdom of Heaven:

> For the day must come when no man need say to his neighbor, Know ye the Lord; for *all shall know Him* [all who have reached the summit of Mount Zion] . . . from the least to the greatest [Hebrews 8:11]. *How is this to be done? It is to be done by this sealing power, and the other comforter spoken of, which will be manifest by revelation.*[8]

Knowledge through our Lord and Savior Jesus Christ is the grand key that unlocks (parts the veil to) the glories and mysteries of the Kingdom of Heaven.[9]

At the summit, no longer as spiritual orphans but rather spiritually begotten children of Christ, with a mighty change of heart, we will again come unto our Heavenly Father. "*And every one that hearkeneth to the voice of the Spirit cometh unto God, even the Father*" (D&C 84:47).

As this great and glorious view of the summit of Mount Zion becomes real in our minds and hearts, we will want to develop the intimate, marriage covenant relationship with Christ that He desires. We will want to expose our hearts to Him and let Him have "full sway" (Alma 42:30) in them. Then the temple will become the most powerful spiritual motivation in our lives, because we will know and have the pure love of Christ that comes through the mighty change in our hearts.

Endnotes

1. The Temple Paradigm

1. Madsen, Truman G. "The Highest In Us," *House of Glory* (Salt Lake City, Utah: Bookcraft Inc. 1978), pp. 102-103.
2. *Lectures on Faith* (Salt Lake City, Utah: Deseret Book Company, 1985), vol. 6, p. 7.
3. Joseph Fielding Smith, comp. *Teachings of the Prophet Joseph Smith* (Salt Lake City, Utah: Deseret Book Company, 1976), p. 162.
4. Madsen, Truman G. "The Temple and the Atonement," in Donald W. Parry, edit., *Temples of the Ancient World* (Salt Lake City, Utah: Deseret Book Company, 1994), p. 72.
5. Widtsoe, John A. "Temple Worship." *The Utah Genealogical and Historical Magazine*, vol. 12, April, 1921, pp. 50-51.
6. Hinckley, Gordon B. "Some Thoughts on Temples, Retention of Converts, and Missionary Service," *Ensign*, November 1997, p. 49.
7. Smith, Samuel. "My Country, 'Tis of Thee," *Hymns of The Church of Jesus Christ of Latter-day Saints* (Salt Lake City, Utah: The Church of Jesus Christ of Latter-day Saints, 1985), p. 339.
8. Lammi, Elmer W. "Moroni Statue Tops DC Spire," *Church News,* May 19, 1973, p. 3.

2. Seeking the Source of Temple Worship in the Holy Land

1. Gailbraith, David B.; Ogden, Kelly; Skinner, Andrew. *Jerusalem the Eternal City* (Salt Lake City, Utah: Deseret Book, 1996), p. 260.
2. Benson, Ezra T. "What I Hope You Will Teach Your Children About the Temple," *Ensign,* August 1985, p. 9.
3. *Teachings of the Prophet Joseph Smith:, op. cit.,* p. 151.
4. Lundquist, John M. "What Is a Temple? A Preliminary Topology," in *Temples of the Ancient World, op cit.,* p. 84.

5. Lundquist, John M. "Temple, Covenant, and Law in the Ancient Near East and in the Old Testament." *op. cit.,* pp. 272-294.
6. *Teachings of the Prophet Joseph Smith, op. cit.,* pp. 57-58.

3. The Mountain of Holiness

1. Thomas, M. Catherine. "The Brother of Jared at the Veil," in *Temples of the Ancient World, op cit.,* p. 389.
2. Parry, Donald W. "Garden of Eden: Prototype Sanctuary," *Temples of the Ancient World, op. cit.,* p. 133.
3. Smith, Paul Thomas. Matthew, B. Brown. *Symbols in Stone.* (American Fork, Utah: Covenant Communications Inc., 1997), p. 15.
4. *Teachings of the Prophet Joseph Smith:, op. cit.,* pp. 158-159.
5. Whitney, Orson F. *The Life of Heber C. Kimball. (*Salt Lake City, Utah: Bookcraft, 1992), pp. 209-210.
6. Gentry, Leland H. "Adam-ondi-Ahman, A Brief Historical Survey." *Brigham Young University Studies,* vol. 13, no. 4, p. 561.
7. Young, Brigham. *Journal of Discourses* (Liverpool: R.D. and S.W. Richards, 1854-56), vol. 11, pp. 336-337.
8. Stone, Irving. *Men to Match My Mountains* (Garden City, New York: Doubleday & Company, Inc. 1956).
9. Ehat, Andrew F. & Cook, Lyndon W. *The Words of Joseph Smith.* Grandin Book Company. Orem, Utah 1993, pp. 119-120.
10. *Lectures on Faith, op. cit.,* vol. 2, p. 55.
11. *Jerusalem the Eternal City, op. cit.,* p. 248.
12. Lindquist, John M. "The Legitimizing Role of the Temple in the Origin of the State," in *Temples of the Ancient World, op. cit.,* pp. 184-185.
13. *Teachings of the Prophet Joseph Smith, op. cit.,* p. 323.

4. Ascending the Mountain of Holiness

1. *Jerusalem the Eternal City, op. cit.,* p. 192.
2. *Ibid.,* pp. 241-242.
3. *Ibid.,* pp. 245-246.
4. "The Old Testament and New Testament Faith." *Heart and Mind* (Grand Rapids, Michigan: Institute of Religious Research. Special Issue 1997), p. 5.

5. Hamblin, William J. "Temple Motifs in Jewish Mysticism,"
   in *Temples of the Ancient World, op. cit.,* p. 444.
6. *Ibid.,* p. 461.
7. Berrett, Lamar C.; Ogden, D. Kelly. *Discovering the World of the Bible.* (Provo, Utah: Grandin Book Co., 3rd ed., 1996), p. 134.
8. Colianu, Ioan Petru. "Ascension," *Encyclopedia of Religion.* (New York: Macmillan. 1987), vol. 1, pp. 435-441.
9. Hamblin, William J. "Temple Motifs in Jewish Mysticism" in *Temples of the Ancient World, op. cit.,* pp. 442 & 447.
10. Thomas, M. Catherine. "The Brother of Jared at the Veil," in *Temples of the Ancient World, ibid.,* p. 389.
11. Thomas, M. Catherine. "Hebrews: To Ascend the Holy Mount," in *Temples of the Ancient World, ibid.,* p. 480.

5. The Camp of Israel: Base Camp of Mount Zion

1. Holzapfel, Richard Neitzel. *The Exodus Story* (Salt Lake City, Utah: Bookcraft, 1997), p. 67.
2. Top, Brent L. *A Peculiar Treasure* (Salt Lake City, Utah: Bookcraft, 1997), p. 2.
3. *Old Testament Student Manual, Genesis-2 Samuel* (Salt Lake City, Utah: The Church of Jesus Christ of Latter-day Saints, 1980), p. 152.
4. Roberts, B.H., edit. *History of the Church* (Salt Lake City, Utah: Deseret Book Company, 1980), vol. 5, pp. 423-424.

6. Equipped for the First Ascent: Initiation to Mount Zion

1. *Ibid.,* vol. 6, pp. 184-185.
2. Charles, John D. *Endowed from On High* (Bountiful, Utah: Horizon Publishers, 1997), pp. 42, 52-54.
3. Widtsoe, John A. "The House of the Lord," *Improvement Era,* April 1936, p. 228.
4. *Teachings of the Prophet Joseph Smith, op. cit.,* p. 328.
5. Smith, Joseph F. *Gospel Doctrine* (Salt Lake City, Utah: Deseret Book Company), p. 15.
6. [Ref. is on p. 89]

7. Macdonald, Joan B. *The Holiness of Everyday Life* (Salt Lake City, Utah: Deseret Book Company, 1995), pp. 4, 8.
8. Whitney, Orson F. "Latter-day Saint Ideals and Institutions," *Improvement Era,* August, 1927, p. 851.
9. Widtsoe, John A. "Temple Worship," *Utah Genealogical and Historical Magazine,* April 1921, pp. 62-63.
10. *Endowed From On High, op. cit.,* p. 38.
11. Wilson, Marvin. *Our Father Abraham* (Grand Rapids, Michigan: Eerdmans Publishing Co., 1989), p. 205.
12. McConkie, Bruce R. *Doctrinal New Testament Commentary* (Salt Lake City, Utah: Bookcraft, 1965), vol. 3, p. 485.
13. *Teachings of the Prophet Joseph Smith, op. cit.,* p. 298.
14. *Ibid.,* 322.
15. *Endowed From On High, op. cit.,* p. 35.
16. Smith Joseph F. *Doctrines of Salvation* (Salt Lake City, Utah: Bookcraft, 1995), vol. 1, p. 156.
17. *Journal of Discourses, op. cit.,* vol. 21, p. 194.

7. The Great Endowment:
The Purifying Power of Mount Zion

1. Welch, John W. *Illuminating the Sermon at the Temple & Sermon on the Mount* (Provo, Utah: Foundation of Ancient Research and Mormon Studies, 1999), p. 85.
2. Neilsen, Donna B. *Beloved Bridegroom* (1999), p. 23.
3. *Journal of Discourses, op. cit.,* vol. 2, p. 31.
4. *Teachings of the Prophet Joseph Smith, op. cit.,* p. 237.
5. Peterson, H. Burke. "The Temple and Its Influence in Perfecting the Members of Church," First Quorum of Seventy meeting, February 20, 1986.
6. Packer, Boyd K. *The Holy Temple* (Salt Lake City, Utah: Bookcraft, 1980), p. 42.
7. Nielsen, Donna B. *Beloved Bridegroom, op. cit.,* p. 99.
8. Welch, John W. "Benjamin's Covenant, A Precursor of the Sacrament Prayers" in *King Benjamin's Speech.* John W. Welch & Stephen D. Ricks editors. (Provo, Utah: Foundation for Ancient Research and Mormon Studies, 1998), p. 308.
9. Millet, Robert L. *Another Testament of Jesus Christ in First Nephi, The Doctrinal Foundation.* Monte S. Nyman & Charles D.

Tate, Jr. editors. Religious Studies Center, Brigham Young University, Provo, Utah. Salt Lake City, Utah: Bookcraft, 1988), pp. 165-166.

10. Brown, Matthew B. *The Gate of Heaven* (American Fork, Utah: Covenant Communications, Inc., 1999), p. 112.
11. *History of the Church, op. cit.,* vol. 5, pp. 215-216.
12. Thomas, M. Catherine. "Hebrews: To Ascend the Holy Mount," in *Temples of the Ancient World, op. cit.,* p. 485.
13. Interpretive adaptation of lecture given by Wayne Brickey, Tel Aviv, Israel, Dec. 29, 1996.

8. A Full View of Mount Zion

1. *Teachings of the Prophet Joseph Smith, op. cit.,* p. 343.
2. *Teachings of the Prophet Joseph Smith, op. cit.,* p. 308.
3. *History of the Church, op. cit.,* vol. 5, p. 527.
4. Ehat, F. Andrew & Cook, Lyndon W. *The Words of Joseph Smith* (Grandin Book Company, 1993), p. 329.
5. Pratt, Orson. *The Seer,* vol. 1. No. 10, 1853.
6. Smith, Joseph Fielding. *Elijah the Prophet and His Mission* (Salt Lake City, Utah: Deseret Book, 1957), p. 46.
7. *History of the Church, op. cit.,* vol. 6, p. 254.
8. Ehat, F. Andrew & Cook, Lyndon W. *The Words of Joseph Smith, op cit.,* p. 329.

9. The Great and Last Promise: Reaching the Summit of Mount Zion

1. *Teachings of the Prophet Joseph Smith, op. cit., p*p. 150-151.
2. Benson, Ezra T. "What I Hope You Will Teach Your Children About the Temple." *Ensign.* August 1985, p. 9.
3. Widtsoe, John. "Temple Worship." *Utah Genealogical & Historical Magazine,* April 12, 1921), p. 56.
4. McConkie, Bruce R. *A New Witness for the Articles of Faith* (Salt Lake City, Utah: Deseret Book Company, 1985), p. 495.
5. *Lectures on Faith, op. cit.,* vol. 2, p. 55.
6. *History of the Church, op. cit.,* vol. 5, p. 389.
7. *Lectures on Faith, op. cit.,* vol. 6, p. 12.
8. *Teachings of the Prophet Joseph Smith, op. cit.,* p. 162.

9. Wright, Lawrence. "Forcing the End," *The New Yorker,* July 20, 1998, pp. 42-53.
10. Nielsen, Donna B. forward by Dr. Robert J. Norman. *Beloved Bridegroom (*1999), p. iii.
11. Adaptive interpretation of lecture by Wayne Brickey on the roof of Simon the Tanner's dwelling, Joppa, Israel, December 30, 1996.
12. Nielsen, Donna B. *Beloved Bridegroom, op. cit.,* p. 39.
13. Welch, John W. *Illuminating the Sermon at the Temple & Sermon on the Mount, op. cit.* p. 63.
14. Adaptive interpretation of a lecture by Wayne Brickey at the Sermon on the Mount memorial, near Capernaum, Israel, December 28, 1996.
15. Hunter, Howard W. "A More Excellent Way," *Ensign,* May 1992, pp. 61-63.
16. Wilcox, Michael. BYU Education Week lecture, 1997.
17. Hinckley, Gordon B. Address at the dedication of the Taiwan Temple, 1984.
18. Evans, Richard L.
19. Frankl, Viktor E. *Man's Search For Meaning* (Washington Square Press, 1985), pp. 56-57.
20. Wheelwright, Lorin F. "O Love That Glorifies the Son," *Hymns of The Church of Jesus Christ of Latter-day Saints, op cit.,* p. 295.

10. Yielding Our Hearts to God: Lord, How Is It Done?

1. Cannon, George Q. *Millennial Star*, April 23, 1894, pp. 260-261.
2. Eyring, Henry B. CES Fireside discourse, September 8, 1996.
3. Derrick, Royden G. *Temples of the Last Days* (Salt Lake City, Utah: Bookcraft, 1987), p. 53.
4. Welch, John W. *Illuminating the Sermon at the Temple & Sermon on the Mount, op. cit.,* p. 172.
5. Hafen, Bruce C. & Marie K. "Bridle All Your Passions," *Ensign,* February, 1994, pp. 14-18.
6. *Journal of Discourses, op. cit.,* vol. 9, p. 3.
7. Savage, Susan, "Temple Snow," *Ensign,* January 1986.

8. McConkie, Bruce R. *A New Witness for the Articles of Faith,
op. cit.,* p. 602.
9. Snow, Lorenzo. *Millennial Star.* vol. 50, no. 25, p. 392.
10. *Teachings of the Prophet Joseph Smith, op. cit.,* p. 66.

11. The Bond of Perfectness:
The Only Way to the Summit of Mount Zion

1. *Teachings of the Prophet Joseph Smith, op. cit.,* p. 330.
2. *Beloved Bridegroom, op. cit.,* pp. 8-9, 31-32.
3. Thomas, M. Catherine. "The Brother of Jared at the Veil" in
Temples of the Ancient World, op. cit., p. 388.
4. Robinson, Robert. *Come, Thou Fount of Every Blessing,* arr.
Mack Wilberg, from *Wyeth's Repository of Sacred Music,* 1813.
Oxford University Press.
5. Roberts, B.H., edit. *History of the Church, op. cit.,* vol. 6, p. 230.
6. Madsen, Truman. "The Temple and the Atonement," in *Temples of
the Ancient World, op. cit.,* pp. 66-67.
7. Bacon, Francis. Quotation from "Of Revenge."
8. MacDonald, Joan B. *The Holiness of Everyday Life*
(Salt Lake City, Utah: Deseret Book, 1995), p. 47.
9. Thomas, M. Catherine. "The Brother of Jared at the Veil," in
Temples of the Ancient World, op. cit., pp. 388-389.
10. *Lectures on Faith, op. cit.,* vol. 4, pp. 14-15.
11. Gabriel, Charles H. "I Stand All Amazed," *Hymns of The Church
of Jesus Christ of Latter-day Saints, op. cit.,* p. 193.
12. Wilcox, Michael. BYU Education Week lecture, 1997.

12. The Wells of Salvation:
Sustaining the Ascent of Mount Zion

1. *Jerusalem the Eternal City, op. cit.,* p. 24.
2. *Ibid.,* pp. 17-18.
3. Tennyson, Alfred Lord. *In Memory of A.H.H. (1850). The Oxford
Dictionary of Quotations* (Oxford University Press, 3rd edition,
1980), p. 535.
4. Bonhoeffer, Dietrich. *The Cost of Discipleship* (New York,
New York: Touchstone, 1995), pp. 149-150.

5. Longstaff, W.D. *Take Time to be Holy*, arranged by John Longhurst (Orem Utah: Sonos, 1991).
6. *Teachings of the Prophet Joseph Smith, op. cit.*, p. 268.
7. *House of Glory, op. cit.*, p. 41.
8. *Ibid.*, p. 64.
9. Featherstone, Vaughn J. "A Haven in a World of Turmoil." Special meeting of the Seventy; St. George and Manti temples. See also *The Incomparable Christ* (1995), pp. 3-6.
10. Widtsoe John A. "Temple Worship," *Utah Genealogical and Historical Magazine,* Apr. 12, 1921, p. 51.
11. *Journal of Discourses, op. cit.*, vol. 9, p. 317.
12. Smith Joseph F. "Salvation for the Living and the Dead," *Relief Society Magazine,* vol. 5, p. 678.
13. Kimball, Spencer W. *Proceedings of the Priesthood Genealogy Research Seminar,* BYU campus, Aug 4, 1977, p. 4.
14. *House of Glory, op cit.,* p. 41.

13. The Salt and Light of the Covenant

1. Widtsoe, John A. *Improvement Era,* April 1936, p. 228.
2. *Teachings of the Prophet Joseph Smith, op. cit.*, p. 258.
3. Kocherhans, Gib. "The Name Melchizedek—Some Thoughts On Its Meaning and the Priesthood It Represents," *Ensign,* September, 1980, p. 16.

14. Views from the Summit of Mount Zion

1. MacDonald, George. *The Gift of the Christ Child and Other Tales,* vol. 1, p. 28.
2. Wheelock, Cyrus H. "Ye Elders of Israel," *Hymns of The Church of Jesus Christ of Latter-day Saints,* 1985, no. 319.
3. *History of the Church, op. cit.*, vol. 5, p. 403.
4. *Ibid.*, vol. 6, p. 50.
5. Millet, Robert L. *Alive in Christ—The Miracle of Spiritual Rebirth,* p. 28.
6. Boyd K. Packer. *The Holy Temple, op. cit.*, p. 263.
7. *Teachings of the Prophet Joseph Smith, op. cit.*, p. 348.
8. *History of the Church, op. cit.*, vol. 3, p. 380.
9. *Teachings of the Prophet Joseph Smith, op. cit.*, p. 298.

Index

A

B

C

S

Sacrament—120
Sacrifice, defined—170, 184, 186
Salt—241-251
Satan, devil—121, 125, 127, 145, 146, 218, 234-235
Savage, Susan, poem by—198
Savor, sweet—170-171
Scriptural Temple, term defined—15
Smith, Joseph, and statements by—18, 28-29, 32-33, 40, 45, 46, 62, 70, 77, 80, 89, 94, 104, 104, 110, 111, 113, 138, 148, 150, 151, 152, 155, 156, 156, 161-162, 163-164, 164, 166, 166, 169, 191, 193, 202, 205, 214, 217, 220, 226, 243, 244, 246, 259, 260, 262
Smith, Joseph F., statements by—81-82, 248
Smith, Joseph Fielding, statements by—154, 236
Snow, Lorenzo, "up only" sign—260
Stone, Irving, book by—41
Stone, white—103-104
Suffering—46-47
Symbolism—94

T

Temple, body as a—79-80
Temple, Jerusalem—27, 50, 52-53, 258
Temple, Solomon's—32
Temples, smaller stake—23
Temple text—178
Temples, topographical in Israel—29-30
Thomas, Catherine, statements by—208, 220
Tree of Knowledge of Good and Evil—145
Tree of Life—118-121, 128, 129, 146
Tribulation—124-126

V

Veiled woman—207
Voice of God—93

W

Washings—73-74
Water—224-240
Welch, John—195
Whitney, Orson F., statement by—95
Widtsoe, John A., statements by—22-23, 80, 96, 106, 163, 234, 246
Wilcox, Michael, statements by—221, 240
Woodruff, Wilford—109
Works—167

Y

Young, Brigham, statements by—41, 61, 109, 113, 152, 152, 197, 236

Z

Zion's Camp—199-200

About the Author

In 1963, Mark H. Greene III was climbing mountains in Colorado for a better view—especially of himself. Little did he know, then, that 33 years later he would be facing the most challenging mountain of his life. It is Mount Zion, the mountain of the Lord's house. Now he knows that if he can reach the summit of this mountain, he truly will see the "great view."

Mark has been an orthopedic surgeon, specializing in hand and upper limb surgery, for the past 17 years in Salt Lake City. He has served in a variety of Church callings, including a full-time mission to Belgium and France. He was recently released from the Stake High Council of the Monument Park North Stake, and currently serves in a favorite calling as a Primary teacher in the Monument Park Twelfth Ward.

After his mission, Mark married the beautiful Jill Stephenson. They have six children: Brian, Lara Evans, Lys-An, Linsey, Leslee, and Stephen. All of these children are uniquely special and have brought Mark and Jill great joy.

Some of Doctor Greene's patients call him "tripplesticks" because of the Roman numeral III ending his name, which represents three generations of *Mark Greenes*. He appreciates this sobriquet because it reminds him of the name he bears and the ancestry it represents. His father was also an orthopedic hand surgeon, and his grandfather was a professor of finance at the University of Utah. He still, on occasion, sees patients who remember these wonderful men.

Mount Zion requires climbing it with others, especially family and ancestors. Then, lasting relationships will develop.

A cherished portrait of Mark's family, shown here, is in the image of a mountain. It represents the bonding relationship of love required to reach the summit of Mount Zion.